MEDIA WAR

Martin Andree teaches media science at Cologne University in Germany. He has been doing research on the dominance of Big Tech for more than 15 years. Leading German and international media, conferences and institutions regularly draw on his expertise, calling for his contributions on this subject. In 2020, he published the highly reputed *Atlas of the Digital World*. He received the Günter Wallraff Special Award for Press Freedom and Human Rights for the bestseller *Big Tech Muss Weg!* (2023), which has also been published in English (*Big Tech Must Go!*). He studied in Cologne, Münster, Cambridge and Harvard.

Martin Andree

MEDIA WAR

Dark Tech and Populists are Seizing Power

Campus Verlag
Frankfurt/New York

The original German edition was published in 2025 by Campus Verlag with the title *Krieg der Medien. Dark Tech und Populisten übernehmen die Macht*. The English edition is distributed worldwide outside German-speaking countries by The University of Chicago Press. All rights reserved.

ISBN 978-3-593-52114-5 Print
ISBN 978-3-593-46229-5 E-Book (PDF)
ISBN 978-3-593-46228-8 E-Book (EPUB)

All rights reserved. No part of this book may be reproduced or transmitted in any form or by any means, electronic or mechanical, including photocopying, recording, or by any information storage and retrieval system, without permission in writing from the publishers. Beltz Verlagsgruppe expressly reserves the right to use its content for text and data mining according to § 44b UrhG.
Despite careful checking of the content, we accept no liability for the content of external links. The operators of the linked pages are solely responsible for their content.
Copyright © 2025. Campus Verlag, part of the publishing group Beltz, Werderstr. 10, 69469 Weinheim, info@campus.de.
Cover design and illustrations: Verena Bönniger, Delicious Layouts, Hilden
Typesetting: Oliver Schmitt, Mainz
Printing office and bookbinder: Beltz Grafische Betriebe GmbH, Bad Langensalza
Beltz Grafische Betriebe is a climate-neutral company (ID 15985-2104-1001)
Printed in Germany

www.campus.de
www.press.uchicago.edu

CONTENTS

Introduction — 7

1. The combat zone — 25
2. The warlords — 45
3. The objectives of the warlords — 61
4. The invasion — 79
5. The occupation — 95
6. The weapons — 111
7. The trap — 137
8. The uprising — 159
9. The capitulation — 177
10. The bitter end — 193

Endnotes — 213
Acknowledgements — 245

INTRODUCTION

"Civil war is inevitable"

That's what Elon Musk wrote on X, referring to the riots, including racist attacks, arson and looting, in the UK on 4 August 2024. More than fifty police officers were injured and hundreds of arrests were made. Subsequently, Musk repeatedly posted content on X that incited people to overthrow the 'tyrannical' British government.

What would this civil war look like that Musk is apparently hoping for and actively supports on his Platform X? Musk supports the AfD (Alternative für Deutschland, Alternative for Germany), a far-right party in Germany and maintains close contact with other right-wing populist movements in various European countries. In the UK, Nigel Farage, one of the architects of Brexit and someone with close ties to Donald Trump, had already taken a position as regards Musk. In fact, he seemed pretty close to striking a deal with Elon Musk. On 16 December 2024, Elon Musk received him at Trump's Mar-a-Lago estate. According to media reports, there were plans for Musk to support his party (Reform UK, previously the United Kingdom Independence Party (UKIP)) with 100 million US dollars.

However, the deal didn't materialise. Musk dropped Farage because he "doesn't have what it takes to be Reform UK's leader".[1] Farage was apparently not radical enough for Musk. Musk preferred Tommy Robinson — a British right-wing extremist whose biography is littered with acts of violence and assault, involvement in hooligan riots, threats of violence, stalking, doxxing, financial fraud, drug possession, defamation, hate speech, incitement to hatred, racism, discrimination, and so on.[2]

As a convicted criminal, Robinson has also served several prison sentences. His *modus operandi* is always the same. First, he verbally beats the shit out of his opponents like a hooligan, but, when convicted, he presents himself as a victim. In other words, he acts like a mega-troll. He proudly called his autobiography: *Enemy of the State*. 'Hahaha, look people, I'm a really evil troublemaker.' He's pretty crass isn't he? But after one of his various convictions in 2023, he published a video portraying himself as a victim. It was called "Silenced". 'How terrible,' he sniffles, 'the evil state authorities have well and truly gagged me!!' And — you can't make this stuff up — he has been fighting for years as a supposed 'journalist' for 'freedom of speech', which he considers to be in grave danger. In 2019, he asked Trump for asylum in the USA in the context of a conviction of his in the UK, the poor guy[3] (yeah right, like you're not allowed to say anything in the UK anymore). Musk apparently thought that this stuff was great. He liked it so much that he shared a link to the "Silenced" video on X, and in January also shouted on X: "Free Tommy Robinson". He later asked the question: "Why is Tommy Robinson in a solitary confinement for telling the truth?" Really, Elon, you want to know why???

Robinson fuelled the violent riots in August 2024 with his posts on X,[4] people were chanting Tommy Robinson's name on the streets. And Musk wrote: "Civil war is inevitable."

This example leads us directly to the 'media war', which is not just an abstract notion. It's a war that's also leading to real riots and acts of violence, such as the storming of the US Capitol in 2021. It's a war in which the power of Big Tech platforms has formed an alliance with populist forces. As Steve Bannon, the thought leader of the global right, puts it:

> "Money and informationa are the twin tactical nukes of modern politics — and he [Elon Musk] can deploy both at unprecedented scale [...]. Musk just spent a quarter of a billion dollars to elect Trump [...] If he puts the same amount of money into all of Europe that he put behind Trump, he will

flip every nation to a populist agenda. There's not a centrist left-wing government in Europe that will be able to withstand that onslaught."[5]

Europe and the free world is currently losing this media war. We are losing it, and we are losing our Western democracies in the process. All of this is only possible because we as a society have not fully grasped yet what exactly is going on. What is this media war all about?

The fight for media dominance

The term 'media war' refers to the ongoing battle for media dominance that is raging in the Western world. It consists of two components. It started a long time ago as an economic war of displacement. Since then, digital platforms that largely originate from the USA have been aggressively displacing and substituting the traditional, editorial media. During the decades of this 'hostile takeover', they established a narrative according to which their platforms offer users 'truly free media'. This narrative was increasingly radicalised over time: the 'lying' editorial media were assumed to be in cahoots with the supposedly 'corrupt elites' of the State, and so on. This campaign waged by the digital platforms against editorial media reached a climax in November 2024 when Donald Trump was re-elected as president. After that, Elon Musk officially announced the 'victory' over journalism on X and declared to the people on his platform: "You are the media now." All of this is a war *for* the media. And we all know who *owns* the media of the future — it is the 'Dark Tech' corporations. By this, I mean the large, monopolistic US tech corporations that started out as idealists in garages decades ago — but then, through a process of 'Darth Vaderisation', went over to the dark side of the force (the whole story is told in detail in my book *Big Tech Must Go!*).

However, we're not only experiencing a war *for* the media, but also a war *in* the media, that is, a battle for dominance and interpretive authority on the platforms, which are increasingly determining political agenda-setting. The debate is becoming more and more aggressive. Hate, incitement and malice are the new reality of digital discourse (▶6). Insults, defamation and accusations are rampant, bullying, rants and shitstorms are spreading. Right-wing populist movements and parties benefit most from the polarising effects of these platforms. The riots in the UK, as well as the storming of the Capitol in the USA, show how easily this verbal war can turn into real violence. And, of course, there is also the real, brutal war of aggression that Putin has been waging for years against Ukraine and thus against Europe. The consequences of this military war have long been visible, also in the neighbouring Western democracies. Once again, it is the platforms used by Russian cyber-attacks, troll farms and fake accounts that are being used to sow doubts within the population about support for the war — and thus *instrumentalise* them for their military goals.

On top of this, the imperialist turn of the new US administration is intimidating. Firstly, military interventions have not been explicitly ruled out, even against allies (Greenland, Canada). Secondly, the US government is forming a coalition with European right-wing populists and has even supported Putin in Russia.

In the war *for* the media, the Dark Tech corporations are winning. In the war *in* the media, *populists* are advancing on all fronts. The key point now is that both movements have openly joined forces. The battle that the platforms have been waging against the 'established media' since the 2000s has been exploited primarily by right-wing populist movements for their own agenda. And it is precisely this synchronisation that is so dangerous, telling people the fairy tale that Western governments 'censored' the 'traditional media' in the past — but now the Trumps, Vances, Musks and right-wing populists of this world are 'liberating' them through the power of 'uncensored' platforms to allow for true 'freedom of speech'. We have all seen in recent months how tremendously successful this synchronised development has been.

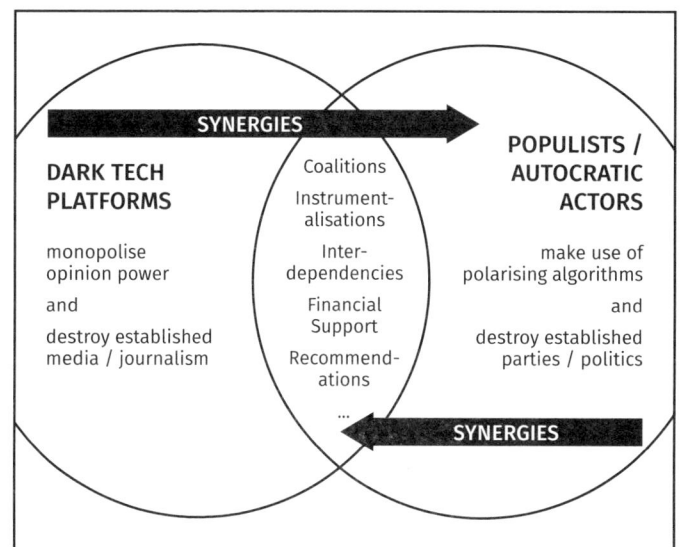

Figure 1: Media War

As we will see in the course of this book, this narrative of supposed liberation is based on a conspiracy theory (▶1). In reality, the hostile takeover of the public sphere by the Dark Tech platforms even leads to severe *restrictions* on media freedom (▶7) — we will come back to this later. One might also wonder why the USA, of all countries, has come up with the idea that it could 'liberate' European democracies, even though the USA only ranks 28th worldwide in *The Economist*'s Democracy Index (Germany, in 13th place, has a higher ranking).[6] We should consider that *The Economist* compiled this ranking *before* Trump's second presidency, during which he is increasingly transforming the USA into an autocracy. The Press Freedom Index shows a similar picture (Germany is ranked 11th, with the USA ranked 57th, behind Romania and Sierra Leone).[7] Trump, Vance and Musk want to teach us lessons on democracy? Sounds pretty absurd.

In reality, democracy in Europe is attacked from four sides: By the tech platforms, by the US government, by the European populist movements and also by the military threat from Russia. In principle, we are observing the synchronisation of two fields: The 'established legacy media' and 'legacy parties' (as the right-wing scene has termed it) are defending themselves against increasingly synchronised attacks from the tech platforms, the Trump administration and their populist allies. All this has also long been supported by a large bottom-up movement in Europe and the Western world, whose new rhetoric we are confronted with on a daily basis through various platforms (such as: "We will no longer let the opinion cartels dictate how we should think and vote! We will send the corrupt elites and the legacy media to hell! We'll get the real truth from the platforms!", and so on).

Month by month, the impact of these attacks gets more powerful. What is particularly frightening is that the attackers, for their part, are openly linking their advance in the media war with concrete military threats. JD Vance had already threatened in the summer of 2024 that the US would leave NATO if the EU dared to regulate tech platforms more strictly.[8]

As we will see later, the platforms of tech companies are the most important weapons in this media war (▶6). In the future, beyond political and economic power, it will be decisive if actors also control opinion power, as Elon Musk does by owning the platform X. In the words of the libertarian mastermind Peter Thiel (himself the ideological foster father of US Vice President JD Vance), we are witnessing a "war" between the old knowledge elites against the new medium of the internet — "a war the internet won".[9]

And what about us? We have still not realised the predicament we are in

As I write these lines, however, many strange things are happening. While threats coming from the USA have become an important topic in Germany, and while the public seems to have understood that the Dark Tech companies are not the cool, benevolent philanthropists that they had presented themselves as for years, we continue to mentally dodge these issues.

In April 2025, YouTube's twentieth birthday was celebrated largely uncritically in the German media. One leading outlet presented the 20 coolest videos from the platform's history in a very positive way. The fact that YouTube's parent company Alphabet has consistently distinguished itself in the past through intentional violations of the law, disregard for constitutional principles, massive data surveillance (even of minors) and aggressive tax avoidance seems to have escaped the attention of many journalists. By now, it should be completely obvious to anyone that Alphabet as a corporation is *not democracy compliant*. US Judge James Donato recently commented on Google's deliberate deletion of evidence from the company:

> "It's the most serious and disturbing evidence I have ever seen in my decade on the bench with respect to a party intentionally suppressing relevant evidence. This conduct is a frontal assault on the fair administration of justice."[10]

Would journalists celebrate a Hells Angels anniversary just as uncritically? And then run a similar headline: "50th Anniversary of the Hells Angels: The coolest motorcycles from fifty years — and the coolest biker outfits"?

Things don't look much better for the institutions. As I write these lines, various new German initiatives are being announced in which we are planning on further expanding our dependence on US Dark Tech companies in the future. In March 2025, for example, the Federal Council recommended that the police in Germany should use Palantir's security software nationwide (Peter Thiel is a major shareholder here).[11] And the German BSI (Federal Office for Security in Information Technology) has announced a strategic collaboration with Google and Amazon, among others.[12]

That means: We actually still don't get it. Although the media war is already being waged on several frontlines, the same media are still not important to us as a society. *Things* are important to us — but MEDIA??? WTF? Who cares? The new German government is currently being formed. As always, officials are once again jostling for responsibility for finance, defence, the economy, the environment, health, education, family or the foreign ministry — important things that important people take care of. But even though a new ministry for digital affairs was created, digital sovereignty does not play any major role. And I bet that, in many Western countries, most people cannot name a single politician with full focus on the media.

External threats — internal threats

The process of forming a new government in Germany has shown that people have at least understood one thing: We must defend our security. Military rearmament has been made the most important priority for the coming legislative period. Metaphorically speaking, on their defensive towers, the lords of the castle have at least discovered the huge enemy army out there threatening them, and they seem willing to defend their property. But unfortunately, *the enemies are already inside the castle and engaged in a lively exchange with their armed companions outside*. It is quite stunning that the lords of the castle don't even seem to notice.

Let's take this bitter pill first: the USA is proving to be a hostile, blackmailing and unscrupulous power these days. The transatlantic relationship, which has been built over decades, is thrown overboard in a matter of days. Alliances and treaties have lost their value to a large extent. From a European perspective, we can't trust the US government at all at the moment. The current US government is actively supporting Putin and right-wing populist movements, quite obviously for the purpose of destabilizing Europe, possibly splitting the EU and deregulating the digital markets to a very large extent in order to maximise the economic and political instrumentalisation of its digital media monopolies.

In contrast to Putin's Russia, there is a fundamental problem lurking here. The USA controls our democracy in two critical areas already now. Firstly, through its monopolistic and oligopolistic platforms. It 'owns' our political public sphere in the digital world — and that is nothing less than *the future foundation of our democracy*. The recent election campaign in Germany has also made it abundantly clear that the USA is openly instrumentalising its ownership of these platforms to influence elections in our country for their own interests and on behalf of their political 'partners' (the right-wing 'AfD').

But beyond that, *the same* tech companies also control the digital infrastructures in Europe. The extent of our dependency is staggering. Huge amounts of sensitive data, both from companies as well as from public authorities and administrations, are stored by the major US cloud providers Amazon, Microsoft and Google. The same situation prevails with Office software with the quasi-monopoly of Microsoft. Our vulnerability to blackmail and dependency is dizzying.

In the past, the question has been raised time and again as to what dangers could arise if the dictatorial Chinese government were to access data from European TikTok users. From today's perspective, this sounds like a joke, considering that the USA is now increasingly slipping into becoming an autocracy. Comparing the USA to China, it poses a much bigger threat to us, as they have access to private and sensitive data from European authorities, administrations and companies to an unimaginable extent (▸ 8)

Perhaps it has now become clear why there is a media war. And any political agenda that understands the scale of the problem would have to treat the issue of digital sovereignty *at the same level of priority as our military defence capability*. Our freedom is currently being synergistically heckled from two sides, in the East militarily by Putin, from the West by Trump, Vance, Tech & co. — with the crucial difference *that this alliance has long since taken up positions inside our castle.*

They hold this power because they already completely dominate and control our digital world. And now we must think further into the future. As a result of the ongoing digital transformation, they are expanding this dominance from month to month, from quarter to quarter, *without the digital monopolists having to do anything actively*. Economically, they are winning this media war anyway, which is why the democratic public sphere will almost inevitably become their prey.

We must then also ask ourselves the question: Which dimension of this war actually poses a more acute threat to the people in Europe? The military threat posed by Putin from the East? Or the war of the media, in which the libertarian enemies of democracy have long since taken up positions in our own countries — and are expanding these bastions with every passing month? Especially as these forces have long since synchronised with Putin.

Let's put ourselves in the mindset of the US government on the basic assumption that they will pursue an aggressive, imperialist expansionist policy in the future (which is more than obvious in view of the current statements on Greenland, Canada, the Panama Canal and Gaza). To put it bluntly: Why should they take military action against other countries at all, as in the old days, if they already completely control the digital infrastructures and media in these countries anyway? If, from the perspective of the USA, one could enforce one's own interests via Trumpist partner organisations such as the right-wing AfD in Germany, which in turn could be 'supported' at will via its own digital platforms, and could thus be kept dependent at will?

A 'media war' is much more promising for such actors than an old-fashioned classic war with military means. And this war has already been openly declared. Let us briefly recall the speech by US Vice President JD Vance at the Munich Security Conference. A forum which in the past has always been about foreign and security policy (i.e. 'important things'). It is important to keep in mind that he spoke during a tipping point in Russia's war of aggression against Ukraine. Above all, he spoke in Europe. And what was Vance's speech in Munich about? He talked about … the MEDIA.

According to Vance, the greatest dangers for Europe do not originate from Russia or China — but from within. Europe, he said, was lagging far behind in the field of "freedom of speech", which was threatened by "censorship". But bright hero figures like Trump and himself could help us to get on track concerning freedom of speech (ironically, he later added that with Trump, there was "a new sheriff in town"; sounds indeed like a fun liberation we are going to have with this new sheriff). In the future we should please work together with right-wing groups like the AfD all over Europe.[13]

The libertarian horror story about evil state censorship was copied directly from US populists by the German AfD. In his interview with the AfD party leader, Alice Weidel, on 9 January 2025, Musk further developed his crude theories: "it's actually quite easy to tell who the bad guys are. It's like who wants to shut down freedom of speech? They are the bad guys, that's very clear." Weidel adds: "Yes. And do you know what Adolf Hitler did? The first thing, he switched off free speech." We also remember the other nonsense argument: Weidel stated that Hitler in fact had been a "communist", had therefore been a leftist. And that also today, all parties in Germany except for the AfD were left-wing or green. That in history, it was always these evil leftists who "censor"; and sure, they are all enemies of free speech and democracy, exactly just like Hitler — and BANG! how nicely that worldview works out here for Weidel and Musk. Wolves in sheep's closing, pretending to fight for freedom of speech and democracy. Everyone else is a 'censor' — everyone else is like HITLER. Sure.[14]

Let's take this a step further and examine the narrative of Vance & co. Supposedly, it is Trump's USA that is 'liberating' Europe from corrupt elites and censorship in this media war. So far, so absurd. Their most important weapon in this liberation movement is, of course, the platforms of the US tech corporations. And the work of destruction that Trump, Vance and Tech are wreaking in the USA has long since begun in Europe — on 'all channels'. It is true that Trump and Vance are currently literally 'only' *ruling* in the USA, not in Europe. But it is *the same* platforms of US tech companies that also dominate our European digital public sphere.

In our own scientific measurement of all digital traffic across all end devices, we were able to show that the mirage of digital diversity is an illusion. It is important to emphasise this point because it contradicts our intuitive perception of the digital world. Aren't there millions of offers out there? A selection so huge that we might even lose track of it? Don't we have a myriad of channels at our disposal that we could have only dreamt of in the past? Actually, if you measure the distribution of attention scientifically, you find that almost all digital traffic is concentrated on a very small number of tech platforms. And even within these platforms, brutal winner-take-all mechanisms apply, with a large share of attention concentrated on the leading influencers, streamers, and creators — who, in turn, dance to the tune of the platform algorithms (▸6). And 'outside', i.e., outside the tech platforms, there is a vast desert of content that is hardly used. Dark Tech corporations have succeeded in sucking most digital traffic up into the silos of their platforms — while at the same time almost completely drying up independent offerings on the free internet. The internet is already an occupied zone and no longer free.[15] And the same principle applies to all countries in the Western world.

This is precisely the unbeatable strategic advantage of this completely new symbiosis of Trump and Tech: they are fighting a media war — and they are doing so via *media that they own and completely control*. These digital 'nuclear weapons' (Bannon) allow them to maximise their own supremacy. And to be equally clear: in Europe we have no pieces of our own on this chessboard. NOTHING. With the exception of TikTok (whose Chinese origins should give us little hope), almost all the major digital platforms in the European media world are owned by US tech corporations. Metaphorically speaking, we are like tiny, completely meaningless fruit flies. We are just passively watching.

Let's take a look at the processes surrounding the formation of the new government in Germany, for example. Although the media war is in full swing, and although we as a society are currently *losing* this war against the USA and the populists allied with it *on a broad front*, it is once again hardly playing a role in political priorities. According to the old patterns, it is once again about important 'things', not about the media: the economy, security, migration, finance and so on.

When historians look back on our time in a hundred years' time, they may say: In March 2025, there was a tiny remaining chance for Germany and Europe to turn the tide against the coalition of Trump, tech, Putin and the populists — but unfortunately it was missed. If our politicians continue to fail to wake up, we can confidently say: "Good night, democracy."

We have long since lost our digital sovereignty

Thus, we are trapped. And it's entirely our own fault. Because this media war started many years ago (▶2). But all this time, we have just been watching idly from the sidelines, focusing our attention on the supposedly 'important things' and, at best, allowing ourselves to be lulled to sleep by the casual future talks of tech evangelists. Now the trap is snapping shut and I don't see how we can get out of it any time soon.

As you can already see, my assessment of these issues is pitch black. As an academic, I have been dealing with the problem of digital power concentration and the dangerous accumulation of opinion power for more than fifteen years. I have been running from pillar to post in this field for many years, in Germany and abroad. But all attempts to generate a social debate on the subject that would lead to us consistently breaking up the unconstitutional media monopolies and regaining our own digital sovereignty have systematically failed.

Here are a few highlights:

- Following the publication of Chris Anderson's digital utopia *The Long Tail* in 2006, according to which digitisation has a kind of Robin Hood effect that takes from the rich and gives to the poor, I scientifically explained in as early as 2010 why exactly the opposite is likely to happen — and why the internet would continue to develop towards a massive concentration of use on a few providers.

- Since 2011, I have tried to generate a debate on the issue of digital dominance through hundreds of major conference papers.

- The first press article on the topic was an essay entitled 'The end of the digital utopia', which was published in 2012. At the time, the editors thought the argument of the article was so far-fetched that the text was published under a funny title.

- Because it was not possible to spark a debate on the digital dominance of tech players, eight more years passed before it was possible to deliver court-proof empirical evidence of digital monopolisation. This proof is so difficult to provide because there are more than 16 million different digital offerings (i.e. apps, websites, platforms) in Germany, which are also accessed via varying end devices (smartphones, tablets, desktops and laptops). This can only be proven by means of a real usage study that assigns billions of individual digital uses (called 'views' or 'impressions') to the individual offerings, measuring it down to the second. I published this study in 2020 together with Timo Thomsen as the *Atlas of the Digital World*. The extent of the measured digital monopoly formation was hair-raising—but once again, nothing happened. Politicians and the media have largely ignored the clear findings of this study.

"Atlas of the Digital World" (2020)

- A condensed version was published in English in the research journal *Social Sciences* for international regulators and experts.

Social Sciences Paper (4/2025)

- As the danger of digital monopolies continued to be a non-issue in the public eye, fears arose that all these scientific efforts might have been for nothing. This was the starting point for a new book, which was published in 2023 under the title *Big Tech Must Go!* The text also contained detailed solutions (which, however, have not yet been taken up). At least, I managed to reach a wider audience with this book, which was of course also driven by the dramatic escalation of the situation in recent months. The book resonated at more than a hundred events, was also published in English at Chicago University Press, triggered a debate and was awarded the Günter Wallraff Special Prize for Freedom of the Press and Human Rights in May 2024.

"Big Tech Must Go!" (2023)

- Together with legal scholar Prof. Nikolaus Peifer, the proposed solutions from *Big Tech Must Go!* were further expanded and elaborated in December 2023 and supplemented with a detailed plan of action, in which even the specific responsibilities (federal government, federal states, EU) were set out in detail—again without success.

- Back in July 2024, when Kamala Harris was leading the US election campaign, I announced at great length in a leading German news outlet that we would be in huge trouble if Trump won the election, and that a coalition of political power and the tech companies was appearing on the horizon.

- In 2024, the German Interstate Media Treaty was under revision, which provided the perfect opportunity for action. Together with Prof. Peifer, a concrete regulation proposal was published in August 2024. Once again, politicians ignored these proposals. In hindsight, it is tragic that this 'last chance' was also wasted. After all, we could have implemented these measures *before* the new Trump administration took office in the USA.

- In February 2025, the 'Save Social' petition was launched in collaboration with many other initial signatories. This petition has since attracted more than 250,000 signatories in Germany and was presented to German political parties in March 2025.[16]

For me, this whole story is also evidence of how far the destruction of our public sphere has already progressed. Remember the funny movie *Don't look up*? In vain, scientists warn of an asteroid impact. In our case: Comprehensive scientific empirical evidence that digital monopolies represented an unconstitutional concentration of opinion power was published in September 2020 at the latest. Nothing happened for five MORE years (!!!!!).

During this time, I tried everything I could think of as a scientist to come up with simple, popular, catchy ways of presenting and expressing myself so that the general public would wake up before it was too late. I have spoken at hundreds of events — at expert panels, with all democratic parties, with media regulation authorities, at schools, at universities, with NGOs, in the digital economy, with tech investors, at start-up conferences, in trade discussions, at all levels from the EU to the federal government to the federal States and State parliaments. I started this journey as a scientist, but then kept trying out new, ever more striking methods to present the issue and to illustrate how great the threat to our democracy and our free world really is.

A battle cry for democracy

This book is now my 'last call', so to speak. The many people who have followed my activities in recent years will have noticed one thing immediately. In 2023, the subtitle of my book *Big Tech must go!* was still positive: *We Will Stop Them!* Of course, the situation was already desolate in 2023, and during those days, I certainly wanted to encourage myself a little against the gigantic superiority of Dark Tech.

However, the extreme dynamics of the last few months have changed everything. And one thing is also clear: this threat will by no means disappear by itself. On the contrary. The anti-democratic warlords are on the verge of achieving their goals. They are finishing the job this very moment. It does not look as if they can still be stopped. Why should they voluntarily stop given how close they are to the finishing line?? Sure, in the face of crisis, at least we now have a debate. But we are still tackling this issue far too slowly. We are losing the media war on all frontlines.

Because that is exactly what is happening right now. In a few years, our democracy could be lost. Are we still able to turn the tide? I assume that, even with maximum determination on our end, the chances are now less than ten percent. Sure, that is depressing. But we have to face the facts now, otherwise we have no chance at all. The drama of current political events has also shaped the provocative style of this book. The text does not merely seek to present the battle for media dominance in abstract terms, but to portray it so vividly that readers can feel it in their own flesh as they read. This book is certainly not for the faint-hearted.

Extraordinary circumstances call for extraordinary measures. If we continue to muddle along as dishonourably as we have done in recent decades, we might as well give up and surrender. It is truly time that we take it seriously — the media war. And it is time that we stop philosophizing and finally, FINALLY!!! take action. We have to start really fighting. Otherwise, it will soon be too late.

 Additional information, including various research projects, and in-depth studies, as well as updates on this book can be found at www.media-war.com

1.
THE COMBAT ZONE

Game over, democracy?

We experience 'media war' every day online. Superficially, terms like shitstorms, hate speech, rants, gaslighting, trolling or doxxing spring to mind. But, on another level, the 'media war' phenomenon emerged many years ago, when digital media began to attract more and more attention and overshadowed the 'old media', i.e. newspapers, television and radio. Since the noughties, we have witnessed the meteoric rise of a handful of monopolistic US digital platforms and the decline of analogue media.

However, the well-known side effects of polarisation, fake news and disinformation are causing massive collateral damage in Western democracies[1] — the media war has increasingly developed into a war for truth, legitimacy and media freedom, which is infecting more and more of the Western world, starting in the USA.

A political outsider has taken full advantage of this dynamic. Donald Trump was surprisingly elected President of the USA in 2016 due to his aggressive use of Twitter, particularly through the systematic spread of lies and ever new, spectacular false claims: "I think that maybe I wouldn't be here if it wasn't for Twitter," he said when he became President.[2] Twitter versus 'mainstream media': the destruction of truth began its journey, the post-truth era began.[3]

Immediately after taking office, he took the media war to the next level by insulting the established editorial media, calling it 'fake news'. In a meme video, he is shown knocking CNN, as embodied by a person, to the ground. Since then, the belief in supposedly 'left-wing mainstream media', 'State-censored editorial offices' or 'lying press' has spread among supporters of digital platforms in the Western world, with increasingly aggressive hostility towards journalists and editorial offices, who are sometimes insulted and treated like criminals.

After his election defeat in 2020, Trump spread the 'stolen election' lie online and incited his supporters to march to Congress to prevent the orderly handover of power to the new government. A little later, his followers actually stormed the Capitol. The attempted coup in turn made the owners of the digital platforms uneasy — they blocked Trump's social media profiles. Although Trump, who was still President of the USA at the time, was fuming with rage, he had no choice but to yield to the power of Big Tech and its platforms as regards his social media profiles.

But it generated a response. Trump, who had been banned from the platforms, prepared his political comeback, launching his own platform, 'Truth Social'. It has particularly permeable outlink structures, allowing him and his supporters to easily distribute content to the leading platforms, thus immunising him from the superiority of the tech companies. In the future, no one will be able to digitally 'silence' him.

At this point, the big tech billionaire Elon Musk arrived on the scene. In early 2022, he declared himself to be a "free speech absolutist", rejected any form of content moderation as 'censorship', bought the Twitter platform on the spur of the moment and largely eliminated content curation structures in the company.[4]

Musk increasingly took Trump's side, officially recommending him and interviewing him on X. At the same time, he increasingly took sides with other right-wing extremist groups and parties on the platform. He even actively campaigned for the German AfD. He rejects protests from advertising companies ("Go fuck yourself!") and later sues them in antitrust proceedings — allegedly he is only concerned with 'freedom of speech'. His view: the allegedly "left-wing" (?) advertising companies need to be prevented from influencing the content of the platform.[5]

Media war: We initially recognised that it was spreading ever wider, encompassing not only the media, but also the economy, politics and the law. The front lines originated in the USA but have long since been successfully imported to Europe, especially by right-wing populist groups such as the AfD in Germany, right up to Pegida, the 'coronavirus deniers' and a 'storming of the Capitol light', i.e. an attack on the German parliament building in Berlin.[6] And this war is being waged about many important things — about our democracy, about legitimacy and truth, about freedom, and above all about power, might and rule.

The digital media revolution

When 'cool digital evangelists' or the 'heroes of the tech industry' have spoken about the digital revolution in recent decades, they have repeatedly claimed that the change we are experiencing today is very similar to the media revolution set in motion by the invention of the printing press in the past. The printing press effectively did away with the supremacy of the Pope and then put an end to absolutism during the French Revolution.[7]

From the perspective of media history, it is at least true that such power struggles for media dominance are to be expected when old leading media are replaced by new ones. However, one aspect is worrying. From the broad perspective of media history, we can assume that, in the case of digital transformation, resistance would be just as pointless from a long-term perspective as the resistance of the old church elites against the printing press or the resistance of the French ancien régime against freedom of the press. Looking to the future, we can safely assume that the era of analogue media is drawing to a close. The media order of the future will undoubtedly be digital. Newspapers, television and radio will continue to melt away. Digital media will 'rule'. In fact, they already are the leading media. Studies indicate that, since the Covid pandemic, more of the general public's attention has been spent on digital media than on all analogue media combined.[8] By 2029, the share of analogue media will fall to less than a quarter in Europe.[9] It's important to note that no outcry in the form of criticism of digital culture, no efforts at 'regulation', no vows of commitment to analogue 'quality media' can stop or reverse this development.[10]

In the current media war, the predominance of digital media will prevail (and to be clear, in this aspect, this war has long since been decided). We would also have to assume that this transformation should massively reinforce and expand the increase in media freedom by comparison with the last few centuries. From a media history perspective, the question arises: What is the new, hopefully better, digital order that this will create for us all? Is it really possible to identify a digital equivalent to the Reformation of the 16th century or the democratic revolutions of the 18th century, as Dark Tech companies' and digital evangelists have always claimed?

And above all, who would then be the digital Martin Luther, the digital Franklin, Rousseau or Diderot? Do these digital figures already exist and should we already recognise them out there on the horizon of this new, improved digital media order? Are they 'freedom fighters' who are campaigning for this new order and using the manifold possibilities of the new, digital media for a new, better world? And are many millions of users, followers and supporters rallying to their cause?

Of course they exist — and now it's getting scary. Here's their rough narrative.

After all, it is precisely the 'heroes' (as they see and portray themselves) in this 'media war', such as Trump, Musk, Tommy Robinson or Alex Jones, Zuckerberg and many more, who are the leading digital 'freedom fighters' of our time. They are all united by the fact that they have been 'courageously' fighting for freedom on the internet for years, for 'freedom of speech' without limits. They have all 'heroically' rebelled against the old, depraved elites who also ruled the old, equally depraved media regime.

While, in their view, the old analogue media regime had been built on a 'State-censored press system' and a broadcasting controlled by the government, the 'digital liberation' has eliminated this 'systematic oppression' of the people by creating new, interactive platforms that have given the patronised and conditioned masses a 'voice' and the possibility of real participation for the first time.

According to their narrative, the 'digital liberation' has also revealed that the social order of the old media regime had never been really democratic at all. It had only been a 'sham democracy'. The subdued masses had 'in reality' been remote-controlled by a conspiratorial collaboration between the censored media and the State power itself.

That's why the new, digital freedom fighters also see themselves as entitled to abolish our sham democracy, which in reality has only ever been a 'disguised tyranny'. In this new digital world, we will be truly free for the first time — and this freedom will be secured by these freedom fighters from Trump to Tech and their international partners.*

You might well quickly start to question this narrative, because you hopefully find Trump, Musk, Zuckerberg and the populists pretty obnoxious. Don't worry, I agree. However, the description above can serve as a condensed summary of the new, digital media order, which was designed to 'liberate' us right from when it began. At least, that had originally been the plan. The early and well-meaning pioneers of the digital revolution had always a liberation in mind — Tim Berners Lee, the inventor of the World Wide Web, as well as Steward Brand or John Perry Barlow. They all fought for a better, free digital world.

At the same time, the above passage in italics serves to illustrate the central dilemma in the current media war. Let's assume that reading the last few paragraphs makes you as sick as it made me — then the obvious question is: how do you intend to put a stop to Trump, Tech & co.?

---

*Author's note: In the course of this book, I will playfully adopt opposing positions from time to time in order to be able to work out the battle lines in the war of the media more strikingly; such passages are formatted in italics in the text.

Do you want to 'regulate' the free internet? Do you want to take freedom of speech away from the people? Don't you think the people on the platforms are mature enough to form their own opinions? What right do you have to presume that they do not? Are you yourself part of the corrupt establishment? Do you — like the Nazis or the communist Stasi in the past — simply want to ban unwelcome statements by decree? And preferably throw people who say unwanted things into jail?

"Uh no," your answer will probably be, "I don't want any of that."

Good. It's also better that way.

Because the aforementioned digital freedom fighters would also take offence if you wanted to say something as bad as that. They would immediately interpret your statement as solid proof that our democracy is *in fact* no longer a democracy at all and that you too are only a democrat in disguise, who is no better than any of those autocrats, dictators and oppressors we have in the world out there.

By now, you should certainly be feeling a little uncomfortable at the very least.

Because you are now experiencing, first-hand, the trap we are all in.

And you will quickly notice that we can neither move forwards nor backwards. Let's play through this on a trial-and-error basis.

Scenario 1, i.e., we go back in time:

I can't get over it — do you want to go backwards in time, back to the world of the snoozers, the old people, the outdated? Do you want to stop progress? Do you seriously want to tell people out there to read 'a good book'? Face it: The analogue world is long gone. Do you really want to side with the losers and the outdated establishment? Do you want to abolish the free web again like the old-fashioned, backward bureaucrats of the EU? Do you seriously think you would be able take back the freedom and digital rights which have just been granted to people? And what would be your alternative? Should the State then support 'boring newspapers' with taxpayers' money? Do you want to go out there and confiscate people's smartphones? Or what exactly did you have in mind?

So a return to the analogue world would be difficult.

Let's take a look at scenario 2, 'going forwards' — this is the rhetoric from the 'digital liberators':

Great, now you've finally got it! Welcome to the digital world of the young, the cool, the opinion leaders, the start-ups, the streamers, YouTubers, influencers, nerds, hackers, geeks and multipliers. Resistance is futile. Technological progress has never been stopped before anyway. Here, in the digital world, you have arrived where the future is. We, the 'digital enthusiasts', are the winners in this battle. It's also better for you to join our cool troll gang, because we'll blow up the old elites anyway, their time is up anyway: BOOOM!!! We will no longer let journalists and editorial offices dictate the mindset we have to live by. We'll get the real truth from the platforms anyway.

Never again will we allow 'corrupt health officials', for example, to take away our basic rights as they did recently during the pandemic. We are much better equipped to decide for ourselves than the lying press, the arrogant experts and these so-called 'scientists'. And by the way: we will launch racist attacks against whoever we want. Nobody will stop us. For example, if the politicians don't deport the immigrants themselves, we'll simply take our fate into our own hands. We'll organise some nice riots via the platforms and torch the refugee homes as it suits us. If the legacy elites falsify our elections, we'll simply storm parliament. And if anyone dares to get in our way: we'll just shoot them down. BANG!!! Because WE ARE THE PEOPLE! Hey, just kidding, aren't you allowed to make a joke once in a while? Don't panic. Goodness, you're not allowed to say anything anymore. It's all censored here, just like China.

Oh, so you don't want that either?

So you'd rather go back? To the old world? Read newspapers? Do you want to censor the web? Patronise people? Deny them their right to judge for themselves? Treat them like kids who can't decide for themselves? Abolish freedom of expression? Or what?

We understand why we're trapped, why we can neither move forwards nor backwards. Yes, we know that our future is digital. But we recognise that neither of these two paths is an option for a peaceful, democratic future. In the course of the book, we will start to understand the alternative options that we could develop, if we really wanted to.

We will also recognise which aspects of the media war have not been decided yet. And we will start to grasp that the dark forces of digitalisation are driving us and taking control of us. In a cynical way, they are turning us into hostages in the name of freedom of expression and democracy. They are instrumentalising us for their anti-democratic works of destruction.

Dark Tech and the populists are setting the rules of discourse

Of course, the above description is simplistic in order to describe the battle zone in which we find ourselves and to illustrate the forces that are currently shaping the media war. Here, we can only gain an initial orientation about what is happening, simply because it is in the nature of things that the confusing situation completely overwhelms us.

It is important to note that we are witnessing the emergence of an international, political mass movement which is complementing the digital media revolution. This movement is presenting itself as part of the myth of alleged 'liberation', which is taking place today in much the same way as the Reformation or the French Revolution did in earlier times. It has an effective, identity-creating myth, an ideologically founded 'grand narrative' (▶3/6). We have noticed the tremendous appeal of this 'grand narrative' both in the US election campaign as well as in Germany and other European countries. We have seen in the USA that the Democrats have barely been able to set out their own political agenda. In terms of their political programme, they now represent a purely anti-Trump party, virtually devoid of their own, positive agenda. Currently, they seem to be mentally paralysed. We experienced almost exactly the same dynamic in the

German election campaign: the symbiosis of the AfD and Elon Musk in particular dominated media headlines and political agenda-setting. By contrast, the 'established parties' were barely able to set their own political priorities in their programmes. This vacuum, in terms of a political programme, from the moderate conservative parties in Germany (CDU / FDP) led to a succession of panicky, knee-jerk reactions from them, as they copied libertarian, nationalistic and Trumpist positions instead of developing an innovative and convincing political agenda of their own (I will come back to this).[11]

Thus, the roles played by the main actors in this battle are clear. The protagonists of this movement, i.e. Dark Tech, Trump & co. are currently running the show as innovators in terms of their political programme. They are the originators of this 'grand narrative', they set the agenda and they have also been successful in defining the new rules for future communication. They are also the protagonists replacing the 'old' discourse of enlightened democracy with a new ideology that is largely derived from the digital dogmas of the platforms (▶3). In the battle for supremacy of the different media channels and platforms, Dark Tech, Trump, but also the populists attached to these movements, are the attackers. They are laying siege to the 'old' paradigm, firing ever new salvos from ever new perspectives against our old media order and our democracy, riding roughshod over anything that stands in their way. Those under attack don't yet really understand what's happening, are looking for guidance, are overwhelmed and are tending to take too long to react. And some of them may still be naïve enough to think that this attack will disappear by itself at some point.

At the same time, the attackers are successfully implementing this new narrative. Wherever they appear, they promise 'freedom' to the stunned listeners. The attackers thus appear disguised as 'revolutionaries' announcing a new and better world. They therefore define the role being played by the parties that are under attack. As they are being attacked, they have to defend themselves, so they *inevitably* appear *reactive*. But by defending themselves, they are *inevitably* on the side of the 'old', outdated media and knowledge order. And thus, they appear by default as forces that *oppose freedom* and *the future* alike.

A dispute between former EU Commissioner Thierry Breton and Elon Musk is a good example of this. For years, Breton had perfectly embodied the role of an old, arrogant, European aristocrat in such disputes, conveying his 'quasi-police decrees' to the platforms through officially typed letters (from a Dark Tech perspective: letters???? LOL!!!). And Musk? He responded digitally, provocatively, via a meme: FUCK YOUR OWN FACE!

We immediately recognise the whole symbolic 'catch 22' nature of the situation. Due to the preconfigured division of roles, a 'commissioner' like Breton *inevitably* appears as a backward opponent of freedom, as someone who has been fast asleep during the last ten to twenty years and has not yet arrived in the digital world. By contrast, Musk's meme in combination with 'Fuck your own face' orchestrates (and proves!) the digital freedom that these supposedly casual 'troll revolutionaries' simply take for themselves. This digital order of battle alone inevitably leads to Breton appearing as an *opponent of digital freedom*, which immediately makes him *suspicious* — and vulnerable in the truest sense of the word. After all, why would anyone seriously be *against freedom*? It can only be someone who is up to no good.

The rest of this constantly retold Dark Tech conspiracy theory is well known. To rephrase the Dark Tech narrative: *In the old days, a cartel of ruling parties and State-controlled editorial offices (the leftwing, corrupt legacy press) held power over the blind sheep and normies (average Joes from the public) out there through terror of opinion and State propaganda. Luckily, those days are over. Thanks to great digital platforms, we, the people, are finally being liberated from the tyranny of democracy. The State and the complicit legacy media can no longer withhold the truth from the people. Thanks to the platforms, we the people have access to any type of information, turning us into enlightened 'independent thinkers'. Finally, we can see through all the rotten lies of the system, as now we can form our own opinions based on uncensored information. And it is only thanks to the same great platforms that we are finally allowed to express our own uncensored opinions for the first time. The State elites and censors are powerless and can't do anything about it.* YOU ARE THE MEDIA NOW was Elon Musk's victory message. He has used the phrase repeatedly since Trump's victory, like a slogan. Again, in their narrative: *A new, libertarian age is finally dawning — for truly 'liberated' people.*

Right now, millions of people believe in this conspiracy theory. And also in Germany, it isn't just voters of right wing parties such as AfD who believe in it. A survey of 1,512 people conducted in Germany in April and May 2024 illustrates this. In the sample, 40 % of those polled agreed with the statement: "Our country is now more like a dictatorship than a democracy." Among AfD voters, that figure is already 81 %. And 51 % of respondents agreed with this statement (91 % of AfD voters): "The population is systematically lied to by the media and politicians".[12]

More and more people spread these kinds of messages via social networks. Anyone who dares to express doubts about the fairy tale of 'suppression of free speech' and these supposedly 'uncensored' platforms is hounded with relentless severity. And the intensity of digital disputes concerning alleged 'censorship' and constraints on 'free speech' shows how radically indoctrinated these supposed 'independent thinkers' have become.

We cannot underestimate the massive significance of these and similar disputes, as they show that Dark Tech, Trump and the populists have not only succeeded in creating a new 'grand narrative' but that they have also created a new form of discourse on the platforms *through which they can define the rules.* They have created and occupied a new ideology of (supposedly!) 'free' discourse, which is so cleverly constructed that it constantly creates new 'LOSE-LOSE' situations for their opponents. The attackers appear to be do-gooders who give people new 'freedoms'. The attacked actors, on the other hand, appear as if they want to take something very desirable and precious away from the people. In the linguistic prejudice of digital ideology, they are referred to as the 'establishment'. The combat term *legacy* describes them in a very similar way as 'heirs'. It pejoratively labels the opponents as actors who have obtained their elite sinecures not through ('digital') merit and effort, but through tradition and privileges.

The attackers have also been able to create another very cleverly constructed 'LOSE-LOSE' situation for their opponents in the way that they launched their assault on the digital battlefields of the platforms. The attacked parties have two options: If they do nothing, they will go down without a fight (and in fact there is no realistic scenario of 'going back', for example to the analogue media order). But if they defend themselves, they will appear as deniers, as backward opponents of freedom. And in this role, they will also inevitably lose.

Thus, we are constantly trapped (we all realise this, often without understanding exactly what is happening). If we were smart and had a quick look at the list of the richest people in the world, however, we would quickly become very suspicious. Apart from Bernard Arnault and Warren Buffett, all of them are tech oligarchs. Never before in human history have single individuals managed to amass more power, wealth and dominance than these 'tech bros' (our chart shows the status quo on the day after the US election). And, facing the world's gaze, the heads of the big tech companies have joined forces with the current antidemocratic US government. The pharaohs and sun kings of yesteryear are minuscule compared to this accumulation of power. Do we really believe that all of these people are planning to 'liberate' us?

It would be wise to also reject the fairy tale of 'liberation' that we are constantly being told. For example, in the year 1996, the internet was still being used by only 36 million people worldwide[14] (!). Common usage only established itself in western democracies after the turn of the century — at a time when democracy had reached its global historic zenith (see illustration). Again, we should

● Tech oligarchs				● others	
1	**Elon Musk**	US	US$ 290.0 Bn	+10.1%	↑
2	**Jeff Bezos**	US	US$ 228.3 Bn	+3.2%	↑
3	**Mark Zuckerberg**	US	US$ 202.5 Bn	±0%	–
4	**Larry Ellison**	US	US$ 193.5 Bn	+5.4%	↑
5	Bernard Arnault	FRA	US$ 173.2 Bn	-1.6%	↓
6	**Bill Gates**	US	US$ 159.5 Bn	+1.2%	↑
7	**Larry Page**	US	US$ 158.3 Bn	+3.6%	↑
8	**Sergey Brin**	US	US$ 149.1 Bn	+3.6%	↑
9	Warren Buffett	US	US$ 147.8 Bn	+5.4%	↑
10	**Steve Ballmer**	US	US$ 145.9 Bn	+2.0%	↑

Figure 2: The richest people in the world (Bloomberg Billionaires Index, 7.11.2024)[13]

be suspicious: What is it exactly that the tech companies wanted to 'liberate' us from? By contrast, since the full penetration of digital platforms (Web 2.0) after the year 2010, we have been experiencing a massive global *decline* in democracy.[15]

In any case, we can reject one claim made by libertarians of Dark Tech corporations and net activists alike: No, the lived reality of Western democracies before the digital transformation bore *no* resemblance *whatsoever* to the era of the inquisitorial papacy, feudalism, monarchy or absolutism. In fact, the whole comparison made by the digital evangelists is nonsensical: if they (rightly) praise the media revolution of the printing press as democratising — why in God's name should we be 'liberated' from this wonderful, democratising media order by the platforms? We were already free.

And fortunately, alternative digital media systems are also conceivable. Of course, there are possible scenarios in which we could take the initiative again and swap roles. We could get back on the offensive and then the enemies of our democratic order would be the ones having to defend themselves. That's exactly what will be discussed in the following chapters. Of course, we would have to

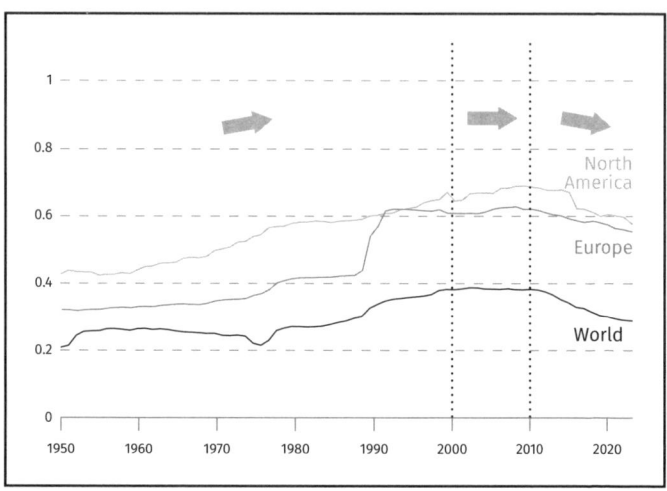

Figure 3: The development of democracy over time (data: V-Dem Liberal Democracy Index)[16]

manage to fight forward again, right on into the digital future. But we can only move forward if we understand the extent to which the supposed 'liberation' of Dark Tech, Trump & co. is actually leading to the systematic *destruction* of media freedom. And we ourselves would have to offer an alternative, better vision of *genuine digital liberation* that points into the future. Unfortunately, we have largely left the field to the anti-democrats and Dark Tech without a fight.

Dark Tech controls the digital public sphere

As we have seen above, Dark Tech and the populists are telling a compelling fairytale about 'liberation', in addition defining the new rules of digital discourse. But the most important thing is: Under digital conditions, the tech giants are also almost completely in control of the political public sphere.

Most of my research time has been spent on the scientific description and measurement of these digital monopolies — the hair-raising results of our measurements have made waves both in Germany and abroad. Our extensive scientific measurements are fully published in the *Atlas of the Digital World.*

A summary of the findings plus the political interpretation was released in the book *Big Tech must go!*

Here are just a few key facts to help you understand the extent of the digital occupation of our public sphere:

- All digital media genres relevant to democracy are occupied by monopolies and quasi-monopolies, such as search engines (Google, 88 %), free video-on-demand (YouTube, 78 %) and social media (Instagram and Facebook, both operated by Meta, together account for an 85 % share of usage time; data according to the *Atlas of the Digital World*).
- Because we measured the distribution of all traffic on the German internet, we were also able to mathematically quantify the extent of the unequal distribution. This is measured by the Gini coefficient, which most people are familiar with from economic analyses of wealth distribution, for example. The Gini coefficient is always positioned between 0 and 1. If we imagine, for example, a country in which everyone had exactly the same amount of wealth, then the distribution of wealth would have a Gini coefficient of 0, indicating an equal distribution. By contrast, let us imagine a country in which the mathematically most unequal distribution conceivable prevails. In concrete terms, this would mean that one single person owns the entire wealth of the country and everyone else owns nothing. In this situation, the Gini coefficient would be 1. As we had performed our holistic baseline measurement of the digital traffic in Germany, we were able to calculate the Gini coefficient for the distribution of traffic on the German internet. Our measurements yielded the shocking value of 0.988.

In Western societies, when we talk about Dark Tech companies and the threat they pose to the public sphere, the debates almost always focus on hate speech, fake news, data surveillance and the like. We hardly ever focus on the problem of digital monopolies. But I would consider this aspect to be the most important one. The deliberate establishment of these monopolies is the major way in which the digital platforms are mounting their attack on our democracy. The narrative that the platforms supposedly give us 'access' to free speech and thus liberate us from the 'tyranny of democracy' ultimately serves as a justification for a libertarian coup that is increasingly undermining the foundations of the democratic state itself—through the occupation of the public sphere.

Sounds exaggerated? The best way to illustrate the problem is to briefly reflect on the origins of the democratic public sphere. The public sphere emerged in ancient democracies as a free space, typically inside the city. In ancient Greece, this was the *agora*, the meeting place in the centre of Athens. In ancient Rome, the venue was called the *forum*. It was a space that, interestingly enough, was both a market for opinions and a market for goods (the *marketplace*). First of all, we see a *public exchange* taking place at this venue. Moreover, the specific venue itself was never *owned* by a single party. Thus, the public square was always run by the *public authorities*. The forum is therefore also public insofar as it was owned and controlled by the public itself.[17]

Thus, the democratic community regulates and protects this public space in its own interests. We the citizens are allowed to determine the foundations of our own democracy, which is thus organised in the public interest. And even if this self-determination and the various checks and balances have become much more sophisticated over time than they were in ancient times—the *principle* of democratic self-regulation of this forum was always a cornerstone of our democracy until the day the platforms gained power over the digital sphere.

When someone like Elon Musk calls the platform X 'The World's Townsquare' (it's their advertising slogan), we immediately recognise a clear attempt to take over the public sphere. Let's paint a picture of what exactly the slogan means. We need to imagine the *agora* in the centre of Athens, the forum in which ancient Greek democracy held its meetings, discussions and votes in order to deliberate together, above all *in the interests of the community*. Like any democracy, this forum was always at risk of abuse. Imagine if an Athenian named MEGA-ELON had simply *bought* the *agora*, i.e. simply occupied and took possession of this public space. He would say something like this: "I *free* you from the oppression of democracy. From now on, I will rule over this square, the *agora*, which incidentally also now *belongs to* me because I have bought it." Is there anyone who thinks that this is liberation? To me, it smells of something that the ancient Greeks already called out by the same name we use today: *TYRANNIS*.

This is precisely why it is so important to fully understand and quantify the scale of digital monopolies. With monopolies and oligopolies dictating the conditions of the digital public sphere, we no longer have truly free media (we will come back to this in detail later on). And some tech oligarchs even openly admit that they intend to dominate the conventional democratic public sphere in the course of this hostile takeover, as they want the hated *legacy media* to disappear.

They can only do this by 'liberating' the people, sending the supposedly 'elitist gatekeepers' (editorial offices and journalists) packing and making the users of the platforms believe that they are now 'promoted', so to speak, and that they themselves have now taken the position of these media. That may feel good at first. But there is clearly a Faustian pact behind it because now *the forum no longer belongs to the democratic community*. The citizens are no longer able to set up the framework of their own democratic discourse themselves — for instance to define the rules by which the individual parties are allowed to speak to each other. Thus, they have lost their control over the public forum. The tech company who owns the platform can decide on these rules in the same way that any supermarket owner can deliberately set the rules for his supermarket. The democratic community no longer has any legitimising power here because this specific democratic forum *now belongs to Elon Musk*. Basically, he can do what he wants with it. And perhaps he has also named it 'X' as a message to us: I (Elon Musk) am simply 'crossing out' the democratic public sphere with two strokes of the pen — and occupying it with my own platform.

You can see why this works like a coup — which was certainly not carried out by force, but 'only' accomplished via network effects and economic power. But it is nevertheless just as effective as a real coup because, as a result of it, *the Dark Tech companies own our digital public sphere and thus control our democracy in future.*

It is important to note that we did not notice this dismantling of the democratically legitimised public sphere in the past because we were so enthusiastic about the alleged 'freedom of the internet' and the new 'access' we had. This is why, in internet activist debates, we not only tolerated this liberation but absurdly even actively demanded it ourselves. David Golumbia summarises this claim, which has been made again and again by digital evangelists and cyberlibertarians, as follows: "Governments do not have the power to manage public spaces." However, this only makes sense under the questionable premise that democratic governments are considered as being 'evil' and the platforms as being 'good'. Golumbia rightly notes, however, that shaping the public sphere has always been "one of the core functions of democratic governance" and poses the logically compelling question: "Are purportedly public forums like X and Facebook even legal to begin with?"[18]

In the old media system, despite all its limitations and imperfections, the citizens were always able get access to information and political discourse through arrangements and structures by which they themselves were able to shape and control our democratic state, its processes, debates, its media and institutions. But, in the brave new world, the citizens will only get access to the political discourse via monopolistic and oligopolistic Dark Tech corporations. And even worse, these tech corporations have now also entered into a symbiotic relationship with the anti-democratic Trump administration.

We now understand why Tech, Trump & co. not only define the new rules of discourse but also control the digital channels themselves and why both forms of domination are mutually reinforcing. Dark Tech and the Trumpists are holding a beautiful pink fluffy bunny in front of our noses like magicians so that we don't understand what's actually happening. The pink fluffy bunny is supposed to be 'freedom of speech' and 'uncensored discourse' (▶ 8). It is a diversionary tactic designed to prevent us from understanding the Faustian pact we are entering into with Dark Tech.

The tech oligarchs 'give' us 'freedom of expression' as a sham 'gift' and we take the bait and enter the colourful, dazzling, seductive cyber worlds of their digital monopoly platforms. The problem is that the network effects kick in immediately. This means that the more people use a platform, the more other people start using it, simply because everyone else is already there. The platform becomes a media standard — like Facebook or Instagram for social media or Google for search engines. This in turn means that it is hard for people to get out of the platforms once the monopolies and oligopolies have established themselves. The effect is called 'lock-in': People are locked into the platforms as if they were in a prison.

And this is precisely the diabolical trap: if you fall for the bait ('freedom of expression') and are 'trapped' in a platform, in a worst-case scenario you will never get out again. Many people know the phrase: "If a product costs you nothing, you are the product". If we study it, we can see that this saying *trivialises* the game that is being played here. The Faustian pact is not primarily about the use of data or economic exploitation processes by the platforms (where people usually answer: "I don't care so much who uses my data, I have nothing to hide"). The Faustian bargain is about much more, because the monopolies enable Big Tech to digitally 'capture' their users. Anyone who falls into this trap may then be condemned to a lifetime of bondage because they might be locked into the platform forever.[19] Not only will they be exploited economically for years and decades via advertising, but they will also be controlled by the tech companies. This is the case as the Dark Tech rulers have full control over the digital machine room: they use algorithms, filters and other means of manipulation to determine which specific content is presented to each individual person over years and decades.

We are the victims of a huge game of deception in which we are 'liberated' by the 'tech bros', only to be locked up and controlled forever. And we currently can't even conceive of any utopian vision of how we can shape a new, better digital world in a different way, so that our democracy would not be annihilated. But that is all up to us. We can give up now and leave the field to the anti-democrats. Or we can fight.

2.
THE WARLORDS

Alliance against democracy

This alliance came together at dizzying speed: first Trump and Musk joined forces at the second Butler Rally (5 October 2024). Then, on the day of Trump's inauguration as US President, the complete subjugation of the tech elite was presented to the world, since they were clearly placed in front of the elected representatives of the people, Trump's cabinet, on 20 January 2025.[1] Beyond Musk's outreach to right-wing populists in the UK and other European countries, he openly campaigned for the AfD during the weeks before the parliamentary elections in Germany. Among other things, he interviewed the party leader, Alice Weidel, on 9 January 2025. Furthermore, it has long been known that Trump has a particularly close relationship with Putin. In October 2024, it was reported that Musk is also in regular contact with Putin.[2]

When I warned, in detail, about the impending symbiosis of Dark Tech and right-wing populism in the German press back in July 2024 (*Süddeutsche Zeitung*), my argument was dismissed on social media channels as baseless conspiracy mongering. However, the real dynamics exceeded my predictions in a quite scary manner in the subsequent months. Still, also from today's perspective, we have to acknowledge that each individual player is not only part of this alliance, but is also always pursuing its own agenda. On top of that, these players will obscure the true nature of this symbiosis and cooperation for obvious reasons.

Nevertheless, it is important that we answer the central question here: Who are the key players in the 'media war'? And above all: what are their goals and ideas? It is a complex coalition of many actors who are essentially pursuing largely similar goals (above all the replacement of democracy with libertarian-authoritarian structures). The following argument is therefore an idealised extrapolation, which by its very nature can only be speculative. It is certainly an alliance that will remain in constant flux in the future. But we need to understand: Who are the most powerful actors in this situation? And what is the system of thinking behind their actions?

First of all, there are the Dark Tech corporations and the oligarchs who own these huge empires — Elon Musk, Meta (= Instagram and Facebook), Alphabet (= Google, YouTube and so on), Apple, Amazon, Microsoft. Elon Musk had already become part of the Trump administration, working as an advisor. Additionally, the Big Tech companies have become part of team Trump during the weeks following the US elections. At the same time, this coalition of Trump and tech is supporting the right-wing populist parties in Europe. And, finally, Vladimir Putin is also part of this coalition of tech and populism. For his part, Putin uses the tech platforms as digital multipliers for his cyber propaganda. And the populist parties in Europe in turn support Putin's agenda on a broad front.

As already mentioned, it is a 'war *for* the media' on the one hand, in which the Dark Tech platforms are trying to knock the 'established media' out of the field in order to take over, monopolise and control the digital media and thus the public sphere. And it is a 'war *in* the media' in which populist parties are trying to defeat the 'established parties'. For this purpose, they primarily make use of the tech platforms, which either actively help them (such as Musk supporting the AfD, for example) or at least provide 'algorithmic tailwind' for their populist discourse (▶ 6). Both dimensions support and reinforce each other.

The first and most obvious question is, of course, which players are driving this development? Who is 'in charge' here and who is just a free-rider? If we take a superficial look at the situation, Donald Trump initially appears to be the leading figure who is abolishing American democracy step by step. This perception corresponds to our conventional thinking. Based on past experiences, we still operate on the mental presumption that asserts the primacy of politics. Historically, democracies have typically been destroyed by *political* forces, such as the Weimar Republic by Hitler and the National Socialists. Yet we know that *history does not repeat itself, but it rhymes*. This book assumes that, right now, an unprecedented, global change is underway that lies outside our conventional mental templates and patterns of thinking — and that is precisely why it is so difficult for us to grasp.

With Dark Tech, a new type of player has appeared on the world stage. In what is a brand new phenomenon, it is bundling economic power together with media power. And it is now also extending this accumulation of power to the political sphere. We can grasp the extent of this dominance by looking at the global top 100 platforms by market capitalisation. In January 2025, US companies accounted for 85.8 % of the global market share, with Europe lagging far behind at just 2.2 % (China still accounted for 11 % and Africa for 1 %).[3]

Thus, the core problem of Dark Tech's accumulation of power is that their business models combine economic power (like the Rockefellers from earlier monopolistic times) and *opinion power*. Thus, it should be obvious, even to very naïve people, that an unprecedented shift in the balance of power is currently taking place and that the old descriptive categories no longer fit.

This could also be supported by the argument that, strictly speaking, we can no longer really attribute Trump to the sphere of politics. Trump is a strange hybrid when it comes to the new order. As a manager and entrepreneur, he emerged from the sphere of business and not politics. Even before his first presidency, he was one of the most well-known media figures in the USA, and one of the most innovative in that he recognised the power of social networks at a very early stage. He quickly found out how to use them to his advantage, especially Twitter. Similarly, when Trump became active in politics, he

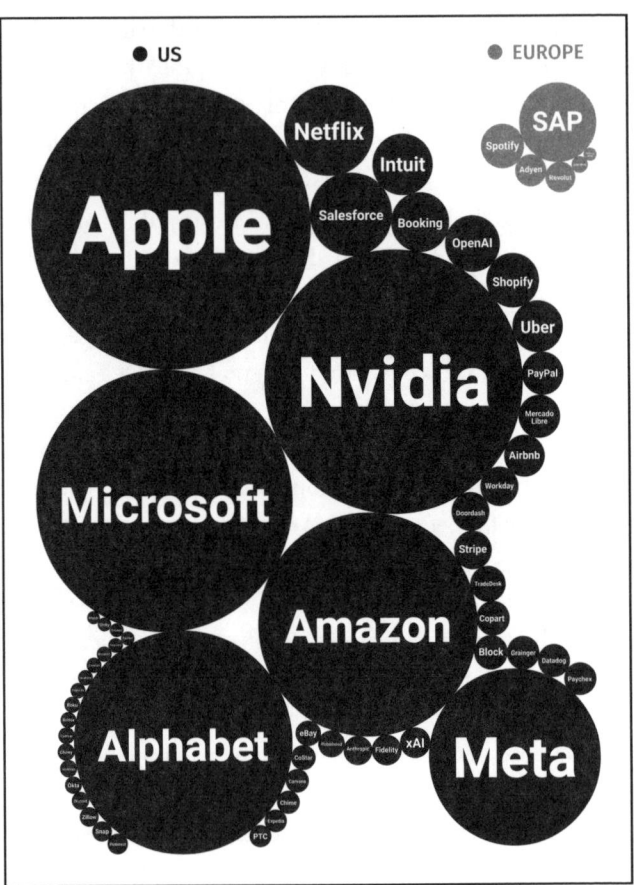

Figure 4: Top 100 platforms worldwide: USA (85.5 %) versus Europe (11 %); shown here without China and Africa (data base: FAZ)[4]

always emphasised that he was not a politician at all, but an outsider, i. e. an entrepreneur and manager. It was precisely this branding that he used back in his 2015 campaign: he started his crusade explicitly *against* politics, promising to 'drain the swamp of corruption in Washington'. From the outset, Trump acted on a mission to instill fear and suspicion into *the paradigm of politics*.

And that's exactly what he has done: as the most powerful influencer in the world, he is completely the creature of the Dark Tech platforms and their algorithms. Accordingly, he has succeeded in undermining a formerly serious, decent and traditional political party, the Republicans, from the inside, and subjugating it completely to himself. Today, this party is nothing more than a meaningless, empty shell — we could also simply call it the 'Trump Party'.

Who is 'in charge' — Trump or tech?

So how exactly should we assess the relationship between Trump and tech? Let's take a closer look at what it looked like in the months leading up to the 2024 US presidential election. Remember how the doddery candidate, Joe Biden, was struggling against his challenger Donald Trump, especially in the disastrous TV duel on 28 June 2024. On 14 July, the failed assassination attempt on Trump at the first Butler Rally further increased the challenger's popularity. Around a week later, Biden withdrew his candidacy and gave way to Kamala Harris, a paradigm change that immediately turned the polls in favour of the Democrats. Harris was then able to further extend her lead since her TV duel against Trump on 10 September. Trump looked old, insecure, confused and battered compared to his opponent. It seemed as if the election had already been decided for the Democrats. But the real and final turning point came at the second Butler Rally on 5 October. Elon Musk appeared on stage with Trump for the first time and has continued to appear both consistently and prominently as part of 'Team Trump' in the subsequent months.

Apparently, Trump was badly shaken after 10 September and he needed a 'useful idiot' right away. He knew that, without a quick solution, the race for the presidency would have been over for him. What he needed now was an immediate, spectacular gamechanger. And he delivered. In fact, Musk, the world's most successful entrepreneur, became part of team Trump. And it was probably Musk who pushed Trump over the finishing line in the end (see graphic). But he is unlikely to have done so altruistically. At some point between

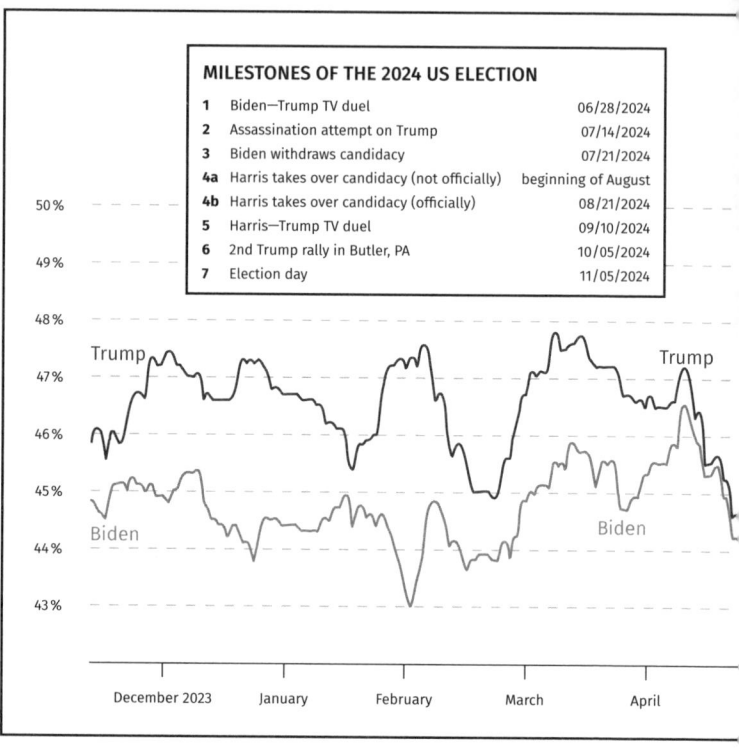

Figure 5: How Trump became President: Aggregate approval ratings over time[5]

10 September and 5 October, the two must have concluded some kind of deal. It might have looked something like this:

Musk supported Trump with a lot of money (more than 270 million US dollars) and additionally considerably boosted his image in terms of youthfulness, progressiveness and power. Trump might have promised him a role in return, in which Musk could first of all help shape the new government and secondly get rid of the countless annoying procedures and regulations that curtailed him as an entrepreneur. At the time Trump came to power, more than 32 investigations and proceedings by 11 government agencies had been in full swing against Musk's company.[6] In addition, Trump may have promised him full access to the US administration's data treasures.

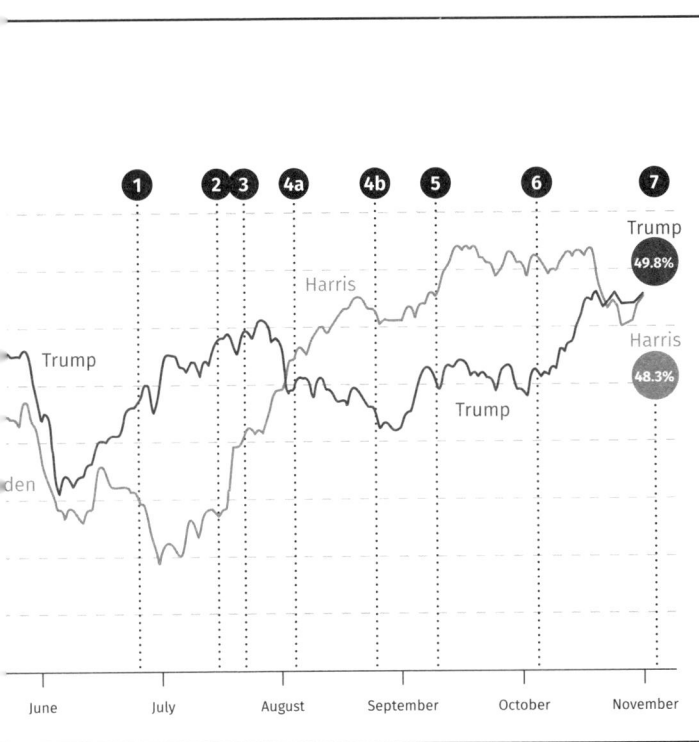

So Musk went along with it and we need ask ourselves: Was he really just Trump's 'useful idiot'? Or is it possibly the other way around: Was Trump Musk's 'useful idiot'? And what exactly is Musk's agenda?

Media War — the four phases

To understand this, we need to outline the battle for supremacy that has been going on for several years between political power on the one hand and the power of Dark Tech on the other. Let's take a look at this from the perspective of today's Dark Tech companies.

1. The UNDERGROUND phase: You know the signs in the rooms of adolescent teenagers: 'STAY OUT!' At this stage, youngsters potentially sympathise with gangsters, try out drugs or do other forbidden things in secret. The Dark Tech companies had a similar attitude in their early days, at a time when they didn't even know that one day they actually would end up 'on the dark side of the force'. For most of them, this was the period between 1995 and around 2010: chaotic beginnings in garages, illegal or at least semi-legal business models, 'mafia' style (the 'bad boys' of the Paypal founders around Peter Thiel literally called themselves the 'Paypal-Mafia'; Elon Musk was one of them. Thiel proudly stated that four of the six founders had built bombs when they were teenagers).[7] Laws were ignored and broken, hacker-style, but hardly anyone cared because the significance of these start-ups was still marginal at the time and their potential was not understood.

2. The ZOMBIE phase: In this phase, between around 2010 and 2020, today's Dark Tech companies recognised the gigantic power of their business models. They understood that the analogue world would gradually be replaced by the digital world and that they had complete control over it. Secondly, they succeeded in enforcing their monopolies and securing them through regulation and legal exemptions (▶5). They also understood that the people out there didn't have the slightest clue what was going on and that they themselves were well on the way to economic world domination, especially as they would also control the political public sphere via digital platforms in the future. Alphabet, Meta and Apple were the leading Dark Tech companies at this stage. In order to extend their power as far as possible without anyone else noticing, they chose a strategy similar to that of the zombie wasp. This type of wasp lays its eggs in a host insect (in this case a metaphor for the State) and at the same time weakens it with poison — the eggs of the zombie wasp then grow inside the still

living, paralysed insect. The host animal gradually dies and is eventually eaten by the hatching larvae. Translated into reality: the Dark Tech companies wanted to siphon off as much wealth and power as possible — and at the same time impose as many costs and damages ('externalities'[8]) as possible on the State for their business models. All this had to happen without the State and the citizens realising what evil game was being played on them. This is why the tech corporations developed their typical 'smoke-and-mirrors ethical bullshit' talk (they just cared for *freedom of speech*, to give people a *voice*, to create *social communities*, to enable *participation*, to build a *sharing economy*, all this *for a better world*, and so on) and their cool disguises (from metal-rimmed glasses and turtlenecks to Birkenstocks, hoodies, T-shirts and baseball caps). Although their misconduct and anti-democratic schemes were repeatedly exposed (Prism affair, Cambridge Analytica, hundreds of lawsuits, etc.), they managed to deceive the people and their governments again and again. It worked so well that, during this phase, hundreds of 'digital evangelists' touted their good works on stages around the world and in ever new bestsellers. As a society, we publicly worshipped the 'tech bros' as well-meaning 'philanthropists' and 'liberators'. Meanwhile, the zombie tech companies sponsored left-wing and conservative parties alike, their lobbyists were invited everywhere, the 'good' digital companies were involved in countless negotiations with the powerful, while nobody noticed the hostile takeover they pursued (By the way: to this day, big tech is allowed to sit at the same table as serious politicians in Europe — as if it wasn't completely clear that these are representatives of companies pursuing an antidemocratic agenda).

3. The TRANSITION phase: Two events in the early twenties changed everything. First, the storming of the Capitol in January 2021 was the first open power battle between Dark Tech and politics. The tech companies pulled the plug on Donald Trump and

blocked him from using the platforms. This was probably the path of least resistance for the tech giants at that time. After all, Trump had already been voted out of office. The 'tech bros' did what they had always done during the zombie phase: they opportunistically adapted to the new political circumstances in order to continue accumulating power inconspicuously to the max. Trump was fuming at the time, but he had to give in. Simultaneously, it was now clear for the first time that nobody was above the Dark Tech companies anymore, not even the President of the USA. This is exactly what dawned on the two most important players of our current times, the first of which was Donald Trump. He founded his own platform ('Truth Social'), which was supposedly 'uncensored' (even before Musk started his involvement with Twitter, by the way). In this way, he was able to immunise himself against any future potential blocking by Dark Tech. He achieved that by creating particularly permeable linking options for content on Truth Social, enabling seamless and efficient possibilities to spread messages from this platform to the leading social media players. In the event of getting blocked, Trump's thousands of followers would have used Truth Social like a 'digital mud slinger' in order to spread Donald Trump's content onto the leading platforms. Furthermore, Trump's appointment of JD Vance as Vice President created a direct link to the powerful libertarian circles of the Dark Tech scene.

The second protagonist who noticed he had a problem in 2021 was Elon Musk. He was already the most successful tech entrepreneur of all time on paper. But unlike Alphabet or Meta, he didn't have his own social media platform. He must have realised, by 2021 at the latest, that whoever controlled the platforms would also control the public sphere in the future. This offered endless opportunities for the owners of these tech platforms to use their power to encroach into the public sphere and politics. But at the time, Musk didn't have control of any social media platform. In fact, there was only one way out — which Musk resolutely used to his advantage. He bought Twitter in October 2022 (the acquisition itself took place in April 2023). This was the only platform that could be acquired at a reasonably affordable price ticket at the time (the final purchase price was 44 billion US dollars). He devised a diabolical strategy to beat his rivals Alphabet and Meta, who were vastly superior to him in this field. Firstly, he launched an ideological 'anti-censorship' war against the leading platforms (especially Meta, i.e. Facebook and Instagram) and positioned X as the leading 'uncensored' news portal. Mind you, he did this at a time when market leader Meta had *reduced* its news presence following a number of scandals, particularly the disclosures concerning the manipulation of the 2016 US election by Russian disinformation.

At the time, Meta outwardly emphasised its goodwill on taking responsibility via moderation efforts in order to improve its damaged reputation. These circumstances provided the perfect opportunity for Musk. While Zuckerberg had just even deprioritised political news in the platform feeds, Musk 'armed' his platform Twitter / X by dismantling moderation teams, increasing the aggressiveness of the tone on the platform and publicly portraying himself as an 'absolutist of free speech'. Thirdly, he began to support the anti-democratic candidate for presidency, Donald Trump. The rest is public knowledge: Trump won the election. The other tech companies happily became Trump's allies and publicly displayed their support for him.

4. The phase of the OUTBREAK: Since Trump's inauguration, the 'media war' has openly broken out. Tech and Trump have formed an alliance and are fighting together with European right-wing populists against democracy and the EU.

Russia's role in the media war

At this point, we see it as important to assess Russia's role in all of this. In the context of his goal of re-establishing Russia's claim to great power after the collapse of the Soviet Union, Putin has used the 'media war' to his own advantage like no other actor. His strategy can be briefly summarised as follows: He is using the infinite possibilities of the Dark Tech platforms to divide Western democratic societies (▶ 6) for his own benefit. The aim is to weaken democratic forces in the USA and Europe while strengthening populist movements. During the US election campaign, Russia consistently launched disinformation campaigns against the Democrats and their candidates whilst at the same time actively supporting Donald Trump. The massive scale of the Russian activities has been widely verified in the context of the US elections in 2016 ('RussiaGate'), 2020 and 2024.[9]

Hundreds of Russian disinformation campaigns have also been uncovered in Europe and Germany. Over the course of the investigations, the TV channel RT DE (formerly known as 'Russia Today') was blocked by the German authorities as of September 2021. Russia's *modus operandi* in Germany is the same as in the USA: populist movements such as the right-wing AfD or the similarly radical BSW (Bündnis Sahra Wagenknecht, Sahra Wagenknecht Alliance in English) are to be strengthened, 'established parties' weakened, people's trust in their own government undermined. The aim is to weaken Western engagement in the Ukraine conflict, for example by stirring up fear of a possible escalation of the war. To this end, troll farms consisting of thousands of fake accounts are being set up to spread false information. Real news websites are often imitated by digital clones. Bots and AI-generated content are used to systematically spread millions of pieces of fake news in order to unsettle and polarise the population as much as possible.[10]

Thus, in this media war, Russia and Putin are pursuing their own specific agenda whilst building maximum synergies with the anti-democratic agenda of Dark Tech and Trump. It is important that we recognise the differences despite all the similarities. Reshaping our media order is the overarching core impulse of the Dark Tech platforms and their anti-democratic, libertarian owners, who essentially want to dismantle the democratic State and maximise their own power (▶3).

Donald Trump represents a hybrid position between Dark Tech and a politically largely vacuous authoritarianism. Tech and Trump are united in the basic goal of undermining and destroying the democratic order. Only this set of interests can explain the bizarre coalitions we face today. Why, otherwise, would a technologically advanced, future-oriented tech entrepreneur like Elon Musk ally himself with stuffy, backward-looking, traditionalist muckraking movements like the AfD in Germany?

How is that possible? Why didn't Musk support a progressive, pro-business, pro-digital party such as the FDP in Germany? For one simple reason: because Musk's/Trump's goal is to destabilise and break up the already weakened EU. This would not have been possible with parties like the free-market FDP or the conservative CDU in Germany. The increasingly autocratic new US government and its tech allies want to force the European Union into full dependence, allowing them unlimited future economic exploitation. And the best thing would be if the EU stops annoying tech companies with their 'impertinent' digital rules and regulations.

Even before his official 'switch' to Trump, Elon Musk had also been in contact with Putin, a traditionalist, nationalist, backward-looking autocrat, for similar reasons. Likewise, Trump, tech & co. fit perfectly with Putin's agenda of reshaping the Russian empire. Anything that weakens European democracies is grist to the mill of his own military imperialist agenda.

The food chain of 'useful idiots'

If we were to imagine the vertical food chain of 'useful idiots', our picture would show Dark Tech 'ruling' from the top, simply because, over time, these corporations will only gain more and more power. For now they still leave Trump at the front of the political stage, also because they have rather low interest in the paradigm of politics itself (▶3). Trump's Vice President JD Vance emerged from the Dark Tech power network and is therefore already in position, ready for the future takeover. At the next level below that, we find the European right-wing populists, the 'useful idiots' of tech and Trump. And Putin is just another parasite, using all these developments to his advantage.

Unfortunately, at the very bottom of this anti-democratic food chain are the many people who allow themselves to be seduced and instrumentalized in this game. We are talking about the legions of 'digitally blitzed' voters of the right-wing populists. From the point of view of tech and Trump, they are just worthless stormtroopers in this latest example of so-called political 'participation' in world history. This piece of theatre whereby people are supposedly politically 'empowered' through the tech platforms could go down as one of the biggest and most egregious smokescreens in the history of propaganda. Trump, tech & co. still need these movements because politically dismantling Western democracies would be impossible without them.

But one thing is certain: once Trump and tech reach their goal, once the structures of the democratic State in the USA are shattered and the EU is crushed to pieces, once the new autocratic order is fully installed, the libertarian rulers' interest in these people will collapse entirely. Anyone who thinks that those libertarian oligarchs will then solve our social problems, i.e. build schools and pay for childcare, hospitals or the maintenance of our streets, must be extremely naïve. Musk, Trump, Zuckerberg, Pichai (Sundar Pichai is the chief executive officer (CEO) of Alphabet and its subsidiary Google as well as YouTube) — they all have ZERO interest in the people they are supposedly 'giving a voice' to. Unfortunately, these populist voters are being instrumentalised and do not seem to notice what a terrible trap the oligarchs have set for them.

Of course, this is all speculation. And there may well be temporary 'setbacks', surprising twists, manoeuvres or resets in the future advance of this coalition. With all of this in mind, a Dark Tech disclaimer is necessary: Of course, Dark Tech is not a uniformly acting block, especially as the Dark Tech companies are also in competition with each other. But, it is also remarkable to note how seemingly 'moderate' Dark Tech companies such as Apple and Alphabet (Google) have offered no resistance to and have completely joined forces with the Trump government. The meteoric rise of Elon Musk shows that surprising shifts in power can also take place within this coalition. Even Musk could certainly also suffer setbacks or even fizzle out in the future, but none of this will change Dark Tech's gradual increase in power and its domination of the digital sphere.

An open question is: who will prevail in this battle for supremacy in the future — Trump or tech? Or, to put it another way, is it possible that Trump will reinstall the paradigm of traditional politics (based on democratic processes) during his current presidency and secure it against the threat of a Dark Tech overreach? In my view, there is little to suggest that such a scenario would materialise. Trump himself has little interest in politics in the sense that he is not really part of the political paradigm. He is a manager and has little faith in political work in terms of committees, alignment and compromise, due processes as well as checks and balances. Indeed, Trump was only able to become US President thanks to the support of Dark Tech.

Furthermore, the ongoing digital transformation dynamic is pushing more and more power gains into the hands of the ruling Dark Tech corporations day by day, month by month. They don't have to do anything. They just need to wait — because they hold all the trump cards. They virtually own the digital world. Thus, time plays in their favour every day, especially as they also control the digital public sphere, which will also continue to grow in importance in the future.

Trump has no direct access here in the medium term. On top of that, the current systematic dismantling of State structures and the constitutional collapse in the USA also comes with the paradoxical side effect of massively weakening the 'paradigm of politics' itself. And finally: Trump is old. His powers will dwindle eventually. That's why there are some indications that Trump will end up being the 'useful idiot' for tech and not the other way around. Only time will tell.

However, probably the most depressing insight from these considerations is that, in the end, it doesn't really matter who prevails here, whether it ends up being Trump or tech. Why? *Because the result will be largely the same.* The decisive factor is that the checks and balances as well as the separation of powers in a pluralistic media landscape are being destroyed *in both scenarios*. Even if, for instance, the Trump government were to break up the digital monopolies according to the motto 'divide and rule', there is still not much room for optimism. In such a scenario, it is unlikely that Trump would resist the temptation to take control of the digital platforms himself with the same aggressiveness that he is currently displaying in the fields of justice, science and others. Nothing is more attractive to autocrats than media monopolies.

3.
THE OBJECTIVES OF THE WARLORDS

The libertarian destruction of democracy

If, in a hundred years from now, people look back on our times, they will wonder how it was possible that a coalition of Dark Tech and populism destroyed Western democracies in such a short space of time. They will be even more surprised that the masterminds behind this hostile takeover had communicated their plans to put an end to our democracy for the sake of economic exploitation openly and transparently for years and even decades. But, for some inexplicable reason, nobody took them seriously. The big digital show of supposed 'liberation' was running continuously on all channels — at TED Talks, at 'cool' tech conferences, in the casual subcultures of hackers, nerds and 'IT freaks'. Apparently, we were lulled into a false sense of security by those cool sounds of the future — scientists, digital experts, journalists alike. And it wasn't until the end of 2024 that we slowly started to realise what was going on. And the total "disintermediation"[1] of our democracy that had been planned for decades is now taking place right before our eyes.

This takeover is being carried out on the ideological basis of libertarianism.[2] In its more harmless forms, libertarianism highlights that the most important good is individual freedom. The influence of the State, on the other hand, should be reduced as much as possible in order to 'free' the individual from the State's 'violent' actions. Libertarianism focuses primarily on the economic sphere and believes in free markets. Companies are assumed to be better suited than the State to organise society and ensure that human rights and freedom are respected. The tendency is to reduce the influence of politicians as much as possible and replace political processes with private sector management. Depending on the intensity, the power of the State to levy taxes, for example, is also called into question. Based on this, libertarianism flows smoothly into anarcho-capitalist ideas, according to which the State should be abolished entirely. In such concepts, "libertarianism also develops ideas of a radical 'secession', through which the welfare state is abolished and a new, liberated order is created."[3]

As a result of the digital transformation, these fundamental concepts have been expanded into new, increasingly radical positions of 'cyber-libertarianism'.[4] Many followers of this ideology typically believe in the following points as if they were religious dogma:[5]

- Acts of democratic governments are criminal per se
- The interventions of the State are acts of violence against the free individual
- Democratic governments are illegitimate
- Democracy is really a fraud
- The State must be abolished
- The editorial media are remote-controlled by the elites of the corrupt State and must not be trusted under any circumstances
- All statements by the corrupt government, the elites and the editorial media are lies and propaganda
- Information is free and may not be 'censored' by anyone
- Technology and digitalisation improve the world through the implementation of the libertarian programme

In the economic sphere, 'cyber-libertarians' have a penchant for particularly unscrupulous actions (we are reminded of the 'PayPal Mafia') and for aggressively maximising economic power, which leads to a paradoxical *elimination* of competition and open markets through the establishment of monopolies (Peter Thiel). Supporters of such ideas therefore want to abolish the State completely or to a very large extent in order to rule themselves. In their view, the State consists of nothing but lazy bureaucrats who stifle innovation and threaten freedom at the taxpayer's expense. This is why they believe that the 'corrupt legacy elites' and the complex democratic processes should be eliminated and replaced with more efficient, autocratic structures, envisioning a 'CEO king' running the State like a business corporation. Right-wing libertarian Curtis Yarvin, who is part of Peter Thiel's intellectual network, has been advocating these kinds of positions since around 2008.[6]

In 2014, former Google employee Justine Tunney called for very similar steps in the paper entitled 'We the people'. According to Tunney, the following three steps should be taken immediately:

1. "Retire all government employees with full pensions.
2. Transfer administrative authority to the tech industry
3. Appoint Eric Schmidt [then the CEO of Google] CEO of America"[7]

Imagine I had confronted you with such a horrible scenario in mid-2024. Back then, you would probably have dismissed it as a ridiculous conspiracy theory. But all the concepts that Trump or DOGE are currently implementing have been openly proposed and discussed by the various 'neo-reactionary' tech masterminds for years and decades.

The grand narrative of the new libertarians

The network of libertarian ideas, symbols and heroes that have spawned this movement is vast and complex. Incidentally, we will find that the most visible thought leaders (with the exception of Elon Musk) are often not identical to the most important Dark Tech managers, from Bill Gates to Larry Page and Sergey Brin to Mark Zuckerberg. This is also understandable. After all, their business models were often as controversial as they were semi-legal in the early years. The digital corporations were confronted with hundreds of lawsuits and they were also attacked repeatedly by previous US governments up to the famous hearings in the US senate. It is therefore understandable that the legally accountable CEOs of Dark Tech companies have avoided exposing themselves by making openly anti-democratic statements or coming up with libertarian coup fantasies. But, if you read between the lines, they have also consistently shown their high affinity for the belief system of 'cyberlibertarianism'.[8] Douglas Rushkoff also refers to this system of thought in Dark Tech ecosystems as "The Mindset"[9].

It is crucial that we understand the ideological dogma that characterises this setting and work out the grand narrative that underpins it. Naturally, this is once again an idealised reconstruction. We can trace the ideological roots of this anarcho-capitalist and egomaniacal thinking back to the US writer Ayn Rand. In her novels, she created lonely heroic protagonists chosen by fate. Typically, they feel misunderstood in the face of the mediocrity that people are displaying around them, but finally prevail against all odds and conventions to finally save the world in the end. The heroic individual is allowed to disregard rules and laws at will, overcoming the lame 'establishment', which cannot understand their genius, for the sake of their mission.

The same pattern was later applied to Marvel's superhero characters — such as Spiderman or Batman. And it is easy to see how so many people love these superheroes simply because they would like to be superheroes themselves. This is because 'normal people' like us have to put up with insults, put-downs and humiliation again and again. At the same time, our instinct is: We will only be able to achieve true 'freedom' when we leave these slights behind us.

It now makes sense that Elon Musk used a superhero costume as his profile picture on X for a long time.[10] And perhaps it also makes sense that so many of the main players in this movement have suffered severe narcissistic slights in their biographies, whether Trump or Musk or Steve Jobs. And it makes sense that there are so many people who identify with the stories of these new 'digital superheroes' who have managed to build their huge, dazzling empires against all odds and amassed incredible wealth and riches.

At this point, we can add another central element to this narrative. The narcissistically offended protagonists always start their hero's journey as underdogs. In the digital world, these are the hackers, nerds and geeks who made the grand gesture of showing the whole world the finger, explicitly including the democratic State.[11] These models of thought always served as a guideline for Dark Tech. It is a well-known fact that the postal address of Meta (running Facebook and Instagram) is '1 Hacker Way'. Mark Zuckerberg himself has written a set of company guidelines serving as a manifesto with the same title (The Hacker Way).[12]

Let's listen, for instance, to the sound of the 'Declaration of Independence of Cyberspace', which the internet activist (and former songwriter of the Grateful Dead) John Perry Barlow published back in 1996. It reads:

> "Governments of the Industrial World, you weary giants of flesh and steel, I come from Cyberspace, the new home of Mind. On behalf of the future, I ask you of the past to leave us alone. You are not welcome among us. You have no sovereignty where we gather [!]. We have no elected government [!], nor are we likely to have one, so I address you with no greater authority than that with which liberty itself always speaks. I declare the global social space we are building to be naturally independent of the tyrannies [!] you seek to impose on us. You have no moral right to rule us [!] nor do you possess any methods of enforcement we have true reason to fear."[13]

This already has the sound of secession, of detachment, of the 'exit'[14], as libertarians like to call it. Let's remember the *coup* we have described above — the hostile takeover of the public forum (▶1) that is taken away from the control of the democratic State. The narrative of this declaration of independence works in exactly the same way. It is also an open declaration of war against the democratic State. It is democracy itself that is referred to as 'tyranny'. It is, so to speak, the blueprint of the narrative held up today by the right-wing populists who supposedly want to liberate us from the 'tyranny of democracy'.

While John Perry Barlow, former lyricist for the Grateful Dead, would probably later have used the excuse of 'having had different intentions' back in the mid-nineties, it is hard to find such ambiguity in another text from the same period. The book *The Sovereign Individual* by James Dale Davidson and William Rees-Mogg, published in 1997, portrays the democratic State as a criminal rogue organisation which, through its monopoly on the use of violence, deprives the supposedly superior, innovative economic elites of their well-earned wealth through taxes in order to redistribute it to the supposedly inferior lower classes (here, too, this is supplemented by a supposed subsidisation of minorities, i.e. black people, gay people, disabled people).[15]

But the new information technologies allow digital elites and entrepreneurs to escape this 'exploitation' through an 'exit', namely through offshore organisations or sovereign microstates. These libertarian individuals become 'sovereign' (from the Latin supernus, meaning 'upper', 'that is located above'). Through their exit, they place themselves 'above' the declining democratic order and at the same time dismantle the sovereignty of the State from which they are withdrawing.

Thus, the 'sovereign individuals' can even benefit financially from the demise of the actual democratic State and skim off maximum profits, without having to pay any taxes or duties. At the same time, their exit accelerates the demise of the State to an increasingly worthless residual body that sinks into anarchy and chaos. According to the authors, the economic downturn of the State is also accompanied by an 'information war'. In the "age of the Information War" the leading digital players are a greater power than "the majority of states with seats in the United Nations", their "logic bombs" being able to "sabotage centralized command and control systems": "Ultimately, this means the end of mass democracy".[16]

Eerily, many of the predictions in the 1997 book have become reality in the modern world. The authors provided a blueprint for the numerous aggressive methods of extraterritorial tax avoidance and profit optimisation that have been used by tech oligarchs ever since.

When it was published, the book also served as an advertisement for a newsletter by the two authors entitled 'Strategic Investment' (with the subscription cost coming to a whopping 995 US dollars a year). They also advertised an exclusive 'Investment Club' for accredited individuals who were willing to invest more than 100,000 US dollars. The book also recommended that participants opened offshore accounts in tax havens as soon as possible, in order to secure their own tax-free zone and thereby be able to establish their own 'microsovereignty' in the world.[17]

None other than Peter Thiel, one of the most influential tech investors, who is also the former PayPal buddy of Elon Musk and foster father of US Vice President JD Vance, has described this openly anti-democratic text as one of his favorite books. He has also invested in 'seasteading', a term used for the attempt to build artificial islands in the sea that are completely independent from any State. As early as 2009, Thiel famously declared that he no longer believes that "freedom and democracy are compatible".[18]

To the same extent that technolibertarians hate the State, they worship entrepreneurs, managers and investors. They despise all professions that, in their view, do not create immediate economic value. Cyberlibertarians have even created their own term for such 'good-for-nothings', namely the *paper belt*[19] — in other words, all those hated intellectuals, academics, scientists, experts, civil servants, journalists and politicians of the old elites. They are supposedly nothing more than paper tigers and smart alecks whose days are long gone. This is also why libertarian heroes don't last long in universities. Part of a 'proper digital CV' is, firstly, being a university drop-out and, secondly, proudly boasting about it all the time.[20]

At this point, we can also consider various statements made by the neoreactionary movement (sometimes abbreviated as NRx). Nick

Land, one of its leading voices and a self-proclaimed 'hyper-racist', envisioned a cynical 'transgression' of enlightened modernity in his book *The Dark Enlightenment*. The democratic State should be 'liberated' from the overly cumbersome processes and a 'CEO king' should be appointed.[21] At the end of his book, he flirts with the idea of eugenics to breed future elites. If we are wondering why, at the Butler Rally, Musk made a point of being not just MAGA (Make America Great Again) but DARK MAGA, it could be understood as a reference to Nick Land's *The Dark Enlightenment*, which was also the source of inspiration for the term 'Dark Tech' used here.

Here we should also consider the confused ideas of 'Longtermism' according to Nick Bostrom. One of the core ideas of this 'philosopher' that is especially inhumane is that rich, successful people (in contrast to less affluent population groups) reproduce 'too little' and that this trend must be reversed (because otherwise the quality of the human gene pool would deteriorate). Furthermore, the future maximisation of human intelligence must be placed in a galactic context. This could be achieved by colonising the universe.[22]

The 'cyberlibertarian' dismantling of democracy is in full swing

Even if we feel a little dumbfounded after this high speed tour through some of the core ideas of 'cyberlibertarianism' as espoused by their 'digital evangelists', it still doesn't take a particularly big leap of the imagination to understand that very large parts of these ideas and programmes are currently being put into practice. In the ongoing US 'coup d'état', large parts of the government authorities are being dismissed and brought into line with the libertarian line via purges. The 'Department of Government Efficiency' (DOGE) is effectively dismantling ever larger parts of the US administration. The consequences could be far-reaching in the future, according to digital expert Sascha Lobo:

"The agreements apparently stipulate that DOGE will be allowed to feed government data into its own AI systems. DOGE is advancing the replacement of the State apparatus with a State AI; I wouldn't be surprised if it ends up being owned by a private individual. The idea is to create an AI technocracy on speed, and it is not yet clear whether it will still be democratic at all."[23]

Furthermore, the judiciary will be largely disempowered or alternatively, the US government will no longer adhere to its rulings and objections. The editorial media and academia are being discredited, silenced and dismissed.

This restructuring process follows the libertarian script. The democratic State is being abolished and replaced by authoritarian and, above all, digital rule. This way, oligarchs and Dark Tech can continue to destroy the State from within and maximise their profits in parallel (remember the zombie wasp metaphor!). After all, it won't be the tech oligarchs who are going to build schools, repair roads, maintain hospitals or kindergartens in the future …

The new 'sovereign' libertarians therefore work like gigantic parasites that position themselves 'above' the body politic and completely suck it dry. It is therefore probably no coincidence that such corporations even mark this 'takeover' in their names and call themselves 'Meta' or 'Uber', for example. The same corporations have also managed, through mechanisms of extraterritorial forms of organisation, not to pay ethically appropriate taxes in the countries in which they operate and to pocket the profits beyond any national border through aggressive tax avoidance tactics. According to libertarian philosophy, they reject the State anyway. That is why other libertarian masterminds have continued to develop more extreme utopias that would allow them to put themselves 'above' the State — to be able to then cash in as much as they can and, if possible, shirk any kind of responsibility.

The models mentioned above can also shed some light on Elon Musk's unusual behaviour. He is known to have fathered 14 children with four women to date. In May 2024, he published a Tweet about this, stating: "Contrary to what many think, the richer someone is, the fewer kids they have", which is reminiscent of Bostrom. He also once claimed, in 2022, "I'm doing my part haha". That would all make sense from Bostrom's perspective. Just like Musk's Mars obsession, which serves the 'longtermist' purpose to "preserve the light of consciousness by becoming a spacefaring civilization & extending life to other planets", as Musk once explained.[24]

None of this is part of a mere pipe dream, it's happening right now — anti-democratic Nietzschean 'Übermensch' type characters are building their own world and leaving everything else behind. On the one hand, 'unregulated Freedom Cities' are planned.[25] On the other hand, the implementation of 'network States' is also in full swing. Balaji Srinivasan, who belongs to the circle of libertarian tech investors like Marc Andreessen and Ben Horowitz, has further developed this vision in his book *The Network State* and is now putting it into practice. More information can be found on the website www.praxisnation.com. Let's take a quick look at this libertarian project:

> "As Nation States falter, Sovereign Networks — aligned onchain communities with aspirations of statehood — will emerge as the next global political paradigm. Sovereign Networks offer a path to crypto's next wave of adoption by integrating onchain infrastructure into the parallel institutions supplanting the global system's core functions. […] Soon, Sovereign Networks will be your most important group affiliation, passport, and community. Sovereign Networks will represent Citizens controlling trillions dollars of assets, represented on their native asset registries. We'll watch the flippening of Sovereign Networks over Nation States in real time. […] Today, we are 13k Praxians living in over 80 countries and 400 cities, and have founded companies worth over $400B. Our community is building a real society online using off-the-shelf tech."[26]

In such network States, corporations and companies, billionaires and millionaires are able to 'network' — and 'free' themselves from the outdated democratic State. It goes without saying that they want to develop their own cryptocurrencies that stem from exactly the same ideology. Who is going to build the schools and roads in the 'real' States once they are in ruins? Who will look after the sick and needy?

The truly astonishing thing about the libertarian movement is that it is quite obviously only the mega-elites and oligarchs who benefit, but the whole thing is presented to the outside world as a 'liberation movement', as if it were about enforcing human rights for the suppressed against dictatorial regimes. "Traditional Nation States are built on 'top-down governance'", according to www.praxisnation.com, which describes itself as the 'world's first Digital Nation'. And here, too, the 'liberation' is explained by praxisnation in terms of a revolution in the media order:

> "Historically, paradigm shifts in political legitimacy have always been preceded by advances in communication technology. Monarchies ruled Earth until a new communications technology escalated the war over the mental stronghold of political legitimacy. The movable-type printing press massively reduced the cost of printing books, pamphlets, and newspapers. Now new ideas could spread cheaply and quickly and compete with widespread oral traditions substantiating the legitimacy of kings. […] Today, technology turns the wheel of history once more. The internet unlocked free and instantaneous communication with everyone on earth: the mind is now accessible by all."

The digital media revolution has not only created the internet and with it the possibility of the network State. Now the possibilities of cryptocurrencies are also being added: "Bitcoin began as a revolutionary technology designed to circumvent government tyranny. [!] 16 years later, we've built an entire parallel financial system." This technology enables "the permissionless [!] transfer of property. Crypto levels-up internet communities, enabling them to fund and build permanent institutions with long term goals. The [state] monopoly on the formation of communities — up to and including nations — is gone".

Digital counter-culture: the figure of the troll

Even very naïve people should immediately realise that concepts of detached, libertarian states or communities such as the 'Network State' are attempts by a tiny elite to maximise the processes of digital exploitation. These are ecosystems made for digital elites, millionaires, billionaires and investors but they are consistently presented as a bottom-up movement, as a grassroots revolution. Let's remember the fairy tales that Trump, Vance and Musk tell us: democracy is in danger in Europe, the media is being 'censored', freedom of expression is being restricted. It now sinks in: They use exactly the same narrative as the other cyberlibertarians. Here, too, digital elites disguise themselves in the trappings of subcultural underground coolness in order to simultaneously destroy the very 'democracy' they are preaching about.

To understand the extent of the threat, we need to add that a completely new digital aesthetic of radical right-wing 'transgression' has emerged to complement these openly totalitarian to fascist libertarian currents of thought and ideas. Here, originally left-wing, democratic anti-establishment narratives that emerged in 1968 have been turned into their very opposite. In this 'reversal', people celebrated their own rebellion against 'political correctness' with relish and 'emancipated' themselves from the supposed 'left-wing mainstream' by openly displaying racism, discrimination, misogyny, anti-Semitism and so on. This often also applies to the theories presented above. Nick Land's book *The Dark Enlightenment* for example, describes the great taboos of the bourgeois establishment in a casually ironic tone of postmodern philosophy: racism, Hitler, hate speech, etc. The argument goes something like this: *anyone who questions anti-racism or tolerance today is persecuted as a heretic by the inquisition of the left-wing establishment.* Therefore, an emancipatory 'overcoming' of these outdated belief systems is deemed necessary — so that we can be racist and intolerant to our heart's content as a result of this 'liberation'.[27]

We immediately notice that this 'liberation movement' has taken hold of ever larger areas of online culture. Angela Nagle has dedicated a separate study to the disturbing aspects of this supposed 'emancipation', such as rape fantasies, threats of violence or the harassment of online victims in the real world through 'doxxing' and shows the unfathomable abysses that open up here.[28] What is important is to notice the specific digital culture and aesthetic with the key figure of the troll. He attacks the victims of his anarchic whims with unrestrained, cynical cruelty, while the online community considers his actions 'funny', gets involved and joins in — utilising the usual, supposedly 'funny' or 'creative' formats of online bullying such as memes and insider network jargon. If the victim fights back, it's all supposed to have been a 'joke'.

It is particularly interesting that the trolls' specific way of communicating creates a counter-model to discourse ethics as understood by Jürgen Habermas.[29] Democratic discourse can only succeed (even in tough debates) if the various participants assume a common interest in dialogue, understanding and rational argumentation — and listen to each other.[30] This is precisely why Habermas also calls the ideal democratic public sphere *deliberative*, thinking of it in terms of a model of collective consultation. In contrast, "trolling abandons both the shared purpose of a communication (to convince one another, to engage in dialogue) and the shared audience", as Adrian Daub aptly describes it.[31]

The communication of trolls is characterised by a cynical nihilism that is no longer concerned with consensus, dialogue and argumentative exchange (such concepts would be derisively rejected by trolls as 'moralising' and 'ridiculous'). For the troll, argument and fighting become ends in themselves. And that's precisely why it's impossible to 'win' against the trolls on the internet. Anyone who has been the victim of 'digital shitstorms' or bullying attacks will tell you this from their own experience: the typical reaction is to stop arguing at some point (we will come back to this later: ▶7). The way in which trolls communicate therefore amounts to denouncing the foundations of enlightened discourse and democracy. It heralds a new paradigm which we will refer to here as 'digitalocratic' and analyse in greater depth in the following chapters.

We would also note that it is precisely these digital formats of trolls that are currently being successfully implemented by Trump, Musk, and the many right-wing populists and politicians on the platforms. The current way in which Musk presents himself (DARK MAGA, dark sunglasses, 'gangsta chains', black clothing, etc.) also stems from this style of communication. We need to wake up: *This is no longer a subculture.* And we can also agree with Angela Nagle: It's not at all "funny anymore". Because: "The culture war goes offline"[32], as she states in the last chapter of her clairvoyant book on the subject.

Let's note this: The amalgam of digital-libertarian ideology and aesthetics has long since grown into a new, currently dominant 'grand narrative' of the oligarchs and enemies of democracy, and it is extremely successful. It is catching on with more and more people, who, in their innermost being, have long since renounced their allegiance to enlightened, democratic discourse — "this means the end of mass democracy", as Davidson and Rees-Mogg unequivocally put it already in 1997.[33]

Freedom curtailed: the instrumentalisation of those left behind

It is important that we also acknowledge the social resonance space for this grand narrative. We live in societies that are characterised by weak economic growth and increasing social division. More and more people feel left behind. At the same time, the social pressure on people to succeed is increasing, further intensified by the new evaluation mechanisms of the platforms (followers, likes, etc.), which are themselves creating 'winner-takes-all' markets: A few 'stars' receive a great deal of recognition while most remain passive and barely get noticed. Both economically as well as in terms of the digital attention economy, the rich get richer and the poor get poorer — with more and more people falling by the wayside. Social inequality increases, and at the same time, more and more people experience insults, symbolic devaluation, humiliation and feelings of powerlessness.

We now understand precisely why these *narratives, which celebrate the overcoming of narcissistic grievances*, are catching on with so many people and why the aforementioned aesthetics of 'liberation' are so appealing to them. They have experienced such rejections themselves, which is expressed in the feeling of 'offended freedom', as the title of an excellent study on this phenomenon by Carolin Amlinger and Oliver Nachtwey has phrased it.[34]

Thus, affected people turn with rage against the 'establishment', against the 'elites', and express the "desire for dis-intermediation, i.e. the elimination of all organizational bodies that can bundle interests and objections and create compromises. Instead, plebiscitary demands are put forward apodictically — grassroots democracy, populism and authoritarianism are closely intertwined here".[35] It is precisely this sentiment that Dark Tech platforms and populists are tapping into. They promise 'direct participation' (i.e.: you are the media now) and provide channels through which those affected can finally vent their frustration, resentment and anger. These are the perfect ecosystems to take revenge on the hated 'elites' they consider to be responsible for their situation — and, depending on the occasion, to unleash their hatred of refugees, minorities and women on the 'uncensored' platforms that 'liberate' them to engage in precisely this type of hate speech.

It is particularly interesting that nowhere in this act of rebellion can the development of a constructive programme for positive change be found. There is no "vision of a better order"[36] at any level. This could also explain why those affected do not seem to notice the actual goals of the libertarian oligarchs who are instrumentalising these feelings for their own interests (maximum personal enrichment through the exploitation of the remaining State structures). Total 'liberation' is certainly a great thing for the exiting oligarchs (they no longer need to pay taxes and can increase the boundlessness of their wealth even further) — but to what end are the followers of this movement actually 'liberating' themselves? In fact, the libertarian offerings of Dark Tech and the populists at this level seem to be merely vehicles for a "destructive nihilism"[37], which is only concerned with "criticism itself, with the act of being against"[38], with liberation 'in itself', so to speak, being completely devoid of any deeper purpose. The authors report on one citizen interviewed: "Civil war is coming soon [!], he is sure, then things will finally be cleaned up. He knows of more and more people who are arming themselves illegally."[39]

Thus, we can detect exactly the same paradox in terms of dismantling democracy in the name of democracy at the level of the recipients: "Libertarian authoritarians fight against a dictatorship from their point of view, they see themselves as heroes in the name of democracy, but undermine democratic norms."[40] In this struggle for supremacy, we find various 'liberator' figures (Trump, Musk, AfD, the platforms, etc.) at the highest levels of society, but interestingly enough, we find corresponding liberators on the level of the broad userbase of the platforms. Thus, both levels are bound together on the basis of *the same narrative* and are now aligned with each other in a large, global movement. Ironically, they share the same goal, to dismantle democracy, even if their motives are different. Given that "their criticism is not aimed at democratic corrections, but at the subversion of democracy and truth", an "anti-politics" or a "counter-democracy"[41] emerges.

It is particularly cynical that the tech oligarchs and their allies, the populists, are instrumentalising the many disappointments and frustrations of people who are struggling with social decline, personal crises, degradation and rejection. They do this in order to further tighten the screws of social exploitation. Given that the affected social ecosystems of the people who feel left behind are closing themselves off ever further, it is particularly difficult to communicate this connection to those affected.

The affected people would certainly also reject my own account in this book as *ridiculous* — because in their eyes I, too, *as a so-called media scientist, am part of the left-wing, corrupt elite* anyway, *who is presumptuously trying to explain to them what their world is like and who apparently doesn't even consider them mature enough to form their own opinion of the situation* — and so on and so forth.

In a TV advertisement financed by the America PAC (conservative political action committee linked to Elon Musk) and glorifying the first weeks of Trump's presidency, the section at the end about Trump praises him as follows: "He is taking on the ruling elite and returning the rule of the people. Under his leadership, we are respected again." This is exactly what the 'suffering souls' of his followers long for: respect and recognition.[42]

The only tragedy is that this will just accelerate their further decline. In no economic system will the broad mass of workers und unskilled employees be more blatantly disenfranchised and dispossessed than in the brave new world of the libertarian oligarchs. What is particularly astonishing is that *the libertarians themselves openly admit this*. Way back in 1997, The Sovereign Individual described how democracy is being dismantled with a blatantness that borders on the cynical. In the book, the end of democracy is portrayed as a huge opportunity to enrich a microscopically tiny upper class. The drastic decline and impoverishment of the so-called "underclass" is presented as inevitable. Almost 24 % of the population would sink below the threshold of "social usefulness" as a result of the upheavals described; this would affect the many people who are even dumber than "pig dribble", according to the contemptuous style of this text.[43] The libertarians could not care less about the fate of those who are left behind by the digital transformation. From their own Übermensch perspective, the broad masses at the 'lower' levels of society do not matter anyway.

4.
THE INVASION

The deeper meaning of digital monopolies

The aim of the libertarians is to dismantle the democratic State and to shift its power into their own tech autocracy. In fact, this is a project that is part of the transformation that the USA is currently experiencing. Once it is complete, power will then lie with a small oligarchy that no longer has to adhere to lengthy democratic checks and balances or 'regulations'.

In the current 'media war', the main weapon that they are using for this purpose is to set up digital monopolies. Over the course of the last fifteen years, hardly anyone has taken any interest in this problem. Even now, in times of panic with regard to the rapid erosion of democracy, there is still no real debate about digital monopolies. Yes, we have somehow understood that it is a nightmare if an oligarchy takes over power in the USA and 'has too much power'. But we still don't have a real debate about monopolies. Why? Because we still don't understand *what monopolies actually mean*. The topic seems 'abstract' to many people. They don't think that it has much to do with the world they live in and the problems of their everyday lives.

For quite some time, I have not been able to explain the dangers of monopolies clearly enough for people to understand the massive impact that they have on their lives. That's why I'm taking a completely different approach here. Please stay with me for the ride because, by taking this little detour, we can fully understand what is at stake for us.

We'll start with a thought experiment. Let's imagine the basic problem of human existence. Anyone who has ever been through a survival experiment or just watched one on TV knows that the world is tough if you're trying to survive the jungle outside. It's not easy to hunt animals, gather fruit, berries or nuts, toil as a farmer out there to grow plants and, on top of that, protect yourself from harsh weather in the wilderness. Out there, human life is characterised by hardship: Hunger, thirst, shortages, emaciation, illness and so forth. This starting position also marks the dream of human existence, namely to find a kind of 'shortcut' that makes it possible to lead a luxurious life without having to work for it.

People have tried out various models to achieve this goal. The one that is best known is the ancient, tried and tested method of *'plunder and pillage'*. The idea here was to attack the neighbouring village at night, kill all the people and loot their livestock, supplies and belongings. An extension of this model could be, rather than killing the people that were being attacked, to enslave them and force them to work for free for the rest of their lives. As in the case of the Roman Empire, the model could be expanded on a huge scale: Entire regions could be subjugated in a bloodlust in order to exploit their inhabitants through military oppression and, by so doing, seize gigantic riches. In Rome, meanwhile, people could wallow in luxury and wealth, without putting in any hard work.

However, the *'plunder and pillage'* method also has considerable disadvantages. If you raid other villages, tribes or peoples, you can expect them to fight back one day. One night you yourself could be attacked and killed. This is why people have, throughout history, come up with new, more innovative and more indirect forms of *'plunder and pillage'*.

One method through which huge sections of the European population were exploited by rulers to their heart's content over many centuries was medieval 'feudalism'. This was based on a sophisticated mechanism of tyranny and monopolisation. Over time, feudalist rulers managed to take control of the majority of fertile farmland. They were then able to 'offer' the starving peasants a 'friendly act of mercy' by 'lending' them the land as a fiefdom. However, they only did this if the peasants politely asked them for this kind favour. And of course, the feudal lords didn't consider themselves to be bloodsuckers, cutthroats, villains or evildoers. On the contrary: the fief itself was called *beneficium* in the Middle Ages. It was therefore a 'boon' that the gracious lord bestowed on the peasants because he was so kind and generous to them.[1]

The monopolisation of the land meant that the peasants had little choice. They could either starve to death or accept this 'friendly boon' from the feudal lord. By monopolising access to the land and making the peasants totally dependent, the feudal lords were able to extract more and more goods and money from them over time. At first, a farmer only had to pay a portion of the land yields, but over time, additional monetary payments were demanded from the farmers. At a certain point, the feudal lords demanded that the peasants perform additional serfdom services. The dependent peasants had to provide carting services, repair the feudal lord's castle walls or serve as soldiers or as men-at-arms in war. Over time, the feudal lords became more and more sophisticated in increasing the level of dependence of the feudal peasants, again through monopolisation:

> "The most typical of all these extortions of the peasants were probably the monopolies that the landlord established in very different forms to their disadvantage. He soon reserved the right to sell wine or beer at different times of the year [...]. More often still, he forced the peasants to grind grain only in his mill, bake bread in his oven and press wine in his press."[2]

Perhaps it has now dawned on you why we had to take this detour. First of all, it was necessary in order to show you that monopolies are not an abstract problem that barely touches our lives. On the contrary: monopolies are, to this day, a kind of *legal form of robbery* if they are not regulated and if the monopolists are allowed to exploit dependencies in an unbridled, extortionate manner. In fact, a monopoly is even more effective for the rulers than robbery. This is because there is hardly any risk for the aggressor. The aggressor no longer has to put his own life at stake. He doesn't have to fear revenge from those who are being exploited. On the contrary: the victim becomes an accomplice (how awesome is that???). This is because the exploited person more or less has 'to blame himself', like the farmer who accepts *the beneficium*, the 'wonderful boon' of the feudal lord, gratefully and voluntarily (!) as a sign of grace. In medieval documents it sounded like this:

> "To the magnanimous [!] Lord [...]. Since it is well known to all that I lack food and clothing, I have turned to your mercy [!] and have freely [!] decided to place myself under your rule [...]. Until my death I must serve and obey you as I am able as a free man [!] [...]".[3]

Ideally, the poor exploited individual didn't even realise that he was being exploited. For centuries during feudalism, the peasants were told that their fate was determined by divine providence and that all their toil and drudgery for the feudal lords would later be rewarded in the form of heavenly joys in the afterlife.

Does any of this ring a bell? Look at how easy it is for us to say about medieval feudalism: "How idiotic people were back then to accept that!" It's easy for us because we look at this mechanism of oppression *from the outside* and immediately see through it. We have to do the same when we analyse 'digital feudalism' but we'll get to that later.

We can extrapolate three basic rules from looking at the dependence of people during the age of feudalism as depicted in the above description:

- *Without having a monopoly on access to land, the rulers would be completely powerless*
  This can be explained by taking the example of the peasants. If enough alternative land were freely available to peasants, no peasant would ever submit himself voluntarily to a feudal lord. The feudal lords could keep their 'benefits' for themselves, would have no support, would be completely powerless, would not receive any more income and would have to toil in the fields themselves, because otherwise they would unfortunately starve to death. Without their monopolies on access to land, their rule would immediately collapse. The monopolies *are the condition of the possibility of their rule*.[4]

- *The more exclusively the monopolist controls access, the more intensively he can exploit his victims*
  This can again be explained by taking the example of the peasants. Even in the feudal era, monopolising access to land was never absolute. Peasants could, for example, run away from their feudal lord. But the risks and barriers were so great (especially as the feudal lord was also a judge on the territory of his land) that this rarely happened.

- *The more important the affected good is for basic existence, the more the monopolist can exploit his victims*
  Again this can be explained by taking the example of the peasants. Without access to land, it's very hard for them to feed themselves and their families, so they are very dependent. Imagine if someone were to monopolise access to water, for example. In such a scenario, the preposterous extent of the monopolists' demands would become immediately clear.

Digital feudalism

You're probably wondering where all this is headed. Haven't we long since overcome feudalism? Haven't we had free and open markets since industrialisation and Adam Smith's 'invisible hand'? No feudal lord can unilaterally rule over us. Our modern economic world is developed via innovation and competition. Any victory or breakthrough in the marketplace is usually only short-lived. If, for example, you come up with a new product that is well received on the market, you always have to expect that a competitor is lurking somewhere with an even better idea, and BANG, the whole game of 'annoying' competition starts all over again. Modern capitalism is therefore *meritocratic*. By contrast, inherited ('legacy') wealth is rather undesirable. Competition means that you only ever belong to the elite for a limited period of time. This is because the best ideas should prevail and these will soon be replaced by new, better ideas. Everyone has a fair chance in open markets.[5]

That would be the case if it weren't for the new 'digital feudalistic rulers'. The age-old dream of mankind (to revel in wealth without working) was by no means over, even after the invention of the free market economy. Establishing monopolies has once again become the path that tech companies have taken to establish their rule. "Competition is for losers," said none other than Peter Thiel.[6] One of the main components of successful digital strategies is to systematically establish monopolies and then secure them with such insurmountable protective walls that, ideally, they can be exploited without any further effort until the day after tomorrow.[7]

While all other market participants have to deal with 'annoying' competitors who are constantly launching new products on the market, undercutting prices and surprising customers with special offers or promotions, the tech companies can earn money in a similar way to the feudalistic territorial lords of the Middle Ages.

Since they own the monopolies, they simply collect access rents for which they don't have to lift a finger. Let's illustrate this with the example of Amazon, the world's largest online marketplace. If you're a manufacturer of products, there is no way around Amazon, because all potential digital buyers are already there. Amazon can therefore demand more and more money from the dependent manufacturers at will, just as the medieval feudal lords optimised their situation regarding land. Amazon earns, for example, through the trade margin on its sales, through the sale of retail media packages to manufacturers, the sale of advertising space on its own platform, through warehousing and shipping via Fulfillment-by-Amazon (FBA), through fees for coupons and deals as well as the monthly subscription costs for the seller account that professional sellers need in order to access the marketplace, and so on and so forth. According to a study by the consultancy Oliver Wyman, 30 % of all manufacturers no longer earn any money on the platform because Amazon is taking more and more margin from them every year.[8]

At the same time, the exploited manufacturers have been feeding Amazon with data for years and even decades. Amazon therefore knows more about buying behaviour towards each product than any manufacturer. And when the 'Amazon monopoly vampire' has sucked every last drop of blood out of a manufacturer, it can simply drop it because it can easily copy the leading brands and bestsellers and produce them by itself and based on its own data treasures. Amazon already has more than 140 own brands. And it is growing and growing and growing.[9]

Just as the medieval feudal lord converted monopolised access to land into access rents, Amazon does exactly the same with its manufacturers. Just as the medieval feudal lord said to the peasants: "Go to hell if you don't like it!", Amazon could say exactly the same to the manufacturers. Like the medieval peasants, however, the manufacturers or sellers can't leave 'feudal Amazon' either, because they have invested years and decades in building their business model on this platform and are completely dependent on it.

Take a look around and you will see that ever larger areas of our lives are dependent on these digital monopolies. How do you want to survive as a small, medium-sized company, if you can't be found on Google? How do you want to survive as a musician if you don't 'sell your soul' to Spotify and Apple Music and don't voluntarily (!) accept being fobbed off with ridiculous amounts of cents? How do you want to be successful as an editor without posting your contributions for free on social media? How can you be successful as an artist without being on Instagram or TikTok every day? How do you want to be elected as a politician without being 'live' on the platforms all the time? How do you want to complete transactions online without offering PayPal as a payment method? And even I, as a 'tech critic', have to offer my books on Amazon because that's where the majority of digital book sales are made.[10] Anyone who thinks that this comparison with medieval feudalism is far-fetched should pause for a moment and consider how extensive the similarities actually are, namely:

1. *Hopelessness* — in both medieval and 'digital feudalism', people have hardly any realistic options that allow them to escape the monopolies. They are completely at their mercy, largely dependent and therefore not free.

2. *Pseudo-freedom* — the feudal relationship was, back then, and is now built on the assumption that the exploited are voluntarily accepting 'benefits' given to them.

3. *Universality* — as in medieval feudalism, all aspects and areas of our digital world are affected today.

4. *Value creation through rents* — monopolists generate their profits in a similar way to the way in which accumulations of capital yield income for their owners (*interest* payments in the case of loans, for example, *rents* and *lease* payments in the case of real estate). The 'digital monopolists' typically demand *rents for access* in a similar way to the way in which the medieval feudal lords collected rents for access to land.

5. *Increasing exploitation* — over time, the 'digital feudal lords' are also constantly devising new levies that we have to pay. We have to grudgingly accept this because we are completely dependent.

6. *Total (private) legal power* — on his territory, the medieval feudal lord was always also the judge and ran the court. Exactly the same principle applies to the platforms, because the tech giants can unilaterally determine the rules through their terms of use; they provide the law, the judges, the 'legal' processes and have full executive authority, all at once. There is no division of powers.

7. *The dysfunctionality of higher authorities* — in the Middle Ages, higher authorities (such as the royalty) were so weak that those who were exploited had little chance of being heard or receiving help at higher levels. Similarly, the institutions and authorities in the USA, the EU, the EU member states, or the UK, for example, are far too weak today to really counter the superiority of the 'digital feudalists'.

8. *Extensive exemption from taxes* — the 'feudal lords' in the Middle Ages were already largely exempt from paying taxes. Then, as now, the feudal lord enjoyed a double immunity — in relation to taxes, and in relation to autonomy under private law on his own territory or within his own platform. "The word [immunity] denotes the union of two privileges: Exemption from certain tax levies, prohibition for royal officials to enter the 'immune' territory for whatever reason. This almost inevitably resulted in the transfer of certain legal rights over the lord's inhabitants."[11]

9. *Deceiving the exploited through ideology* — medieval feudalism lasted for many centuries. Although the system of exploitation is obvious, people considered it 'normal' in the age of feudalism. In the same way, we consider 'digital exploitation systems' to be 'normal' today and don't question them.

Let's go back now to the starting point of this chapter. The first, most important and most powerful weapon in the 'media war' is the establishment of digital monopolies and the control exerted by them. We have taken a long detour to demonstrate that monopolies are not an insignificant, abstract problem for antitrust authorities, economists, competition regulators and detached experts to grapple with.

We need to wake up and recognise that the establishment of monopolies is the main weapon of libertarian and anti-democratic tech corporations, serving a single purpose, namely to economically exploit as many people as possible as much as possible, while systematically disempowering them, depriving them of their freedom and (as we will see later) manipulating and dominating them through the control of the digital public sphere. In this uncontrolled form, monopolies are nothing less than an indirect, sublimated form of robbery and deprivation of freedom.[12]

Let us again recall what we said in the second chapter, in which we showed that the hostile takeover of the public sphere and 'forum' is an anti-democratic act that works like a coup d'état. Let us consider once again the nature of this idealised 'forum'. Typically, this public square inside the city is *both* a marketplace and a meeting place.

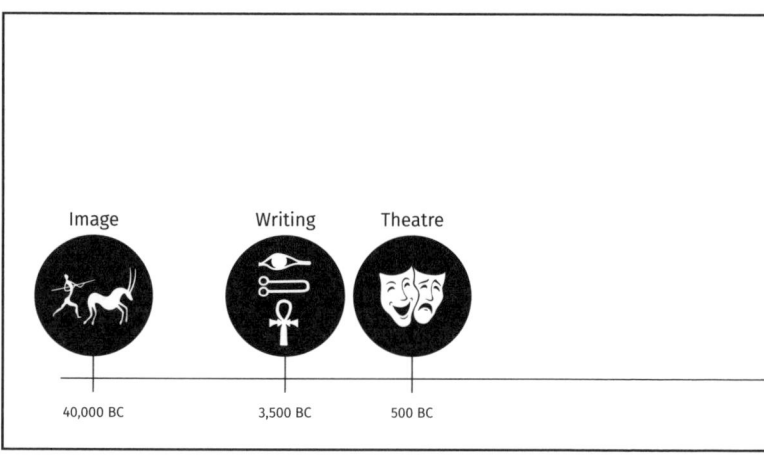

Isn't it fascinating that the tech monopolies have taken control of both in equal measure? Just as Musk calls his platform 'The World's Townsquare', Amazon calls its platform 'Marketplace'. In other words, the public marketplace formerly created by the democratic community now belongs to a private company. The democratic community has effectively been thrown out. This marketplace no longer belongs to the city or the State, but to Amazon. Sociologist Philipp Staab calls this phenomenon "proprietary markets": "the leading companies of the commercial internet […] no longer really operate in markets. *They are these markets*".[13] Or to put it another way: Amazon is both a seller within the market and the ruler of the market itself.

Just as Amazon has now taken over the marketplace, the monopolies and oligopolies of Dark Tech have taken over the most important democracy-relevant media genres (e.g. Google for the search engines, Meta for the media genre of social media, ChatGPT similarly dominates the field of generative AI and so on). Anyone who wants to appear in these media must submit to the rules and algorithms dictated by Dark Tech.

Remember: the goal of the libertarians is to dismantle the State and transfer power to corporations. Now it is clear that the mechanics

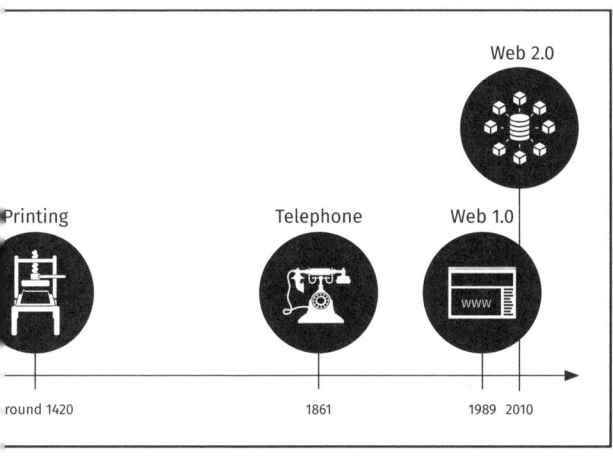

Figure 6: Paradigm shift in the history of the media: Media were always freely accessible, public goods — until they were taken over by platforms (Web 2.0)

THE INVASION 89

of monopolisation produce exactly this result. If Amazon owns the digital market and companies like Meta and Alphabet own the digital media sphere, then it becomes clear that the process of monopolisation in itself massively disempowers the democratic State in line with libertarian objectives.

Digital media genres 'belong' to the digital groups

Just how dramatic this development is becomes clear if we take another step back. Let's consider for a moment the entire history of the media since the first images appeared on cave walls in the Stone Age. At no time since then have media or media genres 'belonged' to one inventor or owner. Writing, the theatre, the printing press, radio or television: they were all 'free media' because they could never be completely controlled by individual providers. Of course, dictatorial regimes have repeatedly tried to control the media by force (such as during the Nazi era in Germany). But the media genres themselves were never owned and controlled by single private actors.

In fact, there was one important historical exception in the history of the media, namely the telephone, which serves to illustrate this issue. The inventor, Alexander Graham Bell, and the company AT&T, had succeeded in registering very far-reaching patents. For the first time in the global history of the media, a private company was able to completely dominate a media genre. However, this was very much disliked by the free-market-minded US government at the time. The US government therefore forced AT&T to open up the patents to allow competition and diversity. Theodore Vail, the President of AT&T, later said: "Society has never allowed that which is necessary to existence to be controlled by private interest."[14]

Since then, this danger has been averted for many decades. Even the 'World Wide Web' was carefully designed by its inventor, Tim Berners-Lee, on the basis of open standards to guarantee that it would remain an independent and 'free' medium. To this day, the 'World

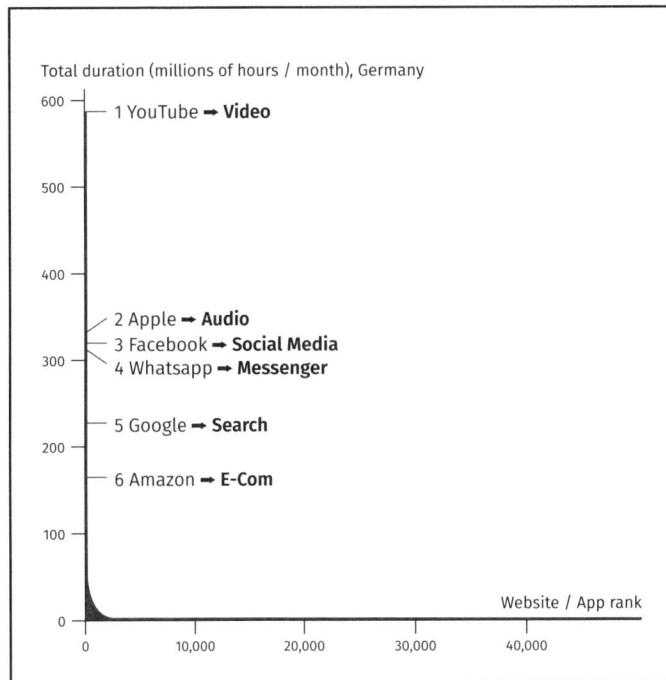

Figure 7: Distribution of total traffic on the internet — the biggest monopolists / oligopolists control entire media genres (data: Andree/Thomsen: Atlas of the Digital World)

Wide Web' is not a company, has no CEO, is managed by non-profit organisations and does not generate billions in sales or profits. The 'World Wide Web' was conceived of as a public good.[15]

And it remained a public good, until today's Dark Tech companies succeeded in drying up the free internet of traffic through the use of network effects and other unfair, often even illegal methods. Today, almost all usage takes place in the silos of their monopolistic and oligopolistic platforms.

The above diagramme shows the distribution of all digital traffic on the German internet across all end devices (smartphone, tablet, desktop). Not only do we see that all traffic is accounted for by very few monopolists and oligopolists. Much worse, the entire rest of the internet has been completely 'drained' (which is why the graph is virtually congruent with the y-axis and the x-axis, so that the line is barely recognisable). This means, for instance, that independent journalistic offers have hardly any chance of making money and surviving in 'digital conditions'. The same holds true for the streaming services of broadcasters, for public service broadcasters, for webshops, for SMEs, global brand groups, bloggers, start-ups, and so on. They all barely manage to get any usage and 'traffic', rotting away in the huge graveyard of offerings we see here. However, if we look at the largest offerings that we've listed here by name, one thing is immediately apparent: Each offer monopolises either media genres (video, audio, search engines) or the market for digital transactions, i.e. Amazon.

Now we need to add one more aspect to understand the huge scale of 'digital feudalism'. Let's remember our third basic rule above: 'The more important the affected good is for basic existence, the more intensively the monopolist can exploit its victims.' The big problem is that *access to media, but also to markets, is a basic requirement of modern life.* How is a manufacturer supposed to get transactions in the digital economy if almost everything has to go through Amazon? And how are people supposed to find information in the digital sphere if not via the media genres that are relevant to democracy, but which are dominated and controlled by monopolists?

This gives us an understanding of the importance of monopolies in the media war. Those who own monopolies and oligopolies that block and control *access* to such public goods have endless opportunities to 'blackmail' the users. This is because access to digital media genres and markets is just as necessary for modern existence as access to clean air, a public network of roads or to healthcare are. Monopolistic control of such goods means that people are very largely at the mercy of monopolists.

Blocking and controlling access to goods that are necessary for existence has always been a tried and tested means of warfare. For example, a castle is besieged until the water or food runs out and the occupants give up without a fight. Dark Tech companies have blackmailed democratic governments dozens of times in the past,[16] basically saying: "If you don't do x or y, we'll shut down our platform for the people in your country." The shameless use of blackmail alone displays the gigantic power of Dark Tech companies. We can be absolutely certain that many democratic governments no longer dare to do anything against this superior power for fear of such reactions or sanctions. And this is precisely what shows who is actually in charge here and who has long since submitted.

Anyone who still thinks that this is an exaggeration should bear in mind that we are currently still in a transition phase. Our world is not yet fully digitised. As already explained above (▶1): If we take the media sphere as an example, we can assume that around 60 % of attention is currently devoted to digital channels. Conversely, this means that around 40 % of all attention is still attracted by analogue channels (e.g. television, radio, newspapers). But what happens when these have largely disappeared? Then our dependence on the digital monopolists will be complete. The dynamics of the digital transformation mean that, with every passing day, the balance of power further shifts in favour of the tech monopolists and only increases our dependency and susceptibility to blackmail.

We are trapped, caught in the lock-in of monopolies, especially as the same tech oligarchs who completely control our European digital markets and media also own our IT infrastructures, data rooms and office software. We will come back to this (▶8).

5.
THE OCCUPATION

Horror stories about European regulation

There is a popular meme circulating on social media with the amusing slogan: 'America innovates, China replicates, Europe regulates'. It is as if, in a concave mirror, it is summarising a series of beliefs that could read something like this: *The internet is free — it should not be regulated! The EU bureaucrats are to blame for the fact that we can't get anything done in Europe. Strict rules only stifle innovation*, and so on and so forth.

As we will see, the exact opposite is the case. It is not that we are regulating Dark Tech but the other way around. Dark Tech is regulating us. But such catchphrases ('America innovates…') are the best way to mask the actual reality and then circulate it as memes on platform feeds. That's why we now even have German politicians who (like Christian Lindner from the FDP, Freie Demokratische Partei, Free Democratic Party) cheerfully suggested that we should dare to be a little bit more like Musk. Lindner, of all people, was the leader of a party that claims to be particularly competent in economic matters. This is astonishing because it is precisely the libertarian oligarchs who are getting rid of the very things that free market advocates otherwise value: Open markets, competition, fair opportunities for all, and a neutral framework that creates a level playing field for all market participants.

In fact, the libertarian tech monopolists have done away with competition more consistently than even a coalition of Marx, Engels, Lenin and Stalin could ever have managed with maximum effort. For decades, free-market and pro-business parties have railed against left-wing socialists and greens for their 'disastrous' economic policies, which allegedly endanger the 'free economy' and 'overburden corporations'. But how is it possible that the very same free market advocates don't even notice when Dark Tech and the US 'broligarchy' dismantle the free market economy in a more fundamental way than the socialists and the green parties could ever achieve? Can't they see that, in the digital markets which will shape our economy in the future, the free economy and fair competition has already been completely dismantled? It is quite stunning that we are experiencing the global collapse of free market liberalism and thus *The Crisis of Democratic Capitalism*, as the British economist Martin Wolf has vividly put it — and of all people, the capitalists fail to notice.[1]

Ideology is to blame for these and similar distortions of perception. The annoying thing about ideology is that we are all, without exception, victims of ideologies, but we are unable to recognise the very ideologies that mislead and deceive us. We can see the mote in the other person's eye, but not the beam in our own. That's why our detour through the feudalism of the Middle Ages was so important. We need to ask ourselves: why did people allow themselves to be exploited by feudal lords for centuries?

If we take a look at the history of feudalism, we can see that, by the 12th century at the latest, some clear-sighted people were already having serious doubts as to whether the feudal system of oppression was really that beneficial for them. And they had the courage to come up with an alternative way of life. They revolted against two monopolies — the monopolisation of access to land by the feudal lords, and, extremely significant in the Christian Middle Ages, the monopoly of access to salvation by the Catholic Church. At that time, these people simply wanted to do their own thing, to lead a godly, pious life, to work hard and to reap the fruits of their labour themselves. By doing so, however, they challenged the order of feudal exploitation. In view of this 'monstrosity', the historian Georges

Duby smugly poses the question: "So these madmen don't know that servitude is the wages of sin?"[2] And indeed: the whole project was perceived to be so outrageous that these ideas were immediately branded as HERESY, and all such efforts were immediately crushed by authorities with brute force. It had to be ensured, according to Duby, "that the line was not crossed between those who have the right to command because they are rich and do nothing, and those who must obey because they work".[3]

Isn't that incredible? All of this happened hundreds of years before Luther succeeded in breaking the Catholic Church's monopoly of access to Christian salvation. It was the same Luther who revealed to his contemporaries the direct connection between the monopolisation of salvation and the economic exploitation processes of the papacy. The entire machine of papal exploitation was only possible by force and by making use of this monopolisation.[4] The liberation of the feudalist economy took even longer and was only achieved after absolutism was done away with in the wake of the French Revolution after the emergence of industrialisation.

Thus, many hundreds of years passed in which the intellectual elites of feudalism, the theologians, lawyers and scholars, made huge scholarly efforts to tell the people out there the most adventurous fairy tales as to why this form of exploitation was, firstly, completely *natural* (as it was intended for them in the divine and just order of things) and, secondly, why all the suffering would pay off for the oppressed peasants in the afterlife at the latest.

The tech oligarchs are blitzing us today in a similar way. Disguised as nerds and do-gooders, they keep on telling us that they just care for *freedom of speech*, that they want to create a *better world*, giving people *a voice* and *empowerment*. For decades, 'digital evangelists' such as Chris Anderson, Jeff Jarvis, Thomas Friedman and Jeremy Rifkin have been telling us, in similar ways, in their bestsellers and at conferences that the expropriation by tech companies is really great for us. *Wikinomics*, i.e. working for free for tech monopolists in *casual digital communities*, will deliver salvation for us all. When regulatory attempts were made to limit the power of the platforms, internet activists were often claiming that such measures *would completely destroy the free internet as we know it* and *evil state authorities were plotting to censor the web across the board*. In that way, legions of hackers, nerds and pirates have defended 'net freedom' in the interests of the tech giants.

It was not only the 'digital evangelists' and activists that were instrumentalised by Dark Tech on its way to power. Influential economic thinkers of the 'Chicago School' such as Aaron Director or Robert Bork helped Dark Tech's case. The two thinkers had claimed that monopolies were really not bad at all for the economy if consumer prices remained low, but actually beneficial for consumers. These and other arguments have since ensured, in the relevant political bodies, that monopolies have been allowed to proliferate and the antitrust authorities have not even intervened against the many killer acquisitions done by the tech corporations.[5]

We can immediately see ideology at work here. If 'left-wing ecologists and socialists' do something that potentially harms competition, the reaction is a huge outcry against 'communism'. But if libertarian tech oligarchs completely abolish fair economic competition, nobody cares. Free market advocates who passionately raise their voices 'against regulation' do not even seem to notice the total abolition of free markets and competition under digital conditions. We can see how ideology determines perception. That was no different in the darkest and most feudal times of the Middle Ages than it is today.

That's why it's time to push all these fairy tales aside. Once again, I am taking a brief detour because nothing helps us to see through our own ideological blindness more than approaching the topic through a comparable case that is outside the scope of our own limited view of the world. For this purpose, I'm using the legal scholar Katharina Pistor's research as a starting point.[6] She deals with the question as to how rulers, oligarchs, the rich and powerful have managed to accumulate enormous amounts of wealth and power in the past.

She develops her model using the paradigm of the so-called *commons*. In the late Middle Ages and early modern period, these were areas of land that were commonly used by all members of a collective alike, such as the people of a village or town, typically to extract resources (e. g. to collect firewood, hunt animals, catch fish, etc.). The *commons* were used by the entire community and were therefore treated as *common goods*.

In 15th century England, these *commons* were then seized by large landowners through processes of *enclosure*. The landlord typically created facts without asking anyone for permission. He usually just fenced off the area he wanted to call his own and marked his claim with a fence, wall or hedge for all to see.

Katharina Pistor now shows that, from the point of view of the rulers, it is not enough to carry out this appropriation, i. e. 'only' to seize the land by force. It also requires a *legal codification* that certifies the land *as private property* for the 'occupier' and his descendants forever, *legalising* the appropriation afterwards and *legitimising* it through specific legal codes in order to safeguard it against possible later objections from third parties.

Katharina Pistor's fascinating insight is that it is not just the aggressive act of appropriation itself that is important. In practice, the appropriation is only completed when knowledgeable lawyers and attorneys help the aggressors convert the occupied zone into permanent property. It is then also the lawyers who invent arguments to somehow *legitimise* the completed aggressive appropriation afterwards.

Let's take a look at the example of the *enclosures* of *commons* at the time. The landlord's lawyers would argue in court, for example, that he was *the first* to take possession of this land (the evolution of the argument under colonialism was that the new 'owner' was the first one who had 'discovered' the land); that he had enclosed his property by erecting a fence or the like; that he had increased the value of the land in question (e. g. by removing stones from the ground, clearing a forest, etc.); that the agricultural use of this land by the landlord is more effective than if it were used for collective farming and is therefore 'a good thing for everyone', and so on. And, of course, it might involve more fundamental attributions or definitions: the legal codes might stipulate that, before the enclosure, the land had only been *used*, but not *owned* by the collective.

Now put yourself in the shoes of the people who were just expelled from the commons — imagine you are sitting in court right now. The landlord who has just taken the access to the land away from you puts forward these or similar arguments. And he might ask you, for instance: "Can you produce any legal documents that prove that this land was really your legal property?" What would your reaction be? That's right! You would freak out: "WTF!!!" But the amazing thing is: even if we (especially looking at this topic from the perspective of today) understand how cleverly this method of appropriation is legally constructed, these completely arbitrary arguments were still effective for centuries and enabled the appropriation of huge territories that were thus smoothly transformed into the property of the landlords. The appropriating aggressors could almost blindly rely on the collaboration of lawyers and legislators. This was particularly the case in the age of colonialism: why else would settlers take on the dangers of such an operation when they were crossing the world at great risk? They could always assume "that an aggressive seizure would ultimately provide them with a title of ownership", according to Pistor.[7]

And here's the thing: look at our time as if you were also looking at it from a distance. Then you will understand: Even today, it's not enough to just establish one's own dominance, for example through monopolistic control of an entire market. Also today, a 'legal code' is required that legalises and legitimises this dominance through specific privileges, prerogatives or exemptions. And also today, we seem to be 'too stupid' to defend ourselves. Not long ago, Eric Schmidt, the former CEO of Google, was talking to young founders who ran start-ups in the field of generative AI. While being recorded on camera, he unabashedly recommended to them that they should simply "steal" intellectual property as much as they liked and then leave it to a "whole bunch of lawyers to go clean the mess up".[8]

As we can see, it doesn't matter structurally whether you are a land appropriating landlord, a colonialist settler or a Dark Tech corporation. The act of appropriation, the establishment of your dominance or the setting up of monopolies itself is worthless unless you establish a *legal code* that will secure your dominance and shield it effectively against future claims: "all they need are the right lawyers on their side to legally code their estates",[9] according to Pistor.

Privileges and preferential legal treatment for the digital oligarchy

The EU has received praise at the international level for having at least wrestled some legal concessions from the Dark Tech companies. However, I would argue that there is a core misunderstanding here. At the fundamental level of regulation, the exact opposite is true: big tech regulates us, it's not us who are regulating big tech. In fact, the lawyers of the Dark Tech corporations have created a series of legal privileges that made their 'feudalistic rule' possible in the first place and fixed it as a 'legal code', as referred to by Katharina Pistor. Let's take a look at this in detail:

1. Service provider privilege

The Dark Tech companies were able to ensure that their media offerings are not regulated as media. As so-called 'service providers' (or 'intermediaries'), they receive massively privileged legal treatment. They are treated as if they were not media, but just something like telephone networks. This is of course completely absurd, firstly because they *are* media, secondly because people also call them 'social media', and thirdly because users regard them as being media and use them like media. What is even more absurd is that, fourthly, these service providers earn money in exactly the same way as editorial media or 'content providers' do. Just as CNN, for example, offers viewers a television programme and shows advertising in between, Facebook or Instagram show a feed, also containing advertising.

Further information: 'Intermediaries' versus 'media'. A multi-perspective investigation into the questionable viability of a regulatory distinction' (MedienWirtschaft 3/2024)

Legally, this is a pure self-contradiction, because even though specific content is being monetised, the Dark Tech companies adamantly deny that they are content providers at all. Yet how on earth should somebody be allowed to monetise content if he is denying that he is a content provider? Up to today, this legal privilege is the foundation of the dominance of the Dark Tech corporations. Its basic assumption (platforms are not media) is, scientifically speaking, just as far-fetched as the landlords' argument that they were the first to 'discover' or 'fence off' the land and therefore it was their 'property'.

2. Liability privilege

Now it gets wild: further legal privileges are now being derived from this arbitrary and scientifically incorrect (!) basis. As the Dark Tech companies are 'only' treated as service providers, they are also exempt from liability for the platform content.[10] A scandal involving the controversial podcaster Joe Rogan shows just how absurd this is: Although Spotify paid the podcaster 100 million US dollars for his content (which it in turn monetises from its users), Spotify cannot be made liable for Rogan's racist statements or factual claims that are false, for example. If Joe Rogan had made exactly the same statements as the host of a television programme, for example, the station would be fully liable.[11]

3. Criminal privilege

The criminal privilege is then derived from the liability privilege. Do you recognise a pattern here? Lunacy A leads to lunacy B leads to lunacy C. Because, as unbelievable as it may sound, platforms are still allowed to *monetise* crimes and criminal content online. They are therefore allowed to monetise defamations of people based on factual claims that are false, racist insults, discrimination, as long as this content has not been removed via notice and takedown procedures, which are generally always implemented too late (there might be differences as to what content is regarded as criminal depending on the country, but the principle that platforms are not liable is the same).[12] Are you aware of any other business model in Western democracies where the economic actors are allowed to convert *specific criminal offences* (!!) into *specific revenues and profits,* precisely attributable to those offences? I know of no case like that. Imagine something like this for drug trafficking, for example: A drug dealer couldn't be legally prosecuted if he didn't produce the sold crack by himself ("Hey, sorry guys, I have nothing to do with the crack, you know I'm just an 'intermediary', a 'service provider'"). With Dark Tech platforms, none of this is a problem thanks to their unique legal privileges.

4. Monopoly privilege

There are strict regulations against the formation of media monopolies in the Western world. In Germany, for example, no provider may have more than a 30 % share of usage in the television category in order to prevent an excessive accumulation of opinion power. Although digital media genres such as search engines, social media or free video-on-demand are just as relevant to democracy as analogue media types, there are no limits here. ZERO. Once again, Dark Tech is massively privileged. The Dark Tech companies can form monopolies and bundle opinion power without any limits, if their monopolies arise naturally (such as the case with the Google search engine, for instance).

5. Instrumentalisation privilege

The issue of instrumentalisation is similar. For example, German TV stations are obliged to report in a balanced manner in the context of election campaigns (according to the principle of 'graduated equality of opportunity'). Once again, 'service providers' are not affected by such rules. Someone like Elon Musk can unilaterally instrumentalise his platform X to recommend Donald Trump in the USA, for example, or to actively campaign for the right-wing AfD in Germany.

6. Lock-in privilege

In most markets, consumers are protected from malicious providers restricting people's freedom of choice and actively preventing them from using other services. By contrast, Dark Tech companies are allowed to protect their monopolies with huge digital 'walls' that prevent users from leaving the platform. For example, platforms are allowed to eliminate 'outlinks', i.e. links through which you would be directed to independent digital offerings outside the platform. Tiktok, for instance, does not allow creators to set any outlinks in the videos. Instagram does not allow direct outlinks either. People interested in visiting an external source have to go through a long, laborious detour that takes about 6–7 steps ('link in bio'), but even then the (external) content is shown in the in-app browser of Instagram. Furthermore, the platforms may even throttle and 'penalise' posts with such outlinks so that hardly anyone gets to see such posts at all. Finally, they are allowed to create barriers through so-called 'closed standards' that prevent users from seamlessly distributing content to other platforms or, for example, transferring followers (with their consent) to other platforms. A little joke on the side: the same Dark Tech managers who actively create these mechanisms of lock-in then show up on conference panels and tell everyone with an innocent face: *we are an OPEN platform…*

7. Expropriation privilege

Dark Tech companies are allowed to use content that is the intellectual property of authors for the training of artificial intelligence technologies. Lawyers in the USA have come up with a really great euphemism for this total mass expropriation of authors, artists and creatives: they call it 'fair use'. Now you might think that's so absurd, it can't be, but that's what it's actually called. Indeed, you couldn't even think of making something like that up. It's a bit like calling colonialist land occupations *fair use* — because the colonialists think that the new rule is 'a good thing for everyone'.

The digital reality: 'US dominates — EU suffocates'

Now that we have hopefully gained sufficiently in awareness (and also understand that the 'US innovates — EU regulates' narrative is just part of a huge advertising campaign by the 'digital feudalist' occupiers), we can take a closer look at the last mentioned example with Katharina Pistor's astute model.

So let's briefly imagine all the content ever created by European authors, artists, influencers, bloggers, creators, but also simply by us European users, as one big beautiful cow. This cow has been virtually released for free exploitation by the various regulations from the DSM Directive (*Directive on Copyright in the Digital Single Market*), the AI Act and the Digital Markets Act for Dark Tech. Although this applies in principle to all participants (and not just to big tech), we also see the typical tendencies towards monopoly formation in this market, which in turn means that this rule, which is called *fair use* in the US, is fair at best for the tech oligarchs and is extremely unfair for everyone else who has no economic access to play along here — and above all for the authors who are deprived of their rights.

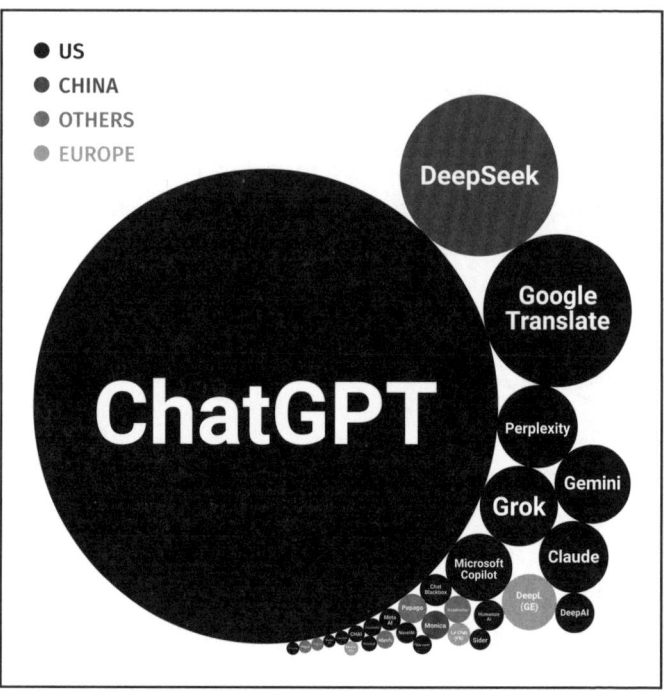

Fig. 8: Market share of generative AI (text generators) by monthly visits, March 2025[13]

Dark Tech can now take advantage of our cow as much as it pleases — and from this cow, in turn, produce and sell burgers, meatballs, hot dogs and so on, simultaneously giving all business models of creative people (i. e. musicians, photographers, journalists, graphic designers, copywriters, etc.) a shot in the neck.

But if our lawyers had been clever, they would have noticed that it's not just our cow that can be freely given away to Dark Tech for alleged *fair use*. There is another, beautiful and fantastic giant cow that belongs to Dark Tech itself — namely the platforms. The trick is that the platforms contain billions of pieces of content that originate from European users. In terms of copyright, this content belongs to us Europeans. Of course, the Dark Tech companies have set a trap for us here too, because they have forced us users to cede all usage rights to all our content via the terms and conditions of use (and because they have access to all this content, they are in a much better position than any other market participant to train their own generative AI technologies anyway). And through their right to define usage conditions, they are able to fence off all this content towards the outside.

Now, if our legal negotiators had been a little smarter, they would have made a counter-proposal, something like this: "Hey dark tech, you're interested in our cow, you want to completely gut it and process it? Cool. Because you have a cow too. In return for processing our cow, how about giving European start-ups and companies fair access ('fair use') to your cow? Meaning: European companies could then receive aggregated and anonymised data from the billions of European texts, images and videos stored on your platforms — and we could develop our own AI technologies on this basis?"

However, NOTHING like this was negotiated. We gave Dark Tech our cow. But we can't get our hands on Dark Tech's cow.

Let's imagine that we would just completely lose it now in the face of all this madness: FUCK IT. And we would rob the Dark Tech cow with the same nonchalance as the Dark Tech companies have been ripping us off for years, even before the cynical *fair use* regulations existed. How would they react? Well, I can tell you. The 'cool nerd-hacker dudes' from Dark Tech would send out legions of their lawyers and bludgeon anything that came just a little bit too close to them with the most brutal legal force. "NOT ONE STEP FURTHER", they will say, "you cannot enter OUR PROPERTY!!!"

These are just some of the preferential legal treatments, privileges and exemptions without which it would be completely impossible for the Dark Tech giants to push all other providers to the wall and continue to expand their own monopolies. So much for 'America innovates — Europe regulates'. And so much for 'The Internet is free — and should not be regulated'.

Even very naïve people should realise that the supremacy of Dark Tech in the digital world would collapse instantly if we were to abolish these feudalistic legal privileges. Should we one day (i.e. very hypothetically) have the courage to liberate the internet, we will make a funny observation and slap our thighs with laughter: the Dark Tech companies, of all people, who supposedly argue so blatantly 'against regulation' and for 'free markets', would fight tooth and nail for these legal privileges and preferential treatments. They would send legions of lawyers, who would defend *these feudalistic misregulations and privileges* to the last drop of blood.

We can also see that perhaps these rules are great for the USA, because that's where the Dark Tech companies are based and rake in their immeasurable wealth. But are they beneficial from a European perspective? Of course not. We have not only put up with all this nonsense but have even voluntarily (!) fixed it as legal entitlements and served it all up to Dark Tech on a silver platter. Unfortunately, we are the ones who were conquered by the tech monopolies in the first place. But on top of that, we were stupid enough to give *ourselves* laws that officially legalise and fix the digital occupation of the media and the digital markets by monopolies. The legal negotiators effectively presented us with all these laws to sign. Metaphorically speaking, these rules say: "Whoever erects a fence around our country also owns our country. Once the fence is erected, they can keep it forever and do whatever they want with it. We will be powerless in the future." And then we signed them.

But it really is beyond the peak of stupidity when the Dark Tech occupiers run around the world telling people: "You'd better leave regulation alone and leave the field to us, because we understand a lot more about it anyway" — and we, the 'digital serfs', *spread* this nonsense *ourselves, and on the platforms of Dark Tech* ('America innovates — Europe regulates').

This applies especially when you ask yourself this question: Who defines the rules *within* the digital monopolies, such as the terms of use? Oh yes, you realise, it's the platforms themselves. Once again, our understanding of monopolies leads to a key insight. Because in conditions in which people have virtually no choice but to use such monopolistic offers, the (otherwise completely harmless) authorisation of all companies to establish terms of use then leads to 'law-like effects'. Lawrence Lessig called the same principle 'code is law' back in 1999. Dark Tech companies thus create their own secondary legal system, which they also place 'above' our State law, and in which they develop their own sovereignty that is no longer democratically legitimised — according to Moritz Holzgraefe and Nils Ole Oermann one of the many aspects in which "digital platforms can be understood as States".[14]

It is clear that the ever-increasing sovereignty of platforms is also undermining the sovereignty and legitimacy of the democratic State. As we have already known since Chapter 3, they want to establish their own state-like sovereignty through their global organisations, which often operate extraterritorially. This is precisely what marks the deliberate and planned anti-democratic aspect of their actions. In any case, it takes a lot of naïvety to post about this topic on the platforms: 'America innovates — Europe regulates.'

6.
THE WEAPONS

Digital manipulation machines

The fact that the platforms are destroying our 'inclusive public sphere' (Jürgen Habermas)[1] and thus the basis of our democracy has been obvious ever since, if not before, Trump supporters stormed the Capitol in Washington in January 2021. These supporters were firmly convinced that the election had been 'stolen' from Trump.

We can also see from such cases: the platforms themselves are the most important weapons of the libertarians in the media war (Bannon even spoke of 'nuclear weapons'). Monopolies allow tech companies to unilaterally control which of the users receives which information. But at the same time, they (and only they!) determine the internal structures, rules and laws that create this media reality in the first place.

However, we have known since Marshall McLuhan, the founder of media studies, that media are never 'innocent'. Previously, it had been thought that media were only a kind of neutral transmitter. In this understanding, the key aspect in the transmission is the content, whereas it would not really matter through which 'carrier' or 'channel' the content was being 'transported'. The very metaphor of 'transmission' suggests a neutrality of the medium.[2]

McLuhan was the scientific pioneer to reveal that this is not true. The different media always have a logic of their own. They therefore function like glasses that colour reality (i.e. the content) depending on which 'media glasses' you are wearing. This has important implications for our current times. At the moment, we are replacing the analogue predecessor media genres (television, radio, newspapers) with digital platforms. Thus, we are actually performing open-heart surgery on our democracy and its fundament, the public sphere. Especially as we already know at this stage of our argumentation: Dark Tech platforms are monopolising public attention after their 'coup' (▶1). Now, they 'own' the public forum in digital conditions. And furthermore, it is also the Dark Tech platforms that unilaterally determine how these new media glasses *colour and format* the messages, information and news we receive.

And again, we hardly have any access to the black boxes of the platforms and the often hundreds or even thousands of algorithms *that produce this media reality according to the wishes and power interests of the Dark Tech owners*. These interests are certainly primarily economic, which is why *the deliberate manipulation of traffic (and not 'neutrality'!) is the basis of big tech's business model* even at this level. However, we will see that these interests are also and increasingly political. It is therefore crucial that we gain an overview of the ways in which the platforms portray content, how they distort and format it. We can quickly show the most important effects in a brief run-through by looking at the various factors that are amplified by the platforms' attention economy. By doing so, we will see that these different aspects reinforce and support each other's effects, rather like a "funhouse mirror":[3]

1. Speed / real time

Let's start with the most obvious aspect: By contrast with editorial media, platforms transmit information in real time. Whoever posts first wins (because the news value is the highest). Of course, a lot of information on the web often turns out to be wrong or at least skewed (see point 9 below). However, because speed is rewarded, the more scrutinising, cautious and balanced voices lose visibility in relative terms.[4]

2. Exponential multiplication of information

The exponentially increasing amount of information on the internet is also proverbial. Allegedly, users cover a distance of around 90 metres a day when scrolling on their smartphones, which is roughly the height of the Statue of Liberty.[5] In combination with the real-time advantage (point 1), this alone means that more individual pieces of information are consumed in the user's overall diet, but at the same time a lot of attention is 'wasted' on incorrect or skewed news. This flood of information alone results in users feeling overwhelmed.[6]

3. Brevity & memification

The combination of the increase in speed (point 1) and the exponential increase in the sheer number of messages (point 2) leads to a number of consequences. In light of the shortening of users' capacity for attention (which is also biologically limited), it results in a shortening of messages, even shorter attention spans and an increased volatility of messages in the digital space.[7]

This explains the many 'innovations' of digital content providers in this field, such as memes, clickbait, listicles, journalistic articles in tiles, hashtags and so on. These are techniques for placing particularly eye-catching headlines, punchlines or other signals in the endless mass of posts, which are 'snackable' and 'thumbstopping', i.e. intended to make users stop rapidly scrolling through the feed for a moment and take superficial notice of the message.[8]

4. Concreteness / 'evidence'

The extreme shortening of attention within the conditions of the platforms creates the common pattern of digital 'revelations', which has been tried and tested millions of times and always follows a similar pattern: You show a photo or a document, for example, and a text accompanying it: "THIS IS INCREDIBLE" — what follows are the alleged terrible facts for which the image provides ULTIMATE PROOF.

You can embed every imaginable fantasy product into this structure. Here are a few examples:

You see a video of two airplanes crossing each other's flight path, but only behind one plane are contrails visible — used as PROOF: "These are dangerous chemtrails!!!! We are all being poisoned!!!!!"

Or: You see a video of an empty office that is claimed to be a government building — used as PROOF: "We pay for all these empty buildings with our taxes!!!!!"

Elon Musk was churning out vast amounts of EVIDENCE for the horrible REVELATIONS of his DOGE team. One post showed an original document from the 'Department of Defense (DOD)', here as the client of 'Thomson Reuters Special Services LLC', according to which the Department of Defense is said to have paid Reuters around 9 million US dollars for a 'social engineering program'. Of course, this fits perfectly with the theory of the 'Deep State', which allegedly works hand in hand with the editorial media to remotely control the people out there. So here we have it, *the ultimate proof of the State-coordinated re-education programmes!*

Musk posted the document with the comment: "Reuters was paid millions of dollars by the US government for 'large scale social deception'" and continued, "That is literally what it says on the purchase order! They're a total scam."

It turned out, however, that (a) the contract had been awarded by the former Trump administration, (b) it was not about Reuters news at all, but about a Reuters data division; (c) the contract had been awarded to develop defence strategies *against* cyberattacks, and (d) the contract had been made public already way before.[9]

The huge impact of such and similar 'revelations' (Musk's post, for example, attracted 35 million views and was shared 76,000 times) can be explained in combination with the brevity of messages on the web (point 1), in other words: the information is condensed into a single, tiny detail that is shown in maximum 'magnification' and ideally activates sensitive 'trigger points' among users. The specific case claims, for example: 'The corrupt elites are misusing taxpayers' money to manipulate us!' — which, on the one hand, triggers emotional reactions in terms of 'unfair discrimination' and 'imposition of elitist paternalism'.¹⁰ On the other hand, balancing contexts and holistic classifications are completely ignored. Due to the exploding number of such messages online, users are completely overwhelmed. They are exposed to a constant bombardment that makes it almost impossible to check all of these supposedly 'terrible revelations' by themselves.

We can also see from such examples why the explosion of 'accessible' information on the internet also brings massive disadvantages in terms of use. We could make better use of our limited attention capacity if we could filter out the high number of such 'spam' messages that ultimately turn out to be false, skewed or, in the best case, irrelevant.

5. 'Back-channel' capability

By contrast with analogue media, on platforms people can give direct feedback via comments. That sounds good at first (and, as we know, was always part of Dark Tech's big 'liberation' promise: all people would now be able to reach an 'audience of millions' for the first time through their platforms). However, just like the acceleration and multiplication of information, this 'back-channel' capability also has a dark side — which we will highlight in the following points.

6. Extremely uneven distribution of attention

First of all, users can only indirectly see that the promise of participation is barely fulfilled by the platforms. This is because there are very few digital superstars compared to millions of users whose content is generally not noticed at all or at least hardly noticed. The 90-9-1 rule of thumb was established early on in research, according to which 90 % of all users consume content purely passively, 9 % like it and only 1 % are active.¹¹

This trend had been confirmed by empirical studies already at the end of the noughties. A tiny number of users create a very high proportion of the content on social media. At the same time, the emergence of a 'digital attention oligarchy' became apparent: Small networks of highly visible creators who support each other, leading to self-reinforcing effects within this digital elite (metaphorically speaking: The rich get richer — the poor get poorer).[12]

A 2019 study on Twitter (now X) showed that 10% of all users create 80% of content. The radically unequal distribution of attention was reflected in this study across all key parameters of digital visibility. A follow-up study from the same year showed that the imbalance was even more pronounced for *political* content (the most visible 10% of users generated as much as 97% of all political content). Another, more recent study also confirmed the general asymmetry in 2021: 25% of all users generated 97% of the content here — the broad masses, i.e. 75% of users, only have a *share of voice* (i.e. a digital share of attention) of just 3%. Users are also aware of this unequal distribution: 21% say that 'nobody' sees their posts, 67% believe that 'only a few people' can see their content; only 11% believe that their posts reach 'many people'. In reality, the platforms give the vast majority of people no *voice*, no *empowerment*, no *participation*, in contradiction to what they are always claiming. We will see later why this is the case.[13]

This massive asymmetry in the digital distribution of attention has extremely far-reaching consequences, especially for young people who are almost exclusively on digital channels. After all, becoming an influencer is the dream job of young people. In Germany, this figure is around 35%, according to a Bitkom study from 2018. In a study from 2023, 43% of all high school graduates stated that they would like to become an influencer or creator.[14] In the USA, the proportion of GenZ members was even higher, at 57%.[15]

The problem is obvious because, under the current conditions of such 'winner-takes-all' markets, typically only a tiny elite of influencers and creators receive the majority of digital attention and the broad masses are largely left empty-handed.[16] The digital world, the preferred habitat for young people, has been designed by the Dark Tech platforms in such a way that a large proportion of them must necessarily fall by the wayside. Incidentally, the same pattern consistently runs through all platform-driven markets and is also almost proverbially known for the field of music, where only a small proportion of artists can live off the income from Spotify or Apple Music, for example, while the majority can barely make any income.[17]

The participation paradox consists in the fact that the platforms (also in the constant digital display of the very few successful 'attention millionaires') suggest: 'Anyone can reach an audience of millions' and AT THE SAME TIME leave the vast majority of digital communities virtually starving due to the extreme spread in the distribution of attention, which in turn inevitably leads to disappointment, to the assessment of 'not being heard or seen', and to many, varied feelings of being left behind and of loneliness among those affected.[18]

Finally, it is particularly fascinating that the same mechanics of digital monopoly and oligopoly formation which we were able to measure at the domain level are apparently also at work within the platforms and lead to the formation of these 'winner-take-all' markets.[19]

7. Focus on people

It is not only individuals but also institutions, brands, companies, universities, authorities and political parties that can create and use their own profiles on social media. However, experience shows that individuals generally have much more 'pull' on the platforms by comparison with organisations. Leading influencers and creators can build up a similar reach to strong media brands and individual star politicians can have followings on platforms that sometimes even outshine those of their own party.

This also has serious consequences. After all, we can also view institutions, organisations, companies, etc. as complex aggregators of views and opinions (which in themselves always represent a kind of opinion 'average'). If such institutional aggregates are reduced in their relative importance, and if individuals are performing much better, this alone leads to a loss of 'breadth' in terms of opinion power — and reinforces the formation of digital elites on a further structural level. In combination with point 5 (strong concentration), this also ironically creates a strong tendency towards the formation of a digital oligarchy. Institutions are being systematically disempowered (remember also the '*paper belt*'!), while a small minority of influencers are becoming 'attention millionaires'. Here, too, the exact *opposite* of what cyberlibertarians describe as the supposed 'democratisation' of political discourse is taking place.

This insight can also help us to understand better why Elon Musk purchased Twitter. Time and again, we have seen derisive reports claiming that the stock market value of X had fallen "by 71%" after the takeover by Elon Musk or the like.[20] These assessments don't get the point. Digital visibility means political power. Maximising his own personal power of opinion is likely to have been a key motive for Elon Musk in this takeover. After the acquisition of Twitter, for example, there were reports that Musk allegedly had "80 engineers" working on increasing the visibility of his posts and ranking his tweets "by a factor of 1,000".[21]

In a detailed analysis of digital visibility on X, the Washington Post was able to show that, in the weeks leading up to the US election, Elon Musk's posts attracted around 15 times more attention than those of Donald Trump in the same period and more than 16 times the attention *of the total, aggregated reach of all US congressional profiles in the same period* (see figure). "In 26 days around the election, Musk fired off 3,870 posts that received more than 33 billion views."[22] That is why Musk purchased Twitter. It might turn out to be the most profitable entrepreneurial act of his life.

8. (Negative) emotions

The platform algorithms love the shouting, ("I'm SPEECHLESS!!!"), attacks, hatred, agitation and malice. The fact that platforms reproduce content with negative emotions more strongly has been empirically proven time and again. A study of 30 million posts from news media on Twitter over a period of ten years (2011–2020) was able to prove the higher virality of strongly arousing negative content (for both 'biased' and more balanced senders) and, interestingly,

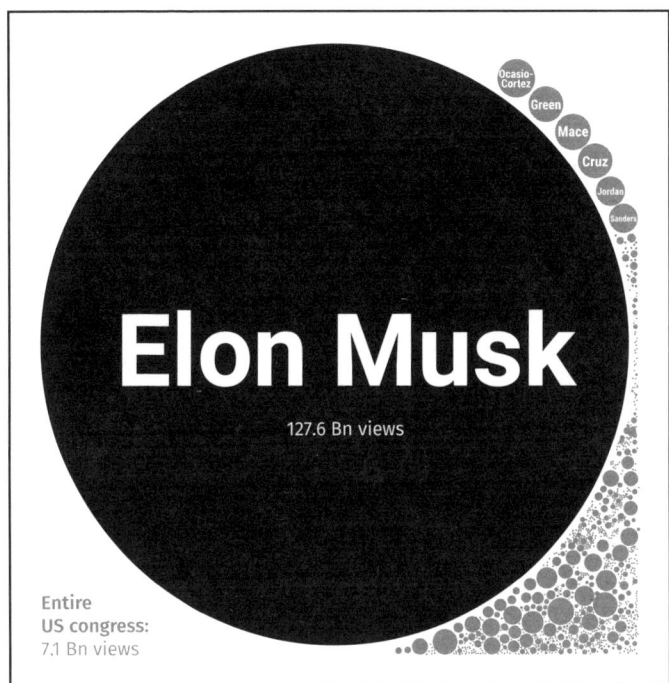

Figure 9: Media and opinion power of Elon Musk on X compared to all members of the US Congress (data analysis: Washington Post)

also demonstrate an increase in these effects over time among the representatives of balanced providers (which suggests that they are 'catching up' with the competition, so to speak).[23]

9. Sensationalism, lies, fake news, disinformation

Entertainment is a central motivation for people to use the media in the first place — and it is precisely for this reason that the media have always been threatened by 'contamination' through lies. For the creators, lies and fake news are initially a great thing because lies are generally much easier and cheaper to produce than true reports (for example, you can save time and money on extensive research), and at the same time, lies are usually much more exciting and entertaining than the mere 'real' reality.

In the political sphere, however, it is desirable to have a shared, true knowledge base on which the democratic opinion-forming of citizens can take place. This also explains why modern democratic societies differentiate between lying discourses, for example, and label them for instance as *fictional*. Anyone who reads a 'novel', for example, allows themselves to be entertained and 'suspends' critical examination (Coleridge), so it no longer matters whether the information is 'true' or 'false'.[24]

By contrast, text genres such as news are read by people on the basic assumption that they are dealing with 'true' information. However, people also want to be entertained when reading the news, which has always led to conflicting goals. That's why there has always been the threat of 'entertaining lies' infiltrating news items right from the outset. However, in the long history of journalistic reporting, new techniques, testing procedures and control mechanisms have emerged time and again, which have repeatedly fended off the (fundamental!) threat to this assumed truth.[25]

A scandal such as the falsified reports by journalist Claas Relotius, which came to light at Germany's news magazine SPIEGEL in 2018, is a good example of how editorial media have dealt with this structural problem in the past. Journalistic texts may (and should!) entertain their readers, but lies and factual claims that are false must be avoided in all circumstances. Because in the case of lies, the short-term media-economic advantage ('more entertaining') is accompanied by a huge media-economic trade-off, namely the destruction of the media brand and its reputation.

In the reality of the platforms, however, it is precisely barriers like these that fall away. Authors of fake news often copy 'real' media brands without restraint, mimicking news logos, using pseudonyms, faking a journalistic CV or scientific background, and so on. Thus, it is important to understand that fake news are the rational and predictable result of the incentives set by the attention economy of the platforms. This is because the authors of fake news can maximise the entertainment value of their content (lies) and maximise monetisation in the short term without accepting any disadvantages in terms of brand and reputation building.

Thus, the tendency towards disinformation or lies on the platforms *inevitably* arises as a result of the regulation mistakes already discussed (full monetisation, no liability) in combination with the platforms' economic interest in maximising user attention. Both factors are dependent on each other and even reinforce each other. Creators can increase the attention maximisation of their content through lies or inventions; these usually turn out to be more sensational, spectacular, exaggerated, etc. and thus receive additional visibility rewards from the platforms.[26]

Because of this, it is not surprising that fake news and lies spread much faster on platforms than true news. They are always fresher than the latest real news and at the same time much more exciting and entertaining, which is why they go viral and get shared by users much more frequently. This correlation has been empirically proven on a broad basis.[27]

A key consequence of this platform logic is that we lose a shared nucleus of social truth in our society. This is because, in the flood of posts, nobody can fact-check all this information anyway. Attention spans are extremely short already. Incidentally, young people are much more likely to exclusively rely on platforms and, relatively speaking, spend much less time on independent websites. If a platform like TikTok no longer allows outlinks on posts, then fact-checking information is also very cumbersome. A new form of knowledge is emerging and we can give it the term 'knowledge without roots'.

Google also offers ready-made short 'snippets' at the top of the page so that you no longer have to look for the sources. The sources also only play a subordinate role in the responses from ChatGPT or the AI texts on the platforms. It's a paradox: digital culture, of all things, in which the supposedly 'liberated', 'independent thinkers' on the platforms like to claim that they would 'rather be doing their own research', is increasingly cutting off any 'way back' to the roots of knowledge. You are stuck in the colourful BLINGBLING of feeds and opinions. There is far too much information, at some point you no longer know what is true and what is not, and it is then that you probably stop caring. We have already lost a common, shared truth, which used to provide a basis on which we were able to have discussions — with different opinions, but still based on the same facts.[28] Today, people live with 'alternative truths' that can no longer be bridged or even connected by discussion or rational argument.

10. Polarisation

Due to the reward structures of the platforms, content that polarises is particularly incentivised. Media scientist Chris Bail summarises his research on these topics as follows: "political extremists are pushed and pulled toward increasingly radical positions by the likes, new follows, and other types of engagement they receive for doing so", which in turn creates a vicious circle of mutual outbidding in the 'digital attention economy'. This leads to a spread that is peculiar to social media, as "it normalizes extremism on one's own side, it also exaggerates the extremism of the other side. [...] Unfortunately, these types of distortion combine to create feedback loops of extremism".[29]

Accordingly, empirical studies show that polarisation is the most important driver for the spread of fake news, but also for the spread of one-sided and biased news.[30] The additional reward of verbal coarseness leads to self-reinforcing learning processes. Even the brutalisation and increase in verbal coarseness can be empirically proven over time (in this dataset over the course of a decade).[31]

11. Social status through digital visibility

In the digital sphere, power and influence are no longer generated by titles, institutions, offices or expertise, but by various metrics that indicate reach — above all the number of followers, likes, shares and so on.[32]

These indicators show the 'value' of an individual in the digital society. In the 'funhouse mirror' of mutual digital amplification (speed, brevity, emotionality, polarisation, lies, etc.), these indicators function like a meta-amplifier. The metrics of digital visibility deliver the central indicators of success and at the same time create a meta-incentive to which everyone submits. This is because all participants in this digital competition are constantly optimising the content of their posts in order to maximise the visibility of their own digital share of voice on a daily basis — and then to mirror these value indicators again back into the digital world like status symbols.

These observations underpin again the *pseudo-voluntary nature of digital feudalistic subjugation* from a new perspective. The digital occupiers merely provide the framework conditions for the (oligarchic) distribution of attention, to which all participants, without exception, *voluntarily* submit themselves. However, they have no other choice but to submit themselves (as they would otherwise disappear into digital oblivion). At the same time, the platforms own and control the central 'currency' through which social status and recognition can be achieved in our digital society.[33] The platforms provide the content-related amplifiers in combination with the associated reward systems. For this reason, it makes sense to extend the lucid metaphor of 'trigger points' to the platform structures themselves. Because, after all, everyone who posts content does not only 'trigger' particularly sensitive, conflict-laden spots in the perception of the other users. On top of that, they also observe and activate the reinforcement mechanisms of the platforms, which can therefore also be described as 'trigger points'. Through trial-and-error processes on the platforms, the creators of digital content learn which content-related trigger points provoke their opponents the most and which infrastructural trigger points they can use to maximise the impact mechanisms of the platforms for their posts.

Of course, under the conditions of monopolies it is more than cynical for the 'digital feudal lords' to say: 'Nobody is forcing people to use our platforms' (of course — they can also bury themselves outside the platforms in the huge digital graveyard). Or: 'Nobody is prohibiting journalists, politicians or users to post well-balanced, level-headed and differentiated articles on our platforms' (sure, you can do that—but it would be futile under the conditions of digital 'amplifiers' and the pre-installed incentivisation economy)

First consequence: Destruction of journalism

The platforms are destroying journalism on two levels. First of all, journalism is losing its financial basis in digital conditions. This is necessarily a result of the dynamics of digital monopoly formation, which we have analysed in the previous chapters. Through their privileges, the many preferential legal treatments and various partly legal, partly criminal methods of monopoly formation, the Dark Tech corporations have largely been able to rid the free, independent internet of traffic. This traffic is now almost exclusively in the silos of their platforms. The tech monopolies are monetised without restraint whereas independent providers hardly stand a chance, which is why we have been observing the decline of editorial media for decades. In our empirical measurements, we were able to scientifically prove the exact extent of the digital monopoly formation down to the last detail.

However, the attention economy of the platforms is also destroying journalism in terms of its content. If we look at the 'amplifiers' analysed above, we can see that the platforms outperform the 'established media' in many dimensions. By contrast with digital real-time messages, for example, the journalists are almost always 'too late'. The really new 'news' can be found on the networks, the editorial news media always lag behind. And then the messages on the platforms are always shriller, starker, more violent, more brutal, more ruthless — especially as platforms do not have to take responsibility for them.

This puts editorial media under enormous pressure (as they are perceived as being 'too late and too boring'). And it is precisely what can be analysed scientifically in great detail when comparing the content of reputable journalistic press brands on the various channels. Under social media conditions, more and more content from these media houses is being translated (by their own online teams) into clickbait perfectly adapted to the platform algorithms (i.e. 'bait' designed to encourage users to click). Thus, journalistic content is becoming more and more indistinguishable from the typical trash and clickbait on the platforms. "This sex problem can turn men into heroes in bed" is an example for such a headline. It's a Facebook post from a reputable German daily newspaper. After all, if you want to survive digitally, you have no choice but to put spectacular, emotional, radical content online as 'bait' in order to generate additional traffic for your own domain.

When it comes to news, the established media are also in a classic LOSE-LOSE situation: if they try to act as quickly as the real-time news on the platforms, for example, they run the risk of making mistakes. When that happens, the libertarian freaks on the platforms cut out just that one half-sentence, that tiny stupid mistake, magnify it a thousand times and let the troll hordes descend on the 'so-called journalists' by the thousands — "I CAN'T BELIEVE THIS …". If, on the other hand, journalists do fact-checks and try to keep a balance, then their content always looks lame and dull when compared to the 'great stuff' on the platforms. Whatever the journalists do, they end up being criticised for slavishly following the waves of excitement on the web, and so on.

Second consequence: Radicalisation of political discourse

Exactly the same problem applies to the 'established parties'. They are in the same LOSE-LOSE dilemma as the editorial offices. Let's take, as a starting point, a characteristic media scandal we had in Germany. For a regional election, three politicians from the moderate conservative party, the CDU, had a funny idea as to how to tackle the Green Party. They took a group picture, in which they were all armed with big threatening chainsaws (the symbol of the libertarians for a radical reduction of bureaucracy and the fight against the supposed 'Deep State'). They posted it on social media with the headine: 'It's time to cut out the Green Waste.' Thus, they perfectly imitated the cool stuff that works so amazingly well for right-wing radical parties on the platforms. They just had to face one problem: the more moderate CDU voters, of all people, didn't think it was so funny. They reacted in an irritated way: 'How can it be that a decent and serious party like the CDU appears like this in public?'

Note: The platforms structurally help the radical parties. When populists like Milei or Musk hold up their chainsaws, it works great for them, because the algorithms boost hatred, incitement and malice, whereas more moderate positions always receive less attention. Thus, as an 'established party', you will lose no matter what. Either you pump up the volume to maximum provocation like the radicals — then you lose, particularly as the 'real' radicals will always be more convincing than their copycats. Or you keep a lower, more balanced profile — but then you also lose, because the 'boring' content doesn't catch on and you are barely visible on the platforms as a result. It is no coincidence that extremist parties and positions are so successful on social media: The platforms are effectively campaign boosters for extremism and polarisation.

It is also interesting that, if we look at the short list of our digital 'amplifiers' and place Trump next to it as a media figure, we immediately see how well McLuhan's model works. Someone like Trump has 'platformed' himself to maximum perfection over the years, so to speak; he has conformed perfectly to the patterns of their attention rewards. This makes him, to a certain extent, completely their creature. Conversely, we can assume that Trump would have become a completely different creature under the conditions of analogue media. Or to put it again in the words of McLuhan: *The medium is the message*!

Trump communicates a lot — he already did so in his early days on Twitter, churning out chaotic amounts on Truth Social. "Flood the zone with shit" was the propaganda credo of his advisor Steve Bannon early on. At the same time, someone like Trump can constantly exploit the real-time advantage and 'throw out' one shocker after another — and at the same time force the media to constantly chase after him. A lot of the content that he puts out is outright lies or just plain bullshit — but hardly anybody cares as long as they are well entertained by Trump. By the time these lies are corrected somewhere,

Trump will have already set off 10 to 15 more 'digital flares'. Hardly anyone uses the fact-checking websites anyway. Far too boring.[34]

Again, we recognize: whoever invents the media structures also defines the thought and communication structures. In fact, Trump has emerged entirely from the platform structures. The journalist Nate White describes it aptly: "Trump is a troll. […] Scarily, he doesn't just talk in crude, witless insults — he actually thinks in them. His mind is a simple bot-like algorithm of petty prejudices and knee-jerk nastiness"[35] (a finding that may once again illustrate why it ultimately matters little who leads this movement in the future — Trump or tech ▶2; in this respect, Trump appears as Frankenstein's monster, created by Dark Tech platforms and their algorithms).

Trolls are, as it were, cynical, furiously fast provocateurs who attack again and again — and like to evade reactions according to the motto: "it was just a joke", or: "don't be like that, I didn't really mean it". Trump, Musk and the digital populists are of course 'super trolls'. They and their 'troll armies' roam the digital world on constant attack. In doing so, they use the libertarian playbook of the transgressive 'counter-culture' (▶3), according to which it is particularly 'cool' to court dictators, bash democracies, degrade women, insult minorities, be openly racist, deny climate change, insult journalists or scientists — and finally use the Hitler salute.

Through the digital structures, the platforms constantly create a WIN-WIN situation for these trolls, which they capitalise on again and again through huge digital attention. They set the agenda (even if most of it is either vile or a lie), which is generously rewarded by the platforms with additional views, comments and shares.

The victims, on the other hand, are constantly in a LOSE-LOSE situation. They have the choice: either they refrain from defending themselves and allow their opponents to beat them up from morning to night. Then it appears as if the accusations against them were true or as if they were too weak to take a stand. But if they strike back, everything is supposed to have been just a 'joke', especially as the wave of excitement has long since moved on to a new topic. Or, as with Musk's Hitler salute, it was all just a 'misunderstanding' (a denial that is also so scandalous that it is itself rewarded with a additional digital attention). If victims even take legal action in the case of punishable offenses such as doxxing, then the whole thing tips over completely and the previously funny attacking trolls become victims: "I'm shocked — XY wants to censor freedom of expression."

Because Dark Tech has constructed our digital media reality this way, it also means that the 'established parties' will inevitably *have to behave in a Trump-like manner, i.e. 'trumpify' themselves, and behave like trolls, i.e. 'trollify' themselves.* A very instructive study by the 'Potsdam Social Media Monitor' evaluated around 75,000 TikTok videos via 30 bot profiles in 2024 before the State elections in three German federal states. The profiles were created in a non-partisan way and without political preferences. However, there was a huge imbalance in the videos suggested to the users in their feeds: 71% of the political videos displayed messages of the right-wing AfD. All the other parties were barely visible.[36]

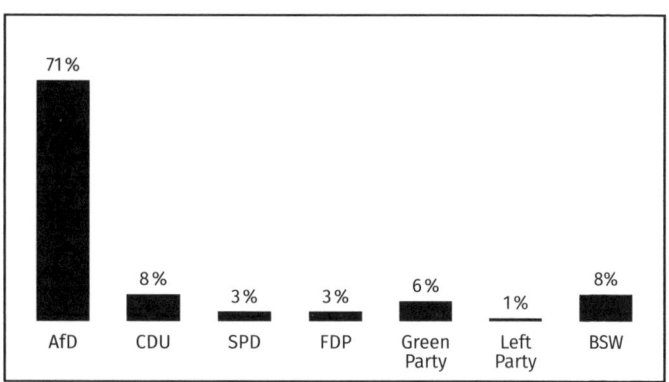

Figure 10: Relative visibility of videos played on TikTok by party (data according to Potsdam Social Media Monitor; Brandenburg, Saxony, Thuringia Augst 2024)[37]

Of course, it is possible that active manipulation plays a role here[38] (which is always difficult to prove scientifically because we have no way of accessing the platforms' black boxes).

However, if we take our own findings on digital 'amplifiers' seriously, then an alternative, albeit much more alarming, interpretation is also conceivable. This type of populism would just represent the 'perfectly fitting' political offer adapted to the polarising platform structures. The tech oligarchs have created the perfect ecosystems for anti-democratic populism and that is precisely why their platforms are so successfully colonised by populist politicians and extremists. Because the content of the populists and the media structures of these platforms are so wonderfully synchronised, we should not be at all surprised if the populists are always unbeatable here. Their spectacular successes would therefore be 'genuine', i.e. not specifically manipulated. However, they would only be 'genuine' insofar as the populists were 'only' the cloned stormtroopers of the libertarian platform programmers — remote-controlled zombies of the Musks, Zuckerbergs and Pichais and their algorithms.

Third Consequence: Elimination of the *paper belt*

If we review the various digital amplifiers mentioned above, we should also notice yet another important implication. Let's briefly remind ourselves of the objectives of the libertarian oligarchs in the media war (▶3): They want to abolish the democratic State, and they want to do so by systematically eliminating the *paper belt* — meaning those damned 'bureaucrats', 'corrupt elites', 'intellectuals', 'professors', 'authorities', 'experts' who only 'disturb' the unrestrained self-enrichment of the oligarchs. Let us briefly consider how these 'smart asses' of the *paper belt* normally communicate. Journalists, for example, who categorise complex contexts and make balanced assessments; scientists, who always doubt everything anyway and often get lost in petty details and boring differentiations; civil servants, who have to adhere to cumbersome processes and procedures; and last but not least, the parties of the old, democratic order, who always had to act via compromises, consultations and committees, constantly balancing different interests.

We can immediately see that the *paper belt* is literally having the rug pulled out from under its feet under the conditions of the 'digitalocratic platforms'. In the 'digital blingbling thunderstorms' of trolls, rants and pranks, the knowledge order of the *paper belt* will continue to melt away on its own. Anyone who still laughs at somebody like the German politician Markus Söder, who turned into a (successful!) food influencer a few years ago in order to be visible on the platforms, has not grasped the gravity of the situation yet. If you are a scientist, journalist, civil servant or politician, the following applies under the conditions of the 'dawning digitalocracy': either you quickly change your aspirations in order to become an influencer or you will increasingly disappear from the social attention radar. Content that cannot be 'memeified' will become meaningless.

Digital transformation of the real world

It is quite fascinating to see that digital structures do not only define the reality on the platforms but also have a tangible impact on reality itself. Trump and Musk have already attracted lots of attention due to their unpredictable behaviour. They act just as erratically in the real world as the trolls on the platforms. As a President of the United States, Trump is racing ahead with hundreds of decrees, breaking taboos every day (e.g. the references to Greenland, Canada, the Panama Canal and Gaza), coming up with new insults, ways of disparaging people and comments that beggar belief. DOGE is responsible for dozens of new 'revelations', scandals, dismissals, closures of administrative institutions and unbelievable allegations every day. The sheer amount of 'news' is far beyond the processing capacity of any human observer. Commentators are always lagging behind. Trump and Musk have copied the mechanisms of the platforms into reality.

And in this reality, those affected are in the same LOSE-LOSE situation: should they go to court and sue every time? But such proceedings consume lots of time and money. Here, too, we have the problem of two speeds: The politicians who do the online trolling act quickly, while the courts (as well as regulatory authorities) act slowly. Here, too, the persons and institutions that are attacked are reduced to a reactive role from the start. Inevitably, they all end up playing exactly the role that the libertarians assigned to the *paper belt*: The role of the 'know-it-all, pedantic killjoy' who can't manage to get anything done by himself but always criticises and complains and, above all, always 'slams on the brakes'.

Indeed, a balanced 'court hearing' would actually have been the ideal form in the democratic public sphere, which Jürgen Habermas also described as 'deliberative'. It would work in a similar way to court hearings that have taken place in the democratic *agora* or *forum* in the past: The public deliberates on a particular issue and it does so according to mutually agreed, fair rules. People treat each other with respect, listen to each other, examine arguments, weigh things up, discuss compromises and reach a common consensus at the end.

However, from the perspective of the libertarian trolls such consultations are just an annoying waste of time. They have long since done away with this type of forum (▶1) and replaced it with the digital platforms, the new, supposed place of 'freedom of opinion' and 'sovereignty of the people'. But 'digital neutrality' is a fiction. The 'amplifiers' described above are increasingly transforming these platforms into a combat zone for a war in which everyone is fighting everyone else. According to Hobbes' *Leviathan*, this was the state of nature — before the emergence of law and government, which pacified this primordial anarchy, the war of all against all.

Trump, Dark Tech and the libertarians are known to hate the State. They are annoyed by court cases and also reject 'encroachments' on 'freedom' (▶3). Let's remind ourselves again of what exactly Musk said at the second Butler Rally:

> "And free speech is the bedrock of democracy. And if people don't know what's going on, if they don't know the truth, how can you make an informed vote? You must have free speech in order to have democracy. That's why it's the First Amendment [which grants the right to free speech]. And the Second Amendment [which grants the right to bear arms] is there to ensure that we have the First Amendment."[39]

Under the conditions of the Dark Tech platforms, the supposed 'freedom of speech' is actively manipulated towards polarisation and aggression by the digital oligarchs, who control the 'engine room'. It is these same digital oligarchs who are also working to completely remove any inhibitions from this battle zone, for example by advocating that racism, defamation and insults should also be allowed to pass as 'freedom of speech' in order to further accelerate the corresponding war of all against all that we are currently experiencing online. Apparently that's no problem at all for Musk. In his statement, he implies that in this media war, all those who are annoyed by people who question this supposed 'freedom' could then simply pull out their firearms and shoot wildly at their opponents.[40] According to this line of thinking, in order to defend their supposed right to 'freedom of speech', even the use of armed force would be acceptable. The fact that this is precisely how freedom of speech itself is destroyed is the subject of the following chapter (▶7).

Users want completely different platforms

The tragedy of all of this is that people would like a completely different media reality for themselves. An empirical study asked people how they experience the viral attention rewards in social media on a daily basis ('actual') and which type of content they themselves would reward with viral, additional attention ('desired').[41]

It is remarkable that, on almost all tested items, we find a massive difference between the ratings for the 'actual' and the 'desired' state of affairs. In other words, the platform reality is very different from what people would like it to be. There is only one aspect where the values for 'actual' and 'desired' are basically identical: Users observe a high viral presence of entertaining content online and they would also like to have it exactly like that.

On all other items, users see through the polarising mechanisms of the platforms, notice the high virality of these posts in the current

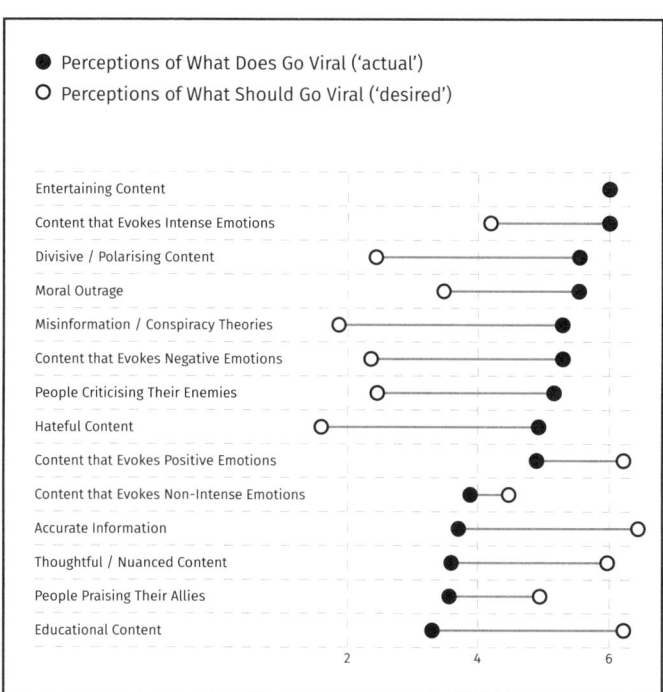

Figure 11: Users' assessment of which content goes viral on platforms (actual) and which should go viral (desired); based on Rathje et al. 2024

state of affairs and strongly dislike it. Thus, we can conclude that users potentially even recognise the malicious manipulation of traffic and visibility by the various amplifiers that we have described above. They understand that we have highly visible content that generates strong feelings, polarising content, moral outrage, misinformation and conspiracy theories, content that generates negative feelings, people who criticise their enemies, hateful content. But, in their digital ideal situation, they explicitly would prefer *such posts* to have *low visibility*.

However, they only see a few positive or balanced posts in the digital 'actual' situation (i.e. content that generates positive feelings; error-free or verified information; balanced and thoughtful content; educational content). But this is exactly the kind of content that they would wish for themselves in the 'desired' digital state of affairs. So, if people could have it their way, these types of content would be virally amplified by the platforms and massively increased in visibility.

In other words, people don't want this flood of hatred, agitation, malice, trash and lies online. If it were up to the users themselves, they would much rather have public digital forums in the spirit of Habermas — with factual, verified information, with informative and enlightening content, with balanced, level-headed and well-considered positions.

However, because the Dark Tech companies control these monopolies unilaterally, they can completely ignore what the communities really want. The users are trapped in the lock-in of the platform monopolies. This is why Dark Dech companies only have to feign 'neutrality' to the outside world and claim that it's all the fault of their supposedly mentally rotten users (i.e. their argument is as follows: 'Our algorithms only react to the demand indicators of our users who are by nature full of hatred, anger and love to see all this shit').

But this is not the case. Whatever the motivations of the platform owners might be, it is not really surprising that they create ecosystems which synchronise well with their own, libertarian troll ideology. This is how they create a system of polarisation that creates the perfect habitat for populism and antidemocratic movements.

Thus, they can direct the 'water' of the platforms onto the 'mills' of their own libertarian destruction in order to create their own political reality. Trump, the German AfD, the Brexiteers etc. are creatures that could only come into being because of this 'digitalocratic' framework. This is precisely the starting point of the technolibertarian and populist symbioses that we are currently observing. The new 'philosopher kings of Dark Tech' have been telling us for many years that this new digital world is 'inevitable' and that resisting it is 'futile'. And it is quite scary that Dark Tech has both the financial power plus the control of the platforms to turn these predictions into reality.[42]

We can now see the outlines of this future, 'digitalocratic' order, which is replacing and 'overcoming' the democratic media order of the 'old' analogue media. This 'digitalocratic' order has the following features:

- The public sphere is controlled by digital monopolies.
- The State has been largely dismantled, as are mechanisms of democratic media and market supervision ('regulation'). Instead, the digital sphere is controlled and shaped by the Dark Tech corporations — they are the ones who 'regulate' the digital world by defining the structures of the platforms plus the terms of usage.
- At the same time, the opinion power of the *paper belt* (scientists, journalists, experts, institutions, etc.) is being reduced and replaced by an oligarchy of 'attention millionaires' (Musk, Trump, etc.) and digital opinion leaders (influencers, streamers, creators, etc.).
- The discursive goals of exchange, rational argumentation, joint consultation and consensus-building (Habermas) are being abandoned, as is a shared factual truth as the basis for opinion-forming.
- Instead, troll figures have taken over, achieving maximum attention on the platforms through nihilistic cynicism and translating the same mechanisms into the reality of political action.

Unfortunately, this new 'digitalocratic media order' is the exact opposite of what people themselves would want for their own democratic society. It is important that we go beyond McLuhan at this crucial point. Of course, media shape the way we think, as implied in the slogan *the medium is the message*. But it is not the case that these media structures represent a quasi-inevitable fate for human beings. It is not true that we are fully at the mercy of such structures with no option to change or reformat them according to our own preferences. If we stay with the metaphor of this book, in this scenario (i.e. of being fully at the mercy of this new 'digitalocratic media order'), the media war would already be lost. But fortunately, as long as democracy still exists, we can still shape our media by ourselves because all these media structures are ultimately very dependent on the frames, rules and regulations that determine who has a say in the digital world. We could abolish the privileges of the tech oligarchs and give the communities a real voice.

If we wanted to, we could create a new, democratically legitimised digital media order. We would have to dare to rise up and shake off the 'digital occupation' by the monopolists. We would improve our digital media and shape our democracy of the future according to our own ideas and wishes. And we would dare to create our own new, grand narrative: "In dark times, the world was once ruled by an anti-democratic clique of Dark Tech and populist trolls. Fortunately, we dared to rise up and liberate the people from the coercive rule of the digital oligarchs and their autocratic buddies. We took back power over our media and were able to put democracy on a new, better digital foundation, which we as a community have been allowed to govern ourselves ever since."

The reverse may also come true. If we don't do this, the Trumps, Musks and their populist allies will not disappear because the advance of the new, 'digitalocratic order' is giving them more and more tailwind every day. They will continue to gain ground. Then we will become powerless and impotent hostages of the new 'digitalocratic order'.

7.
THE TRAP

Why absolutism of freedom of speech is a self-contradiction

Elon Musk claims to be a 'free speech absolutist' but I bet that not even Elon Musk himself believes this nonsense. Imagine he were to buy a very expensive diamond ring for one of his partners for a hundred thousand dollars. However, it would later turn out that the ring was not made of platinum (as the seller had explicitly stated), but only of silver. And that the gemstone was actually just crystal glass. Let's assume that Elon confronts the seller about the fraud and demands his money back. But the seller would explain to him, in a completely relaxed manner, that he had a different opinion on the matter. *Hey, Elon, you shouldn't act in this embarrassing, moralising manner, relax a little and stop getting all worked up. It's my right of free speech to call this platinum. Or do you want to censor me???* And perhaps the salesman would quote Elon himself: *"Go, fuck yourself!"* Then it is clear: the fraudulent seller of the diamond ring would not get away with his troll discourse, be it in the USA or in Europe. In the USA, for example, very strict rules apply to advertising statements or product claims. If Elon Musk buys a heat shield for one of his space projects for many millions of US dollars, he can be sure that the advertising claims about the special material ordered are true.

People are therefore protected against false factual claims and lies in advertising. The far-reaching rights to protect freedom of expression do not apply in such cases. Incidentally, this comparison should also give the radical advocates of freedom of expression pause for thought. According to their narrative, it is precisely the 'corrupt, censoring elites' who are so 'presumptuous' as to declare people 'incompetent' even though they are able to 'do their own research' and so on. Isn't the legislator's intention here the exact opposite? Isn't this essentially about protecting consumers from fraud — especially those who lack power and assertiveness?

The self-proclaimed 'absolutists of freedom of expression' should of course now react in shock and demand the immediate abolition of these terrible, oppressive rules. They are now welcome to quickly reach out for their cell phones and post on the platforms: "I'm SHOCKED!!!! In the USA, advertising statements are CENSORED by the State!!!!" And we immediately realise: such an accusation would obviously be madness. *Luckily*, the various markets are *regulated* against fraud in the interests of consumers. Manufacturers even have to provide detailed proof about the claims made about their products when in doubt. Often even scientific evidence. And remember the rejection of science by the libertarians (paper belt!): Are the scientists who substantiate such product claims really 'corrupt elites'?? Yes, it is a blessing, manufacturers and sellers are actually 'censored' throughout by regulations, and that is a wonderful thing for us consumers ☺. And if fraudulent suppliers violate these laws, they face severe penalties.

By the way, if you think my argument (that these regulations are 'State censorship' of free speech) is too far-fetched, then I have another shock moment for you in stock. After all, various circles of technolibertarians, digital anarchists and net activists (▶3) have repeatedly brought precisely such connections into play in order to immunise all kinds of economic fields against 'State regulation and intervention' with reference to 'freedom of expression'.

This has often been the case with cryptocurrencies, blockchain and the associated financial transactions. The title of a publication by the most important net activist group in the US, the Electronic Frontier Foundation (EFF), praises the cryptocurrency Bitcoin as an important "step toward censorship-resistant digital currency".[1]

Once again, the libertarian argument is to reject the 'interference' of the democratic State and its 'corrupt elites'. But here too, consumers are merely to be protected from fraudulent cut-throats. According to a study by the World Economic Forum, around half of the US population lacks basic financial knowledge on simple aspects such as understanding even how an interest rate is calculated.[2] Let us also consider the asymmetry of power and knowledge in a field that is difficult to understand, such as cryptocurrencies and blockchain. Is it really a 'presumptuous' and 'insolent' reflex of 'corrupt elites' if they try to protect consumers against fraud? Are users really being 'treated like children' by consumer protection measures?

A sideways glance at the well-known crypto-anarchist and weapons activist Cody Wilson can also demonstrate how far the 'absolutists of freedom of speech' can take this discourse. Using a colorful amalgam of various 'net freedom narratives' ('open source', 'peer-to-peer', 'free', 'open', 'decentralised'), he also casually defines all forms of State intervention and regulation as evil 'censorship'. His non-profit organization, 'Defense Distributed', publishes blueprints of weapons, all 'open source' of course, as 'Wiki Weapons'. One of his books is called *Come and Take it: The Gun Printer's Guide to Thinking Free*.[3]

Finally, imagine another situation. How would you feel if someone came by your house in broad daylight and stole your car *while you were standing there watching*? Of course you would protest loudly and threaten to call the police, but the thief would casually explain to you that this theft was completely legitimate as a 'free expression of opinion'. *He would say that you should not 'censor' him and deprive him of his freedom — and above all, you should stop being so embarrassing and moralising.*

This is exactly what happened to millions of artists, creatives and authors early on when Dark Tech tried to nullify their copyrights and make money from the stolen intellectual property. This dispute is particularly ugly because Dark Tech has once again brilliantly implemented the method that imperialist autocrats have been practising forever. They have always liked to turn dependent and exploited peoples against each other. Legislative procedures in the USA, which in the past were intended to protect authors, artists and creatives from intellectual theft, were attacked by massive interventions by 'net activists' and NGOs, who claimed that such 'censorship' measures would effectively shut down the 'free internet as we know it'. Many participants may not have been aware of the instrumentalisation of such groups by the interests of Big Tech. However, we must add the inconvenient truth that "such resistance was part of a corporate-funded and coordinated campaign and conducted by the largest technology monopolies, especially Google, Facebook, Twitter, and others, along with their lobbyists", according to David Golumbia's analysis on the subject.[4] Similar scenes have repeatedly played out in Europe.

The limits of what can be said — in the USA and in Germany

We realise that the very idea of an 'absolutism of freedom of speech' is pure nonsense — sorry Elon. In general, every type of freedom typically becomes problematic when it comes into conflict with other aspects of freedom and conflicting rights.[5]

This is why, also in the USA, not every kind of communication is allowed as 'free speech'. We already mentioned false factual statements in advertising; we can add the unauthorised use of copyrighted content. Child pornography is also prohibited, as are specific incitements to commit crimes or suicide, defamation of character based on false statements of fact; there are also restrictions on the use of photographs of people without their consent or the disclosure of private or intimate content.

We also note that all these restrictions on freedom of speech and opinion in the USA also apply in Germany and the EU. Here, we should therefore be wary of generalisations too. Certainly, *freedom of speech* tends to be defined in broader terms in the USA compared to Europe. However, images of nudity, for example, are often handled *more restrictively* in the US than in Europe (interestingly enough, such constraints are put in place less on the basis of laws than through voluntary self-restrictions). In addition, there are currently various massive restrictions on freedom of the press, media, science and opinion being imposed by the current Trump administration, which, in this form, would be unthinkable in Europe or Germany (including restrictions on press access to the White House, planned budget cuts for public service broadcasters, cutting funding for universities as 'punishment' for 'unwanted' political statements by students and 'politically undesirable' scientific research and teaching, and so on).[6]

There is another way in which freedom of speech and media freedom is better protected in Germany than in the USA. In Germany, the party who loses a lawsuit also has to reimburse the legal costs. In the US legal system, there is no such reimbursement. Often, weaker parties fear those legal costs so much that they allow themselves to be intimidated or accept settlements when there are strong asymmetries of power and financial strength.

If we compare the general situation in the USA and Germany, the main difference in the German legal system is that, according to Article 5 of the German Constitution, "Everyone has the right to freely express and disseminate his opinions in speech, writing and pictures." However, in cases where expressions of opinion violate other rights or freedoms, these rights play a slightly different role in Germany compared to the USA. In Germany, Article 1 of the Constitution always applies: "Human dignity is inviolable. It is the duty of all state authorities to respect and protect it."

This means that, in the case of personal insults, racist discrimination or incitement to hatred, the right to freedom of expression must be carefully weighed against the protection of human dignity. However, the Federal Constitutional Court has provided clear guidance here: "Since human dignity, as the root of all fundamental rights, cannot be weighed against any individual fundamental right, freedom of expression must always take a back seat if a statement violates the human dignity of another person".[7]

Of course, the specific contexts are also taken into account when considering individual cases. After all, in the process of forming public opinion, the possibilities of aggressive criticism of power, politics and government must not be restricted too narrowly. At the same time, however, the right to freedom of opinion is not a "licence to defame or degrade others. The constitution sets limits to public disparagement or incitement to hatred and does not exclude public figures and public officials from this", according to legal scholar Klaus Gärditz.[8]

Accordingly, we can conclude: There is no absolute freedom of expression anywhere, be it in the USA or in Europe, and for good reason. Otherwise, no one would be safe from fraud and serious damage to their own personal integrity. Nevertheless, in Germany too, we find very strong legislation protecting freedom of speech. Even the deliberate spreading of lies can in most cases not be sanctioned in a country like Germany. Limitations compared to the USA only arise in a small number of cases. In the final analysis, there are barely any restrictions on freedom of expression in Germany too. After all, anyone can continue to denounce, expose and criticise anything. In Germany, you should just refrain from the most vulgar defamation, sexist disparagement, racist discrimination or hate-filled threats of destruction.

On sober reflection and consideration, I cannot make out any serious threat to freedom of speech in Germany. The fact is, however, that for decades the 'tech bros' have been telling us fairy tales about how they are 'liberating' our media system with their platforms or why 'censorship' was a major threat to our society — a narrative that the right-wing populists have now completely taken over from Dark Tech. In this narrative, they are now completely aligned as 'partners'.

Censorship as an obsession of Dark Tech and populists

Certainly, the belief that today, our media are 'censored' has become the obsession at the centre of this very prevalent conspiracy theory, which right-wing populists are now spreading everywhere in Western democracies.⁹ Their entire fairy tale of alleged 'liberation' would immediately collapse if those people did not seriously believe that they are the persecuted 'victims' of terrible 'dictatorial oppression' (along the lines of, 'it's just like in North Korea'). As with any narrative, also this one needs a villain, and that is 'censorship' here.

In the eyes of the 'deplorable persecuted victims', any form of lack of interest means censorship anyway. A personal example: In the introduction to this book, I wrote about how I have been doing research on digital monopolies for 15 years, but that the topic had no relevance in the public eye for about 13 years. Now, I could also say: "The corrupt State cartel has CENSORED me!" At the same time, I could also have said: "Sensational revelation — THE MAINSTREAM MEDIA ALWAYS WANTED TO HIDE THIS FROM YOU!!!!" But that's nonsense. Nobody was interested back then. It has nothing to do with censorship.¹⁰

Particularly interesting is the psychology of this worship of censorship. First and foremost, people want to play the 'censorship card' to look like a victim. It feels great to be a victim. Immediately, you're more important when you're being 'censored', aren't you? When the unique, 'mindblowing', top-secret information that you hold in your hand is so important that you have the entire State apparatus against you. In order to get into the coveted censorship zone, people are typically communicating as aggressively as possible. This then leads to the characteristic sadomasochistic actions of the 'independent thinkers' on the platforms, with maximum 'attention payback'. First, the digital trolls repeatedly beat up everything that gets in their way. Here are a few highlights of the insults against German politician Renate Künast, who was called a "bitch", "dirty sow", "hazardous waste", "piece of shit", "dirty cunt", "paedophile", "lobotomised", among other things. If you raise your voice against these insulting trolls, they typically respond something like this: *You ridiculous weaklings, stop peeing in your pants!!!* But once it gets to a point of legal action or a complaint is ruled, the very same trolls suddenly discover their very sensitive, vulnerable side. They speak candidly about their worries and fears and portray themselves as martyrs. Just like with Donald Trump, we see a continual, senseless lashing out. But when confronted with the consequences of their actions, they claim to be the 'unfortunate victims' of an 'unprecedented witch hunt'.

This is particularly absurd because it's *the same* trolls who typically like to call for 'tough action' with 'merciless severity' on all kinds of issues: Refugees should be 'deported immediately', useless civil servants should be 'kicked out' (remember the chainsaw!), authorities need to 'crack down' on lawbreakers and criminals. But woe betide you if you don't give the trolls your full attention or even fight back. Then the same tough wielders of chainsaws turn into snivelling, whining, sensitive wimps. What an incredible show! We note: without this obsession about censorship, the libertarians' whole sadomasochistic giga-theatre game of 'massacre' and 'martyrdom' would implode immediately. It is precisely this thrill that they love, where they can switch back and forth at will between their two favourite roles, namely 'Conan-the-Destroyer' and 'Jesus-on-the-Cross'. And the best thing for them is: They are guaranteed maximum attention on *both sides* of the equation again and again, because they always operate in the perfect sweet spot of the 'platform trigger points'. And that's why every restriction on media freedom, no matter how tiny, is constantly blown up as 'proof' of the terrible 'censorship', leading to ever new waves of outrage on the platforms. You could certainly write a whole book about this, but here are at least a few reflections.

The introductory remarks show first of all that, on sober reflection, there are no serious restrictions on democratic freedom of opinion, including in Europe and in Germany. In Germany, you are allowed to criticise whoever and whatever you want. After all, it is called freedom of opinion and not freedom of discrimination, defamation, of incitement to crime. We still have the important sentence in Article 5 of our Constitution: "There shall be no censorship". This sentence applied before the invention of the internet and it still applies.

In the German constitution, 'censorship' is meant in the narrower sense and means *pre-censorship*, according to which, for example, a publication would only be permitted after approval by the authorities.[11] Such procedures were common under absolutism as well as under National Socialism. However, such censorship in the narrower sense (as "planned, systematic monitoring of public communication" by authorities[12]) does not exist today. It is precisely the hallmark of our open media world that all content can be published without prior review or permission, regardless of whether it is analogue or digital media.

Cases of platform moderation or fact-checkers should also be classified with caution and not hastily labelled as 'censorship' because, first of all, the content concerned is usually first published by the platforms (because it is NOT censored, i.e. checked in advance!). Inside the platforms, the posts generate the lion's share of attention during the first few hours after publication anyway. Thus, even in the case of very severe, criminal content, moderation almost always intervenes (unfortunately!) far too late. And, in the case of fact-checkers, the original content usually stays online and is only supplemented by an attached counterstatement that enables the audience to consider the topic from another point of view by adding complementary information.

Explicit bans, such as child pornography or the protection of children from traumatising depictions of violence, are firstly rare but also typically characterised by a very high "conformity" with the "prevailing social values",[13] and it is precisely this situation that is clarified in the German Constitution by article §5.2 with regards to potential limitations. If you look very hard for traces of 'censorship' in our media world, the only thing that really comes to mind are automated platform filters (ironically it is precisely these processes that *do not* take place in the supposedly '*State-censored elite cartel media*', but on the platforms).

Actually, I myself consider the situation in such cases to be suboptimal (because the affected users have too few rights vis-à-vis the 'digitalocratic rulers', which is particularly evident in the case of profile blocking). But even in such cases, it's typically a game of 'catch me if you can' in the reality of digital media. After all, users are aware of these filters and usually circumvent them by typographical paraphrasing (e. g. 'N*z*' instead of 'Nazi'). Of course it might happen that profiles are blocked in extreme cases. But even in these cases, you have to bear in mind that there is usually a huge scandal connected with that (which also means that there are correction processes in place in the public sphere). We must also bear in mind that people have never had as many different channels to express their opinions as they do today. Should such restrictions arise in isolated cases, those affected today typically have the opportunity to express their opinions through dozens of alternative channels.

Why unlimited freedom of opinion *restricts* freedom of expression

However, the most important argument FOR a careful consideration of the various conflicting rights is that the technolibertarian interpretation of media freedom leads to, of all things, RESTRICTIONS in media freedom. Elon, if you ever read these lines, you need to be very strong …

The 'media freedom absolutists' are ignoring one crucial point. There are two basic conditions of digital communication that have driven the decline und brutalization in the quality of our public discourse. Firstly, their 'liability privilege' (platforms do not have to take responsibility for the content), often in combination with the anonymity of senders. Because the actors (creators and platforms alike) have little fear of sanctions, they can communicate much more aggressively than they would under normal circumstances (▶5). Secondly, the platforms' algorithms reward hate, incitement and malice with additional attention (▶6). The combination of both conditions is leading to the rampant escalation of hate speech that we are currently observing on the platforms.

This is not a marginal phenomenon. In fact, it affects and burdens large sections of the population in Western societies. This can be illustrated by a representative survey of 3,061 internet users that was carried out in Germany at the end of 2023. 49 % of respondents stated that they had been insulted online, while 41 % had been the victim of disinformation concerning themselves. 29 % reported that they had been sent unwanted nude photos, while a quarter reported threats of online violence and sexual harassment. 'Doxxing', i.e. the publication of personal information such as a home address, typically with malicious intent, is a particular problem, affecting 22 % of respondents.[14] This situation is intimidating an increasing number of users to such an extent that they are dropping out of public digital discourse. This can lead to complete silence — 24 % of all respondents reported that they had temporarily stopped using, deactivated or even deleted their digital profiles, while 21 % had stopped sharing content. The proportion of people who shared their political opinion less frequently online (57 %) or participated less often in discussions (55 %) is even much higher.[15] The aggressive trolls on the platforms have thus achieved their goal: ever larger parts of the digital communities are being muted and deprived of their voice — a phenomenon also known as 'silencing'.

And here comes another terrible realisation for Elon. Because even Elon should understand that the right to freedom of expression naturally also entitles people to develop *opinions on the democratic organisation of freedom of expression in the media*. The situation at hand is very clear: 82 % of those who participated in the survey believe that online hate threatens diversity on the internet because it intimidates and represses people.[16] Pay attention now, Elon: 90 % (!!) of German citizens believe that online hate should be deleted if it violates the law.[17] That is an extremely broad majority and, to quote Elon, the 'people's voice'. Elon, what are you going to do now as an 'absolutist of freedom of speech' and fighter against supposed 'censorship' when 90 % of people think that such deletions and 'interventions' against criminal content are necessary???? It is particularly instructive that, conversely, only 30 % of respondents believe that online hate should be tolerated in more harmless cases in which the content does not (!!) violate the law and 66 % oppose this.[18]

This means that the entire model of 'free speech absolutism' collapses like a house of cards. Firstly, people have clearly stated their opinion that they do not want this 'absolutism' being abused by being considered as giving everyone a blank cheque to perpetrate unrestrained verbal violence against others. On the contrary, 'liberation' from the limitations of freedom of expression paradoxically produces a massive *reduction in* freedom of expression because the effects of 'silencing' *exclude* huge sections of the entire population from political discourse. This in turn means that a maximum of freedom of expression for society as a hole can only be achieved by striking a balance between freedoms on the one hand and protective mechanisms on the other.

And there is another aspect we need to add. The survey mentioned above also shows that politicians in particular, but also politically engaged people, are affected by this hatred. But this is precisely where 'silencing' must be prevented under all circumstances, as the German Federal Constitutional Court also emphasises. "Socio-political engagement can only be expected if sufficient protection of the personal rights of those who are engaged and publicly involved is guaranteed".[19] Time and again, we see how committed politicians give up, especially as the verbal violence on the platforms repeatedly spills over into their personal lives.

There is a central insight that we can obtain from these complex considerations on a complex topic. Donald Trump, Elon Musk, Mark Zuckerberg and JD Vance all talk about *freedom of speech* as if it were a concrete 'thing' and, above all, a thing that is exactly the same thing for everyone in the world. But that is not the case and, in this simple (or naïve) sense, *freedom of speech does not exist at all.* On the contrary, freedom of speech is always a delicate compromise in a complex act of trade-offs. In case of doubt, conflicts with other freedoms and other rights have to be balanced out. In this process, the negative effects of freedom on freedom of speech itself also have to be taken into account (i.e. if the freedom to insult others leads to intimidated users falling silent). And finally, this balance MUST emerge as a result of democratic negotiation processes through the procedures, checks and balances we create for ourselves as a society. The balance struck in shaping freedom of expression must always *be democratically legitimised*. But this is no longer the case when 'tech bros' like Elon Musk can unilaterally decide on these matters through their digital 'house rules'. And that is exactly what is happening right now, since they have managed to occupy our public sphere through a kind of coup (▶1). The result, as we are witnessing, is actually the exact opposite of freedom and freedom of expression.

Media freedom that we shape ourselves

We can supplement these findings by approaching the same question from a completely different perspective. We can also ask ourselves: How did media freedom *come about* in the first place? Here, we can come back to the French Revolution and view it from a completely different perspective. In Europe, it marked the transition from the unfree media order of absolutism to the free media order of modernity. Under absolutism, pre-censorship prevailed: Authors needed approval from authorities *before* publication. For the many people of today out there who claim that our media order is 'unfree', let us briefly recall what censorship meant back then. The 'Storming of the Bastille' symbolises the overcoming of absolutism. Back then, the Bastille was the State prison of the absolutist rulers. It was notorious for the terrible and inhumane conditions that prevailed there for the inmates. In the 30 years between 1750 and 1779, i.e. before the French Revolution, "383 of the 941 booksellers, printers, journeymen, peddlers and authors imprisoned for such offences between 1659 and 1789 served a term in this state prison." And further: "The total number of those imprisoned for writing, printing or selling forbidden texts amounted to 40 % of all inmates of the Paris fortress in the second half of the century".[20] Only the French Revolution and the Declaration of the Rights of the Man and of the Citizen of 1793 freed society from this absolutist control of the media.

It is to British media scholar Richard Barbrook's credit that he has reconstructed the two-hundred-year history of modern media freedom using France as an example.[21] What makes his argument so illuminating is that it identifies around ten successive, very different models of 'media freedom' over this period. We can see why, fascinatingly, this is the same insight which we also gained before by taking a different route ('freedom of speech'), as seen above. After all, the term 'media freedom' would also imply that there is only one media freedom, one 'thing' that would be the same for everyone and at different times. But that is not the case.

Barbrook begins directly after the French Revolution with the Girondinist model of media freedom, whose public sphere is characterised by printed publications. These were produced by hundreds of journalists, who, at the time, usually owned a printing press themselves. This situation had specific advantages in terms of media freedom. The 'journalist-printers' were financially independent and a wide variety of publications (i. e. pluralism) was guaranteed (because there were no consolidated media groups at the time). However, this set-up also had many disadvantages. On the one hand, ownership of a printing press was a prerequisite for access to publicity, and on the other hand, there were typically conflicts of interest because these publishing intellectuals were often part of the revolutionary elites themselves. Another disadvantage was the excessive focus on the centre of Paris that resulted in the neglect of the periphery of France.

Barbrook shows how each reorganisation of media freedom over time has introduced new gains, but also new shortcomings. For example, the increasing consolidation of the press in big media companies brings many advantages, such as increasing (internal) diversity due to the growing number of journalists, greater reach due to improved distribution and, above all, lower prices, so that more and more sections of the population were able to gain access to the public debates. But, at the same time, it led to journalists becoming increasingly dependent on their employers (in comparison to the self-employed 'journalist-printers') as well as an increasing concentration of the media into a few powerful media corporations.

The observation that media freedom is always the result of complex trade-offs applies to all aspects. Although the advance of privately financed media corporations delivered a high degree of independence from State power and politics in a positive sense, it also came with new dependencies. These media corporations were dependent on advertising revenues and were thus typically less critical towards economic power, but also towards financial capital. The new audio-visual media led to a considerable expansion of reach as well as free access to the public sphere for the broad masses. On the other hand, the technological limitations of the few available frequencies brought about new disadvantages of media concentration and monopoly formation, especially under conditions of State control of the frequencies. On the one hand, the ensuing emergence of public service broadcasting provided additional diversity and at the same time an increasing independence of media content from the interests of the advertising industry and finance capital. However, on the other hand, it promoted and deepened the points of contact with State power and the emergence of a tendency towards an elitist 'mediaklatura' within the public service broadcasting media sphere, which, in turn, prompted the emergence of pluralistic regulation authorities independent from any State control as a corrective reaction.

From the point of view of the defensive democratic State, restrictions on media freedom are also understandable. For example, when France faced the threat of being invaded by Nazi Germany at the end of the 1930s, the old Jacobin model of media control was reactivated. State control of the media and censorship had also previously served to protect the French Revolution from internal and external attacks. Similarly, at the end of the 1930s, the adaptation of those models served the purpose of safeguarding the French public sphere against manipulation (through the use of propaganda) and sabotage in a period when the threat of war was imminent.

You are the media now? Why this is a lie

Barbrook's text was published in 1995. Thus, from today's perspective, we might at first 'naïvely' add the effects that the digital transformation had on media freedom to his historical overview. On the one hand, we would refer to the increase in existing offerings and the new opportunities for participation on the positive side. On the other hand, we would draw attention to the considerable negative effects that are caused by the growing information overload of users, firstly with regard to fake news, and secondly concerning hate speech and hostile attacks.

This continuation would be 'naïve' in the sense that the digital transformation would appear to be just another arbitrary step in the evolution of media freedom. But, at the same time, we would have overlooked the one crucial point in which the current situation differs fundamentally from all previous reorganisations of the media landscape. In all stages of media freedom analysed by Barbrook, the public sphere of the media was shaped, without a single exception, by *the democratically legitimised State itself* via ever new negotiation processes, reorganisations and optimisations. Media regulation itself is then organized by bodies that are independent of the State and pluralistically composed of various social representatives. Thus, the democratic State even protects the free media against itself, i.e. State power, and guarantees the independence of media regulation — ensuring that the various control bodies are democratically legitimised at the same time. The democratic community is allowed to shape the media, but the State itself has to stay outside these regulatory bodies. And we must not forget: By setting up such complex checks and balances, the democratic State has always shaped and secured the public sphere of free media, which at the same time forms *the basis of its own existence*.

From today's perspective, however, the fundamental difference is that the platforms have succeeded in achieving a hostile takeover of the digital media sphere. By doing so, the formative power and the sovereignty of the democratically legitimised State has been undermined and to a large extent nullified. As we have shown above (▶1), the Dark Tech corporations now *own* the 'digital forum'. As a democratic community, we no longer have a say.

At the same time, however, Dark Tech presents this revolution to us as if 'the (one and only) media freedom' had 'actually' been realised for the first time in human history thanks to the advent of the 'empowering' social media platforms. In stark contrast to Barbrook's insight (there is not *one* media freedom — only ever new forms of media freedom as a result of complex social negotiation processes and checks and balances), Dark Tech claims, as it were, that they are now giving you 'real' media freedom for the very first time. They pretend to give us the ultimate salvation. The old (in their narrative, 'manipulated', 'corrupt', etc.) media have been overcome. Their narrative runs something like this: Here you have our great platforms. You don't need the media anymore. Because: YOU ARE THE MEDIA NOW.

What is fascinating is that, behind this narrative of liberation, there is also a media critique that repeatedly retells the 'fairy tale' that platforms are not media at all, but neutral, transparent mediators or 'intermediaries' (▶5). Digital platforms have always conveyed this mantra in various guises, in order to stand out against analogue media (television, radio, newspapers, etc.) that appear as 'artificially fabricated'. In contrast, the digital platforms claim to be perfectly 'permeable, neutral interfaces' that have nothing to do with the content. From a media studies perspective, this denial of fabrication should make us extra wary. And we can add a crucial aspect here. Because in the long history of the media, this figure appears again and again. The archetype of this media fairy tale derives from the Old Testament. Moses descended from Mount Sinai with the stone tablets containing the Ten Commandments. And then told everyone that it was not he himself who had carved these laws in stone, but that God himself had given them to him up there on the summit of Mount Sinai. And everyone should obey these laws, he said, because they came directly from God and he himself had nothing to do with them.

The figure of this *self-denial of mediality* is also called 'acheiropoieton',[22] which in Greek means 'not-made-by-hand' (a-cheiro-poieton). The platforms have been telling us in a similar way for decades that, unlike the editorial media, for example, they are not 'hand-made', but 'only' neutral intermediaries. The trick serves a similar purpose as it did for Moses: the other, competing media are *defamed* as being 'mere fabrications', using a similar approach as to why Moses rejected the golden calf as a 'delusion'. Anyone who falls for such 'mere fabrications' (according to the fairy tale) is praying to Baal, a 'false' god.

The 'acheiropoieton' has functioned in that way as a deceptive manoeuvre for thousands of years, also for media. We can briefly demonstrate this using media of the modern era: photography promised to create images through content-neutral transmissions that were for the first time drawn by the light and not by painters (*The pencil of nature*, according to the famous description of William Henry Fox Talbot from 1844); the phonograph promised a content-neutral reproduction of sound experiences; the telephone promised a content-neutral transmission of the voice over long distances, and so on. Of course, each medium forms a specific narrative of its own supposed neutrality. And the purpose is obvious: It suggests legitimacy where, in reality, there is always only a vacuum, only an illusion, a void.

The worst thing is: once an acheiropoieton has established itself, it creates a fatal reversal of the burden of proof for the people who are dominated by it. We can illustrate it by once more returning to our Old Testament example. Imagine you wanted to deny the validity of these Ten Commandments for yourself — how would you go about it? How the hell are you going to prove that these tablets did not come from God but (according to your assumption) were simply inscribed on the tablets by Moses himself?

Today, the platform owners tell us the same thing that Moses told the Israelites back then: "We have nothing to do with the content — we are just neutral intermediaries, it is the direct and authentic voice of the people that becomes visible there." Yeah, of course. And because it feels good for the people on the platforms, they believe it in the same way that people believed Moses back then. And the exact same thing is happening now: Now we are the ones stuck with the burden of proof: Are the platforms really 'neutral'? But how are we going to prove whether they are or not, if we cannot get access to their black boxes? How would you prove the same thing for the stone tablets, if no witnesses were present when Moses received them on Mount Sinai?

But within the digital platforms, the owners are in full control of the engine room, making executive decisions on algorithms and determining for all of their users who will get to see what content. Although it is so difficult to prove, various study designs have repeatedly shown their manipulations (these are particularly obvious for the optimisation of economic profits). But this is exactly what, from the perspective of the digital platforms, must in all circumstances stay invisible, as otherwise the illusion of neutrality would collapse immediately. When Musk says (20.12.2024), "The goal of X is to give power back to the people"[23], this is a form of deception that only goes unnoticed if you really believe that these platforms are 'only intermediaries' (or, in the case of Moses, if you believe that the Ten Commandments really come from God himself). The 'independent thinkers' on the digital platforms, of all people, who in their paranoid thinking otherwise sense betrayal, conspiracy, deceit and lies by corrupt elites behind all phenomena, believe the promises of the alleged 'sovereignty of the people' made by the 'digital oligarchs' with maximum naïvety and blind faith. In contrast to this blind trust, the "central principles of parliamentary control, representation, delegation or intermediation through organisation are almost obsessively opposed".[24]

After Trump's election as US President, Elon Musk wrote on X (6 November, 2024): "The reality of this election was plain to see on X, while most legacy media lied relentlessly to the public. You are the media now."[25] This is the pure and complete illusion of the acheiropoieton. It suggests redemption for the people: before, in the order of the 'old media', there were supposedly complex mechanisms of media control and cumbersome social negotiations on freedom of speech or opinion power, all of this being 'controlled' top-down by hostile 'elites'. Now, in the state of digital redemption, we are giving you absolute control of the media for the first time in human history — for absolute freedom of expression and absolute neutrality.

Sounds great, doesn't it? But only if you believe it. Because, in reality, these media are just media like all other media. And while, in earlier, analogue times, the complex creation of this media reality was openly negotiated by the democratic community and visible to everybody who participated in that discourse, the tech companies are shifting the same processes into the black boxes of their platforms and control it in a truly top-down way. It is only by making these things invisible and via the illusion of the acheiropoieton that *they are now able to rule*: they determine who sees what content. They filter, boost, dim, amplify, select and manipulate.

This shows us how incredibly powerful the suggestive powers of the acheiropoieton are — because the same people who feel betrayed by 'corrupt elites' suddenly experience themselves as 'liberated' by the platforms and blindly trust their owners, *even though since years and even decades, the same libertarians and oligarchs have been completely open about their visions of autocratic rule and their plans to abolish our democracy* (▶3).

Elon Musk, the 'liberator of the suppressed people', has a slogan that he has kept posting on X in all kinds of contexts for a while — it reads: *VOX POPULI, VOX DEI*. Of course, this too is meant to suggest to people: To the liberator Elon, nothing is more important than the voice of the people (a voice which he enables through the acheiropoieton of his platform X). Vox populi, vox dei.

But perhaps the catchphrase is a private joke and also contains a deeper meaning. Perhaps he is also implicitly telling us what is really going on, namely that the voice of the people is being fabricated on platforms today in a very similar way as the voice of God was fabricated in earlier times. To put it simply: In earlier times, people were influenced for millennia by false prophets and priests who wanted to make people believe in all seriousness that they knew what the voice of God was saying, and that it sometimes even spoke through them — when in reality, they were simply telling the people the things that turned out to be most advantageous for themselves. The 'voice of God' was always just their instrument through which they ruled.

And today, in the 'digitalocratic order', people allow themselves to be ruled in exactly the same way by 'absolutist digital platform owners', who lead the people to believe in all seriousness that 'the voice of the people' can be heard ('uncensored', as the digital platforms owners would put it) in the networks. And yet, the reality is that it is only the platform owners sitting in the 'digital engine room' who are remixing what is most advantageous for themselves from 'the voice of the people'. The 'voice of the people' is just their instrument through which they rule.

For those who'd like to believe it — vox populi, vox dei.

8.
THE UPRISING

Is it still possible to save democracy?

If an opossum is threatened, it plays dead. This specific type of behaviour was even turned into proverbial wisdom, as in "to play possum". For the opossum, this is a tried and tested method of fighting for survival. The attacker often loses interest and eventually retreats. However, the 'playing possum strategy' can also lead directly to disaster. For example, if you don't pay your bills and ignore the piles of reminders and authorities who threaten to seize your assets, at some point you will find yourself stuck between a rock and a hard place: do you go to jail or do you go underground? The lesson is clear: Playing dead is always pretty idiotic if your opponent refuses to go away. And there is one thing we can be sure of: actors like Dark Tech, Trump & co. will not disappear on their own. They'll devour anything that is in their path. You might choose to play dead, but, in response, they will just eat you for lunch. And they won't stop until we stop them.

But because we have been pursuing the 'playing possum strategy' for many years now, we are left with two choices:

1. Either we do what is actually necessary: we protect our free media and democracy. We dare to rise up and shake off the 'digitalocratic' domination — but we will need to make huge sacrifices to do this.

The alternative scenario is:

2. We submit and let Dark Tech and 'Trumpism' take power.

Given that scenario (2) is of course much worse than scenario (1), let's start with the 'positive' solution. But first we need to swallow a bitter pill. As a society, we have to admit to ourselves that we have completely messed this up. And now that the enemies of democracy have long been striving to batter down our city gates, we can no longer afford to indulge in any illusions.

It's time to face reality:

- The US has left the transatlantic alliance and the partnership with European democracies. They are gone.
- The US treats Europe as an adversary (and adversaries of Europe such as Russia as allies); it acts in a hostile and unscrupulous manner
- Europe can be blackmailed by the US in two ways: first, because it cannot defend itself militarily; second, because it is completely dependent on the tech monopolies. Through these tech monopolies, the US has control of the digital public sphere in Europe. Another particularly dangerous aspect is that the same US tech companies own almost our entire digital infrastructure. The systems we use for our administration, institutions, healthcare, financial transactions, our economy and our security. We are extremely vulnerable and completely dependent.
- The US is turning into an autocracy. They no longer respect the rules of the past. Even military activities against former partners are conceivable (e.g. Canada, Greenland etc.). This means that all existing treaties and agreements with the US, but also with Dark Tech and other US companies, will become worthless in case of doubt or dispute. Only the law of the jungle will apply. We couldn't trust the anti-democratic tech companies one bit in the past. And this is even more applicable to the new combination of Trump and tech.
- The US intends to turn Europe into a kind of dependent colony. They already use right-wing populist parties as partners and they actively campaign for these parties, thus intervening in European

elections. This is precisely why Dark Tech, Trump and the populists are running their synergistic 'liberation' campaigns, in which they claim they want to 'save' the European population against supposedly tyrannical and despotic governments.

- The imperialist method of tech and Trump is consistently based on the principle of blackmail. The tariffs of the US government are the most obvious instrument. But the monopolies are even more dangerous. They allow almost infinite possibilities for exploitation, as they enable access for example to media genres (social media, search engines, free video, etc.) but also to digital markets (Amazon). We are equally dependent at the level of digital infrastructures.
- It is also important to note that the US government has already made it patently clear *that it will bring together the two dependencies (defense / tech monopolies) and use them against Europe with severity*. For example, JD Vance, the current Vice President, had already stated before the election: If we Europeans dared to regulate the platforms more harshly, the US would withdraw its support for NATO. Thus, our military dependence is played out against our digital dependence — which in turn means that, without military sovereignty, there will be no digital sovereignty for us.

This analysis inevitably leads Europe towards two central actions:

1. We must secure our democracy and our freedom against its enemies. At the simplest level, freedom means physical integrity, i.e. protection against violence and coercion. We must therefore ensure that we can defend Europe through its own independent military and without any support from the US.
2. We can no longer depend on the US for essential goods, access and infrastructure — we need our own infrastructure (e.g. cloud solutions) and our own digital media and markets.

If we are already mentally acknowledging our own shortcomings, we should also be humble enough to admit that the Chinese have completely understood these issues and their ramifications for decades, while we, especially our leadership in politics, science and journalism, have spent decades in complete naïvety and cluelessness.

Decades ago, the Chinese were clever enough to allow Western IT companies entry into their market on condition that they would have to use local infrastructure. This step enabled China to build up its own digital expertise. Local people in power understood very early on: If they were to allow Western powers to control and dominate their digital media and infrastructures, then their dictatorial rule would soon be done away with. That's why, finally, they raised the *Great Firewall* and then sought to achieve 'digital sovereignty'. It certainly feels extremely cynical for me to write this because it is evident that the underlying motivation for China to achieve digital sovereignty was *to secure their dictatorship*. But we have to admit that they have been extremely successful in doing so. We ourselves, on the other hand, have gone nowhere with this issue. If only we had defended our European democracy with a fraction of the zeal that China used to secure its dictatorship against external dependencies, we would not be in this situation.

It will be a gigantic challenge to resolve this issue. The European island of democracy is now an annoying disturbance for neighbouring autocratic governments. Russia has its troops in the east anyway and will try to annex as much of Europe as possible by military force. It will continue to expand its offensive in Ukraine and it will certainly continue to aggressively shift its interests further to the west, to Moldavia, Georgia and so on. From the west, the US will try to weaken western Europe as much as possible, ideally by splitting up the EU, in order to exploit it economically as much as possible through governments created by their dependent, right-wing 'partners'. And we can't expect any help from China either.

Freedom in Europe – the basic conditions and prerequisites

So how can we save our democracy? The important thing is that we have to work on two frontlines at the same time. On the one hand, we need to reduce our dependencies so that we can never again be blackmailed at will by the US government. And, at the same time, we must tackle the mammoth task of developing and implementing our own digital alternatives to regain democratic control over our own political public sphere.

In view of the strength of the opponents and their vast superiority, this will be a massive undertaking. It is a disadvantage for Europe that it is not a country but an association of nation states. The European Union is organised democratically and, on top of that, it comes with the complexity of having multiple nation states. It is therefore wrong to play down European 'sluggishness'. Of course, in such a situation, we are acting much more slowly than autocratic regimes, including the new and increasingly autocratic US government. The same disadvantage also applies to the complex democratic processes within the nation states of the European Union.

If we want to have a real chance, we have to fulfill three prerequisites in advance.

- Firstly, we must ensure that we take a cross-party approach. Facing this massive threat, we should stop the usual haggling between political parties. For Germany, for example, this means that, on this topic, it shouldn't matter whether you adhere to the views of a conservative, a leftist, green, or a free-market political party. For truly democratic parties, the democratic foundations of our society are not a point of discussion anyway. That is why all moderate, democratic parties should work together and agree on cross-party cooperation in this field.
- Due to the complexity in terms of who has responsibility for what, we must simultaneously integrate all political levels in a way that would allow us to act with maximum speed. In Germany, this

means smooth cooperation between the national level and the federal states (especially since almost all topics concerning media law are decided at the level of the federal States, not in Berlin). On top of that, we need to integrate and mobilise the European Union as much as we can because only the combined power of the EU can provide the required international bargaining power. In the last resort, it is the only level on which we are able to negotiate with Dark Tech and Trump.
- Furthermore, we should try to involve potential additional partners that give us more weight — i.e. London and the UK, Switzerland, but also Canada, Australia and other partners. The more countries that join in, the better!

Liberation from the 'digitalocracy'

Once we have met all these requirements, we must immediately tackle the most important issues.

1. Secure our own defence capability
In the area of defence, we need to become independent from the US because the topic of digital sovereignty is related, as described above. No matter how this is implemented (I am not an expert in this field), one thing is certain: we can no longer duck out. We need to take action. And fortunately, these issues are currently being tackled.[1]

2. Abolish Dark Tech privileges — open up digital markets
At the same time, we must abolish all privileges and preferential legal treatments that enable and secure the monopolies of the digital oligarchy and mean exploitation and deprivation of liberty for all of us.

In my book entitled 'Big Tech Must Go', I have already set out most of these proposals in detail. Subsequently, with the support of an expert on regulation, Prof. Nikolaus Peifer, the Director of the Institute for

Media and Communications Law in Cologne, these solutions were further fleshed out so that they could be easily translated into legal regulations (see references in www.media-war.com).

2.1 Abolition of the 'lock-in' privilege
In department stores, operators are not allowed to prevent shoppers from leaving the store if they wish to. Platforms, on the other hand, have the privilege of being able to largely 'lock in' their users. We therefore need to open up the platforms. From now on, they should be permeable in all directions. This means that content creators should be able to place external links wherever they like: at the level of the headline, in videos, in texts or images. Additionally, platforms should no longer be allowed to reduce the visibility of content with outlinks. And on top of all that, very large platforms would be obliged to offer their content via open standards. All of this will create a level playing field. By opening up the platforms, we will reverse the situation. The internet's focus will finally return to content and much less on access through the platforms and their control on visibility. Eventually, just as with emails, it will not matter so much which of the competing providers is used to transmit content. The reason is obvious: all email providers use the same open standard. And that is precisely why there is still competition and diversity when it comes to email providers today. We will establish the same pluralism at the level of platforms.

2.2 Abolition of the monopoly privilege
In the sphere of analogue media, monopolistic conditions are already ruled out today. In Germany, for example, the leading TV channel RTL would never be allowed to control 90 % of audience attention. For the TV market, the maximum market share cap is set by law at 30 percent. In the same way, we need to abolish the monopoly privilege for digital media — by simply applying the exact same market share cap of 30 percent to digital media genres that are relevant to democracy (i. e. search engines, social media, free video-on-demand

and generative AI). In all fields where monopolistic or oligopolistic conditions exist, the platforms would have to be opened up to third-party providers.

2.3 Abolition of intermediary privilege

Dark Tech can only maintain its monopolies and at the same time push the editorial media out of the market because its lawyers have managed to push through laws stating that their offerings are not media at all. The central issue is the regulatory contradiction concerning monetisation: The platforms are treated like networks (e.g. telephone networks) but earn their money just like editorial media (they offer concrete and specific media content, which they select and play out for individuals and monetise through advertising). This is obviously inconsistent. Platforms should therefore need to decide in future: Either they start making their money like networks (i.e. not by monetising content) or, if they don't want to be treated like networks, they need to be treated for what they actually are, namely content providers (i.e. editorial media). But then they must bear full responsibility for the monetised content like any other content provider.

2.4 Abolition of liability privilege

This would also mean that their liability privilege would be abolished. By contrast with other (editorial) media companies, they should no longer receive preferential legal treatment. Anyone who takes on economic responsibility for specific content must of course also be liable for the same content. We should deprive platforms of their legal privileges, which have allowed them to burden society with the huge costs and damages of their business models ('externalities') to date.

2.5 Abolition of criminal privilege

Logically, this would also lead to the criminal privilege being abolished. It is completely unacceptable anyway that, in our economy, Dark Tech companies are allowed to earn money on the back of specific criminal offences. Of course, this might vary a bit depending on the country. But if national laws prohibit acts of racism, discrimination, defamation or (as in Germany) Holocaust denial, it should no longer be possible for Dark Tech to monetise such illegal content in that country. None of this has any impact on media freedom. It only affects Dark Tech's limitless possibilities for making money. Even with such limitations, the platforms would still be free to continue showing criminal content — but they would have to do that in specific unfiltered feeds which are not monetised, whether by advertising or any other means. They would be free to find other solutions as they please, i.e. monetise as the 'networks' they claim to be. But we would no longer allow them to make money from criminal acts.

2.6 Abolition of instrumentalisation privilege
As in the editorial media, we must also heed the principle of 'graduated equality of opportunity' in the digital sphere, especially as the monopolistic and oligopolistic threats are much more pronounced there than in the analogue world. This means that the owners of Dark Tech should no longer be able to use their own platforms to instrumentalise them for one-sided political purposes. Elon Musk would be free to continue supporting right-wing parties and interfere in elections, but he could no longer do such things on his own platform X.

2.7 Liberation of unfree users: "You are the media now", for real
In future, those who operate platforms and enjoy their many benefits should no longer be able to systematically disempower the people who create these platforms through their content, as the Dark Tech companies do by not giving their communities a 'voice' in how their platforms are designed. Users should be given this voice in the future. Platforms should therefore be obliged to set up oversight boards made up of elected representatives of content creators, elected representatives of platform users, digital experts from the field of the digital economy and regulation, and finally representatives from the platform's management. In future, these oversight boards should decide

on the community standards, the principles according to which content is played out within the platforms and on key issues concerning the self-regulation of the platforms, such as the possibilities of objection by users, appeal bodies, processes and the organisational composition of the 'judges' in the event of disputes. Platforms that do not agree to such oversight boards should be welcome to change their business model. To put it bluntly: Anyone who wants to be an 'open platform' must accept this representative participation and give their users a true voice. If you don't want to be an open platform, you will have to create the content yourself in future and pay fees for it.

Kickstarting the free, European internet

Only once we have opened up the digital markets to diversity and competition will alternative offers get the fair chance that they never had under monopolistic conditions. That was precisely the reason why dozens of subsidised attempts to create a 'German search engine' or a 'European YouTube' never worked in the past. We could have done without the State subsidies and funding programmes altogether, as those alternatives had no chance under the conditions of the digital monopolies.

Once we have deprived Dark Tech of all its feudalistic privileges and preferential legal treatment, the monopolies of the digital oligarchy will collapse instantly. Once we have opened up the digital markets to competition, the traffic on the existing alternative offerings will automatically multiply. Ideally, it will increasingly become like the market for email providers: What would matter most would be the content and not the distributing platform. Conversely, projects such as a platform operated by public service broadcasting would also have a real chance under conditions where open standards prevailed.

This is how we would create a full digital reset in Europe. We would bring together the coolest 'digital superbrains' in a task force and connect new ideas quickly with investor circles. And financial investors as well as capital markets would be the first ones to grasp that Europe was now getting serious about opening up the digital markets to competition.

It was during my presentations at tech conferences that I learned that nobody understands the extent of monopolisation better than investors, of all people. There, I was told, in response to my presentations: "It's great that you've measured all of this scientifically. But everyone here is already aware of this. For example, we wouldn't give money to someone who invented a new search engine. We all know that the search engine market is occupied by Google's monopoly. For us investors, these are 'no-fly zones' — we would never go in there." By opening up our digital markets, this would change radically. Existing alternatives and new ideas would receive huge amounts of funding from private investors and venture capital — because Europe is a huge, attractive market.

At the same time, we could certainly poach some superbrains from the US. Even if Dark Tech has happily joined forces with the Trump government, there will be many great people from these companies who no longer want to sacrifice their lives and energy for Trump and his abolition of democracy. We could make them great offers — and they could contribute all their know-how to a democratic internet that belongs to the people.

Securing infrastructure against blackmail by Trump and tech

Finally, we need to carry out a quick analysis: Where can hostile forces from the US hurt us most? Where is our dependency greatest? What could they use against us in worst-case scenarios? The situation is particularly bad for our digital infrastructure. The extent of our dependence is staggering. Huge amounts of sensitive data, both from companies and administrations, are stored with the major US cloud providers, i.e. Amazon (AWS), Microsoft (Azure) and Google

(GCP). Experts estimate that the proportion is significantly higher than 70 %. The same situation prevails for office software — the share of MS Office (Microsoft) is around 85 %.

This excessive dependence on the digital monopolies was already evident during the peaceful Biden administration. For example, Broadcom (respectively VMware) has demanded "up to twelve-fold price increases" from its customers, which also affected "federal, state and local governments" in Germany. In addition:

> "In the period from 2015 to 2021 alone (seven years), the federal administration's expenditure on Microsoft has increased almost fivefold. Exploding IT costs are to be expected in public administration. In 2023, the federal government departments increased their expenditure on software licences from around 771 million euros in 2022 to over 1.2 billion in 2023. This corresponds to an increase of 441 million euros or around 57 percent."[2]

We are already utterly exposed to the whims of a malicious US government. What's even more blatant is that it can already access all our data on US cloud services LEGALLY.

> "With the surveillance law 'Clarifying Lawful Overseas Use of Data Act (CLOUD Act)' passed in 2018 — during Donald Trump's administration — US authorities have unrestricted and worldwide access to all data stored in data centers of US companies. US authorities, such as the NSA, CIA and others, therefore have legitimate access to all data stored in US data centers in Germany or the EU. This means that European companies and organizations, but also private individuals who use American cloud services or software solutions, can potentially be monitored and manipulated by US authorities. Industrial espionage cannot be ruled out either."[3]

Incidentally, the fundamental problem of these dependencies has at least been recognised in the EU — and a 'EuroStack' project is planned, which is intended to transfer us to digital sovereignty at a cost of around 300 billion euros, even if it will take until around 2035 before it is finalised. We can only imagine what could happen (and could go wrong) between now and then.[4] By now, we should all have the courage to IMMEDIATELY terminate all existing contracts between European as well as national authorities or institutions with US cloud service providers and also ensure that data from German companies is no longer exposed to risks in the future. We can only become digitally sovereign through our own IT infrastructure.

Revenge from the USA will follow

If we do all of this (secure our own defence capability, open up the monopolised digital markets and carry out a European digital reset, plus secure our own digital infrastructure), if we really get serious with our democratic uprising, the revenge from the US will certainly be terrible. The digital monopolies are their 'holy grail' because that is precisely how they will be able to dominate and exploit us in the future. This is precisely why the tiny restrictions in current European digital regulations are being presented in the US as if the EU were brutally 'ripping us off', as if they were in fact 'hidden tariffs' and so on — even though all of these existing regulations are toothless tigers against the complete monopolistic digital occupation of Europe. The US objection to a ridiculously low penalty from a completely intimidated European Commission was as follows:

> "This novel form of economic extortion [!] will not be tolerated by the United States. Extraterritorial regulations that specifically target and undermine American companies, stifle innovation and enable censorship [!] will be recognized as barriers to trade and a direct threat to free civil society. [!]"[5]

It is remarkable that various aspects of the libertarian political 'struggle for freedom' (censorship / free civil society) are woven into the argument here, although the European ruling was only dealing with violations of competition law.

The official announcement from the US went on to say, ominously, that even such a small reaction as the one we are dealing with here would set off a "death spiral". By contrast, our measures proposed here would be no small matter. Opening up digital markets to competition would cost Dark Tech and the US hundreds of billions in revenue and forever thwart their plan to turn Europe into a dependent digital colony.

In this scenario, we would therefore get to know the combination of Dark Tech, Trump and the right-wing populists for *the first time as they really are*. Remember the uprising against the feudalistic order from the 12th century that Duby reported on (▸5)? It would be *exactly the same scenario today*. The act of revolt itself would be monstrous, almost unimaginable: the subjugated digital serfs would question the supposedly 'natural' ruling order of the monopolies and free themselves from this feudalistic dependency.

The 'digital feudalist rulers' would react to any attempt at 'liberation' with the utmost severity. Let's take Germany as an example: Dark Tech companies such as Microsoft, Apple or OpenAI could immediately stop promised regional investments in the various German regions. Alphabet or Meta could dismantle their strong presences in Hamburg, and so on.[6] Certainly, Dark Tech would immediately mobilise the US government. The US would impose massive tariffs and perhaps even import bans on German and European goods.[7] Would we have the determination to accept these losses? Would our digital sovereignty be more important to us than German automotive industry sales, for example?

Bear in mind that Trump and Dark Tech have an array of different levers at their disposal to immediately take down our rebellion in our fight to secure our own democratic sovereignty. The options for the US government to damage us by accessing our IT infrastructure are virtually limitless. Even customers of European providers of business software (such as SAP) could be affected if their customers' data is hosted by US cloud services. The possibilities for sabotage are therefore limitless for the US: Data access can be blocked, data can be deleted, temporarily disappear (e. g. to blackmail us), data can be manipulated, data can be passed on for the purposes of industrial espionage, sensitive health data can be leaked, government databases or payment systems can fail and so on.

Depending on how far we escalated the level of our fight for digital sovereignty, the US would also be able to unleash migration flows (of numbers in the tens of millions) on Europe depending on the US's future engagement (respectively non-engagement) in the Ukraine war.[8] Already, Trump is engaging in amicable exchanges with Russian dictator Putin and we have no idea how this partnership will evolve. Furthermore, the US could, for similar purposes, act as a catalyst in terms of further conflicts flaring up in the Middle East.

Furthermore, the US could use their own platforms to further frighten millions of people in Europe and they could further ramp up their active campaigning for their right-wing populist 'partner' parties. Already, they quite openly state that they want to 'liberate' Europe from its current democratic governments. Tech, Trump and the populists will tell people all kinds of horror stories about how 'our uprising' is just a multi billion-dollar 'scam' by corrupt elites who want to siphon off the funds used for digital sovereignty to 'enrich themselves at the taxpayers' expense' and so on. We are well aware of Trump and tech portraying themselves as 'victims', for example of a 'witch hunt' (Trump) or 'brutal' censorship (Zuckerberg). We can only imagine the waves of propaganda with which they would hit us if we were to challenge their supremacy.

This is especially the case as they are able to mobilise masses of people through their own platforms. We would immediately have a right-wing populist mob on the streets, 'independent thinkers' who, while being 'remote-controlled' by Dark Tech and the oligarchs, believe they have to defend 'freedom' on the internet and drive out the 'elites' (whereas they do not seem to notice that they are being instrumentalised by a new, anti-democratic mega-elite). They would then be happy to start the 'civil war' in Europe that Musk has long been talking about. That would all be in the name of fighting for 'freedom of speech' of course. The prospects are not good, as you can see. In addition, they could even threaten to shut down their own platforms, the supposed 'last bastions of freedom'. Interestingly enough, they have already used similar threats in the past.[9]

Why the uprising is still worth pursuing

Sure, this will all be mega tough. The situation is tragic to the extent that these and similar measures could have been implemented comparably easily some years ago, when Dark Tech was not as dominant and Trump did not hold power in the US.

If we were to act with determination, we would certainly suffer as a society for several years. We would have to make sacrifices and cut back in order to defend our democratic sovereignty. But if we were to succeed, things would turn in our favour after just a few years. For the first time, we would be able manage our digital markets by ourselves. We would not just be fobbed off with the tiny crumbs that are left for us under the conditions of the monopolistic Dark Tech occupation. We could rise up to the challenge of becoming competitive in the markets of the future. Sure, there would be plenty of hitches and bumps during the transition phase, but the race to catch up would also make all of us more competent concerning digital matters. This drastic 'cure' would literally *force us* to turn from 'digital challengers' into 'digital champions'.

Let's never forget: Europe has a huge domestic market. If we shake off the digital occupation, capital and investments will follow immediately. Investors will immediately support alternative ideas with large sums of money — out of pure selfishness. Our digital economy will boom. But the best thing is: we will save European democracy and persistently secure it against the terrible threats from the East and the West. The best thing will be: from this new, digitally sovereign Europe, we will be able to support the many people who are threatened by the autocratic developments in the US.

Let's never forget: the US once saved us from the terrible threat of totalitarianism in Europe. Isn't it time for us to return the favour to the US? Our alternative platforms, unlike the Dark Tech offerings, will then be democratically legitimised. Such platforms can play their part in enriching the largely destroyed democratic public sphere in the US with sustainable, balanced and secure alternatives. And we will find other areas in which we can help the US fight back against the threat of turning into an autocracy. Metaphorically speaking: Let's just create a democratic 'Marshall Plan' for the US 😊 — and give them back what they have given to us in the past.

9.
THE CAPITULATION

Our life in the 'digitalocratic' occupation zone

You're probably now thinking just how hopeless all this seems, how deeply dependent we are and how Herculean the effort would be to free ourselves from the deadly grip of Dark Tech and the libertarian populists.

Of course, the alternative would be to simply give up and settle down in the 'digitalocratic' occupation zone. However, we should then take a quick look at what is likely to happen to us in the future. Of course, this is pure speculation. But we have a pretty good idea of how Dark Tech and Trump tend to behave, especially as our assumption is that most of the things that are currently happening in the US will also become a reality in Europe. What is particularly interesting is that their approach in the real world is exactly the same as the mechanisms they use on their platforms. Typically, they promote and boost the content that benefits them while, at the same time, they reduce the visibility of content that goes against their interests.

And this boosting and dimming is exactly what they are already doing. On the negative side, there have been numerous public humiliations. Let's remember who was and who was not invited to Trump's inauguration dinner. We know that the top political officials from the EU were apparently not welcome, but the various right-wing populist European allies of Tech and Trump were invited alongside the digital oligarchs. They selected their 'partners', such as Tino Chrupalla (AfD), Nigel Farage (Reform UK), Georgia Meloni from Italy, Eric Zemmour (leader of the far-right party, Reconquête, from France),

Tom Van Grieken (leader of the nationalist party, Vlaams Belang, from Belgium), Santiago Abascal (from the national conservative party, Vox, from Spain) and so on.[1] A little later, JD Vance visited Europe and gave his speech at the AI Summit in Paris, but did not stay for the speeches given by French President Macron and of the President of the European Commission, Ursula von der Leyen. We saw a similar pattern of behaviour at his visit of the Munich Security Conference.

The same applies to public attacks on individuals — often on alleged 'liars' and 'censors' in the field of the Covid-19 pandemic, such as Fauci in the US or Drosten in Germany, but also on other 'hate figures' in the field of climate change, inclusion, research into fascism and so on, according to the narratives spread by the 'media war'. The 'elites' of the *paper belt* are punished in a similar way. The 'so-called' scientists are discredited and people with opposing opinions are harassed and threatened.

The same applies to politicians. Musk's insults aimed at German politicians Habeck or Scholz ('fool') and Keir Starmer from the UK are well known. And, of course, journalists and editorial media will be equally hunted. On the one hand, the digital transformation and the dominance of Dark Tech monopolies are depriving the journalists and editorial media of their financial basis. On the other hand, they are also being massively attacked by Dark Tech and populists in terms of content, constantly being accused of 'manipulation', 'lies' and 'censorship' for every detail, no matter how marginal.

In other fields, there is the symbol of the *'chainsaw'* and the narrative *of cutting all the 'overgrown' state interventions: The lazy bureaucrats, civil servants, and good-for-nothings will disappear. They have never worked a single day in their lives anyways.* And the supposedly *'left-wing'* NGOs and other institutions will be denied access to political commissions and decisionmaking, their funding will be cut off, subsidies will be phased out.

Lawsuits against editorial offices and scientists

Unfortunately, Trump and Dark Tech hold yet another wild card in their hands. Let's recall the liability privilege, according to which their own platforms cannot be held responsible for the statements and content they carry, not even if they make money with precisely this content. Conversely, editorial media are liable. But it is the supposed 'liberators' of the media, the self-proclaimed champions of 'freedom of expression', who have recently started suing the players of the media 'establishment', who — unlike them — *are* legally liable for the content.

In fact, we see a new era dawning here too. In recent months, Trump has sued a whole range of media outlets, authors and academics:[2]

- *CBS News* was sued in Texas for an allegedly biased presentation of Kamala Harris: the amount in dispute is 10 million US dollars;
- A lawsuit was launched against the local newspaper *Des Moines Register* based in Iowa as well as Ann Selzer, head of a polling institute (the point of dispute is the publication of a voter survey in the run-up to the US election with surprisingly positive predictions for Kamala Harris)
- Another lawsuit was launched against ABC News because of a statement about Trump. In this case, the intimidated broadcaster has agreed to an out-of-court settlement and will pay 15 million US dollars to a charitable organisation yet to be named by Trump or his team, as well as one million dollars for the legal costs incurred
- A lawsuit is planned against the *New York Times* and the publishing house Penguin Random House over two articles and a book in which Trump is portrayed as an unsuccessful entrepreneur; 10 billion is said to be at stake here
- The strategy of intimidation is apparently now also being pursued in Europe: in the Netherlands, a journalist was sued by X,

apparently in response to a previous request for the personal data that the company holds about him (to which consumers are entitled under European data protection law)[3]

As the journalist Andrian Kreye has vividly explained, these are so-called *SLAPP suits*.[4] The acronym stands for 'strategic lawsuit against public participation', which serve the purpose of intimidating people and silencing criticism. As already mentioned, such proceedings in the US offer much more extensive possibilities for damaging an opponent in civil law than would be possible in Germany or Europe: "this ranges from the criminal offense of defamation to claims for damages and accusations of betrayal of secrets".

Of course, on top of that we have to consider the massive asymmetry of power and financial resources that they can use against victims. So much for the idea that the US is 'ahead' of Europe when it comes to freedom of expression. The opposite is the case: critics are fighting a financially overpowering opponent who also has very extensive political power. The fear is that this approach could even involve government institutions such as the FBI against the media, authors or scientists. Kreye quotes a statement made by Kash Patel, who has since become head of the FBI, in a podcast with none other than Steve Bannon. He announced a vendetta: "We're going to come after the people in the media who lied about American citizens, who helped Joe Biden rig presidential elections. Whether it's criminally or civilly, we'll figure that out."[5]

All this is particularly disconcerting when we consider that a feature of the digital media reality is that it is hard to sue the Dark Tech owners of the platforms for liability claims. In other words, editorial media, authors and scientists are exposed to massive risks in the future whilst platform owners will be immune from such legal claims to a large extent.

The basic trend is important: we must assume that, in the future, Trump, Dark Tech and their populist allies will use every conceivable means to inflict as much damage as possible on the *paper belt*. In

Europe and Germany, scientists, journalists, experts and institutions of the supposed 'elites' would be systematically deprived of visibility, funding would be stopped, budgets cut, jobs eliminated, critics sued, threatened or silenced, just like they have been in the US.

The active promotion of autocrats and opportunists

By contrast, the autocrats, i.e. Putin, but also anti-democratic or right-wing actors such as Orbán with whom deals can be made whenever desired, will be promoted by Trump and tech — above all in order to constantly re-legitimise them and weaken the democratic forces in the world just as consistently. And, of course, the broad front of right-wing populists will be promoted by Dark Tech.

Particular attention will be paid to the broad field of opportunistic forces. These are actors who, from the point of view of Trump and tech, are characterised above all by the fact that they are beyond the clearly defined 'enemy image' of 'elites' and 'leftists' and are therefore particularly well suited to being quickly transformed into 'strategic comrades-in-arms'. This card can be played wonderfully on a geopolitical level for example.

The perfect prey for such types of campaigns could be the United Kingdom. In fact, Elon Musk has already put a lot of energy into destabilising Keir Starmer's government. The motivation behind this is probably to prevent the EU and the UK from moving closer together again. We must not forget that Trump and conservative think tanks from the US promoted Brexit,[6] which was also strongly driven by disinformation campaigns on Dark Tech platforms. From the perspective of the EU's enemies, it would be ideal if a transatlantic free trade zone without tariffs were established between the US and the UK, including a competing low-tax environment on the doorstep of the EU in the UK and a deeper partnership between Wall Street and the City of London.

Under no circumstances would these actors like to see any

rapprochement between the UK and the EU, especially in the field of digital regulation. For big tech, the idea would be to transform the UK into a kind of deregulated outpost of the US in order to weaken the EU as much as possible. The current UK government's solidarity with the EU is certainly encouraging considering the ongoing threat in Ukraine but let's see how long this mood lasts over the coming months and years. Who knows, maybe Boris Johnson is already planning a comeback. Maybe the US will choose other stooges. We will see.

In a similar way, the US can try to identify other opportunistic powers and allow them to benefit from its 'good deeds'. Switzerland, for example, could also be a candidate. Switzerland often positions itself as 'neutral' in such matters in order to turn geopolitical opportunities into cash and profits. Accordingly, Switzerland has already shown itself to be surprisingly 'open' in relation to the new Trump administration. In an official letter to the US government, they unabashedly pandered to Trump and emphasised their shared views in areas such as tech regulation or climate protection and clearly distanced themselves from to the EU. In the paper, Switzerland positioned itself against the EU and as a "true friend" and "natural partner" of the US.[7] No comment.

The US can use various instruments of selective 'business development'. In this sense, tech companies now prefer to place their investments in Republican-dominated Texas and stage this in a publicity-effective manner through joint appearances with Trump — in order to 'punish' Democrat-dominated California at the same time.[8]

The exact same principle would be applied here in Europe or Germany, for example by relocating European headquarters to the UK, Switzerland or 'friendly' countries such as Orbán's Hungary or Meloni's Italy and thereby penalising affected European countries in the process. The same principle can easily be implemented inside the nation States at the level of the federal States — obedient federal States and regions would be 'rewarded' with investments while financial commitment would be reduced in federal States that criticise tech and the libertarian domination.

Trump and tech will therefore look everywhere for figures who can play a role in supporting their agenda and dividing democratic structures or regions, according to the motto: 'divide and rule'. They are already finding such figures in the sphere of the 'established' media, who benefit from their support for the technolibertarian agenda and at the same time legitimise anti-democratic libertarianism. Last year, we noticed an astonishing incorporation of right-wing populist ideas into the Germany's powerful media ecosystem of the Springer corporation, including an interview with CEO Mathias Döpfner, who described JD Vance's speech at the Munich Security Conference in the *Financial Times* as "inspiring". Many people in Europe had "deliberately misunderstood" Vance, said Döpfner.[9]

Similar figures can also be found in the 'established' parties. Do you remember when Musk announced his alliance with the right-wing party AfD ("Only the AfD can save Germany")? In a seemingly desperate post, Christian Lindner from the moderate free-market party FDP quickly pandered to Musk on X, saying something like: 'Hey Elon, why are you doing it with the racist AfD? Why wouldn't you rather do it with us, the pro-business FDP?'

Due to the overwhelming power of tech and Trump alone, there are such 'opportunities' for them lurking everywhere. Their objective is clear: By creating divisions between more and more key stakeholders, European democracy is further undermined. I could discuss dozens of examples here, but I will choose just one. At a time when every thinking European should be aware of the EU's total dependence on Dark Tech IT infrastructures, we read in the news:

> "Poland has agreed on AI cooperation between Google and the Polish Development Fund. This was announced by Prime Minister Donald Tusk after a meeting with the head of Google. […] The agreement covers the use of AI in energy, cybersecurity and other areas, Alphabet and Google CEO Sundar Pichai said in Warsaw on Thursday. According to Tusk, the agreement will create a framework for greater Google investment in Poland and

strengthen the country's security. According to Pichai, Google could thus contribute to an 8 percent increase in Poland's GDP. He emphasized the country's potential as Google's largest technical center in the region."[10]

As already mentioned: in March 2025, the German Federal Council recommended that the police in Germany should use Palantir's security software nationwide in the future. And the BSI (Federal Office for Information Security) has announced a strategic collaboration with Google and Amazon, among others. You can't make this stuff up.

Establishment of local political partners

At the same time, Trump and tech are already supporting partner organisations in Europe. In the political sphere, they are already in close contact with right-wing populist parties. Thanks to their lobbying activities, they have a seat at the table in every conceivable political and, above all, digital policy committee. Moreover, the tech corporations are involved on many topics and issues through NGO-like institutions where, in many cases, the public as well as affected politicians do not even realise that these institutions are funded and controlled from afar by Dark Tech.

But they are also penetrating other parts of the public sphere where you would least expect it. Many of the leading digital conferences are privately financed, for example by the various exhibitors who are present on site. Well, who do you think is spending a lot of money? Of course, the Dark Tech companies are extremely active at these conferences. But of course, exhibitors and sponsors get preferred slots on the stages. Take a look at a festival like 'Online Marketing Rockstars' in Hamburg, with about 70,000 people participating, and who has what 'share of voice' on the stages. Here's what's truly bad about this: people who attend these events think they are getting 'neutral' content (one could joke that the content is as about as neutral as the platforms …). But the line-up on the stages is also determined by the amount of money exhibitors are willing to give to the organiser.

The same applies to various associations. Take a look at how the various working groups and committees of the supposedly 'neutral' German digital economy association Bitkom are staffed. You will immediately recognise the massive dominance of big tech. It would be interesting to know the proportion of funding that Bitkom receives from Dark Tech sources but, unfortunately, that infomation is not disclosed. It is concerning that Bitkom is also deeply involved in organising the 'Digital Summit of the German Government', for instance.

In addition to the platforms, they are building up their own publics, organisations, associations, NGOs and partnerships with universities, while at the same time gradually dismantling the old, supposedly 'corrupt elites' (i.e. scientists, experts, journalists and so on). They are being replaced with the successful mercenaries of the platforms. In a famous interview with Joe Rogan, in which Mark Zuckerberg criticised the allegedly 'brutal' censorship of the Biden government (yeah, of course, 'poor' Zuckerberg), he also described how this old elite is now being abolished and replaced by a 'new class of creators', the users and influencers from social media.[11]

We can look to the US to get a feel for who will dominate public discourse in the future: "The 2024 election was the influencer election."[12] Social media giants, streamers and influencers such as Joe Rogan, Alex Jones, Adin Ross, DC Draino and Dave Rubin drove the discourse, fuelled by meme sites and aggregators as well as new 'public intellectuals' such as Steve Bannon and Curtis Yarvin, the 'tech-monarchist philosopher king of Substack'. Trump's 'cabinet of horrors' also shows where the journey is heading, for example with Defense Secretary Pete Hegseth, a former Fox News presenter who is tainted by various reports of alleged sexual assault and alcohol abuse[13] or Health Secretary Robert F. Kennedy Jr., who used to be a heroin addict and has attracted attention for spreading conspiracy theories.

The enthronement of a new 'digitalocratic' elite

Thus, the old 'elite' of the 'establishment' is being scrapped and replaced by new, digitalocratic opinion leaders. A significantly large following on the platforms can only be achieved by people who spend an equally significant part of their lives on the platforms and invest their energy there, in the 'media war', for the 'digitalocratic cause'.

Trump, Tech & co. will decide who gets access in the digitalocratic future — exemplified by Trump kicking 'established' media (NBC, NYT, NPR) out of the Pentagon Press Corps in early February and replacing them with technolibertarian 'alternative' media (Breitbart, One America News, NY Post).[14] Other examples were when Musk used his reach on X to promote the far-right AfD or call for the overthrow of the British government.

Thus, we are giving up the meritocratic and content-driven media order of democratic enlightenment. And just by participating, we are supporting the new, digitalocratic media order in two ways: Firstly, we are all already working 'for free' for the platforms. We live in total dependency on the incentives of their media order, to the reach, likes, shares and followers we get on their platforms (this also applies to me, even as a tech critic). At the same time, we are strengthening the monopolies and thereby further cementing their dominance.

Our role in this mirrors the reality of the digital attention economics as described above (▶ 6): We replace the value of content by the reward metrics of a digital following and network effects. In the future, 'truth' will mean that many people on the platforms believe something to be true. (Trump cleverly used this principle as the name of his platform, Truth Social). The digitalocratic rulers are the platform operators who make us dance to tune of their algorithms like puppeteers.

So we rush from post to post in this 'digital occupation zone', from scandal to rant to accusation to slander, to the next 'incredible revelation', the 'unbelievable scandal', the 'shocking affront', watching how this person is 'grilled' and the other 'destroyed'. We can no longer keep up, we no longer even understand what is true and what is false. Let's listen for a few minutes to the 'liberated' sound of the new digitalocracy — in this case we hear the voices of Mel Gibson, Joe Rogan and Alex Jones:

> *Gibson:* I have three friends. All three of them had stage four cancer. All three of them don't have cancer right now at all. [...]
> *Rogan:* What did they take?
> *Gibson:* Jesus. They took some ... what you've heard they've taken.
> *Rogan:* Ivermectin? (Gibson nods.)
> *Rogan/Gibson:* Fenbendazole.
> *Rogan:* Yeah, yeah, I'm hearing that a lot.
> *Gibson:* They drank hydrochloride, something or other.
> *Rogan:* There's studies on this now, where people have proven that ...
> *Gibson:* People drinking Methylene Blue and stuff.
> *Rogan:* Yeah, Methylene Blue, which was a fabric dye.
> *Gibson:* Yeah!
> *Rogan:* Yeah, it was a textile dye. And they find it has profound effects on your mitochondria.
> *Gibson:* Yep. This stuff works, man.
> *Rogan:* There's a lot of stuff that does work, which is very strange. Because, again, it's profit. When you hear about things that are demonised and that turn out to be effective, you always wonder, well, what is going on here? How are our medical institutions, how have they failed us so that things that do cure you are not promoted because they're not profitable. [...]
> [Interlude]
> *The [Biden] government fears Alex Jones, who has the largest audience in the country. He's bigger than any of the networks, the biggest megaphone in the country ... The Deep State hates Alex Jones with a vengeance ... Alex Jones is the most extraordinary person I've ever met.*

Jones: Alright, I want to talk about something really, really positive here. Dealing with the great awakening, one of the main ways the globalist, technocrat, WHO, de-population system attacks us [...] And now it's all in the studies, one hundred percent confirmed.[15]

Let us briefly remind ourselves that the 'independent thinker' Steve Jobs was already on a similarly erroneous path that ended quite tragically. In his rejection of science and medical experts (watch out for the *Paper Belt*!) he treated his aggressive cancer by first doing his own research — and then following "a strict vegan diet, with large quantities of fresh carrot and fruit juices", followed by using "acupuncture, a variety of herbal remedies" and other similar treatments.[16] Surgical removal of the ulcer would have been easily possible after the initial diagnosis. However, Steve Jobs refused professional treatment and unfortunately realised his mistake when it was already too late. Perhaps one might say that was then his own fault. But in many cases, innocent people die as a result of this type of madness. Food influencer Maxim Lyutyi, for example, starved his newborn son to death because he wanted to feed the child with sunlight. He was absolutely certain that the baby would receive all the energy it needed for sustenance from sunlight. He thought this was proven, true knowledge — but he was wrong.[17]

Again and again this insanity is reiterated in the spectacular glare of the platforms: *Merkel is a reptiloid, Bill Gates wants to implant microchips into our bodies via covid vaccinations, chemtrails are poisoning all of us.* They show us 'alternative facts' —*finally revealed: the unbelievably awesome cancer remedy that the mainstream media won't show you*!!!! Or *the 100% certain way to get rich instantly. The 15 reasons why climate hysteria is made up.*

In the future digitalocracy, these voices will increasingly dominate and become ever stronger, simply because they own the digital reach. As these voices rule, the Trumps and Musks, the Zuckerbergs and Rogans, the Pichais and Thiels will continue to further push these movements that are favourable for their digitalocratic agenda (even if the reasons might vary). Both sides benefit from each other in this digital attention economy. As the digital public sphere belongs to them, the tech oligarchs will ensure that those opportunistic actors who are the first join forces on the various fields of 'opportunities' and 'partnerships' can win a small slice of the huge pie and then become part of this new, digitalocratic elite themselves. By doing so, they repeatedly create a classic prisoner's dilemma: the first actor who collaborates typically wins the game. Those who don't collaborate or even criticise have their visibility dialled down.

The German Springer media group is an excellent example of how, from an entrepreneurial point of view, you 'successfully' surrender in this prisoner's dilemma. Springer's CEO Mathias Döpfner excels at this game even though (and this is fascinating) he is clever enough to fully recognise the sickening downsides of this game!!!![18] That's probably why he has consistently been the first one to switch sides and yield to Big Tech's overtures. In 2021, for example, Springer announced a deal with Facebook that, according to industry rumours, would bring the company revenues in the triple-digit millions over several years. The entire German sector was entirely shocked as it had been the same Mathias Döpfner "who, as president of the German Newspaper and Digital Publishers' Association (BDZV), had warned fellow media companies against entering into bilateral and specific deals with Facebook; from the perspective of Facebook, such deals would be well suited to undermine the new 'ancillary copyright for press publishers' that would soon come into force" — bilateral deals would enable Facebook to get away with only minor payments to the publishers.[19]

Similar actions followed later. Even though OpenAI had used press texts on a large scale (without any permission from the copyright holders) to train its own generative AI and although all the media corporations protested indignantly, the Springer Group was once again the first German media company to announce a bilateral deal with OpenAI in 2023.[20]

Similarly, it's the very same Springer media which is also leading the way in giving an advantage to right-wing populist content in the battle for digital reach. For example, some weeks before the 2024 election, Springer's daily newspaper, *Die Welt*, published a controversial opinion piece by Elon Musk with a recommendation for German voters to elect the right-wing AfD. Döpfner is on good terms with Musk, which is why it would seem likely that he arranged the article behind the scenes — even though that was publicly denied by Springer.[21] The controversial article created a huge media scandal in Germany that earned Springer and *Die Welt* enormous additional viral visibility on the platforms and also generated many new digital subscriptions.[22] And again, according to the attention economics of digitalocracy, we see that setting fire to democracy pays off, in this case when it goes along with new digital reach and conversions, all in the name of 'freedom of speech'.

And as sad as this seems, the Springers and Döpfners of this world are only showing us what *our own future* in the 'prison of digitalocratic oppression' looks like. Sure, from a limited perspective, we can despise their egocentric political 'flexibility' towards power. But on the other hand, perhaps these opportunists are simply that much smarter than we are. They realised many years before we did: Resistance is completely futile. The outcome of this media war has long since been determined.

We should acknowledge without any envy: Thanks to such clever 'deals' with the 'digital occupiers', the Döpfners of this world have at least succeeded in coaxing a few million dollars out of the petty cash of the new 'digitalocratic feudal lords' before they voluntarily moved into their 'cyber prison'. What about us, on the other hand? In most cases, we voluntarily allow ourselves to be locked up by the feudal lords without any recompense from their side — *for free*. "What do you want?" the new feudal lords will ask us later in astonishment when we no longer want to live there. "You have voluntarily agreed, subscribed, opted in for this."

Unfortunately, by then it really will be too late. This will be our new reality, a reality in which Dark Tech and their partnering autocrats largely dominate the digital media world and thus the basis of our future democracy. It will be a setup in which they also control ever larger shares of the economy simply because their monopolies are the access 'choke points' (as per the book called *Chokepoint Capitalism* by Rebecca Giblin and Cory Doctorov) to the public sphere, to the digital markets and to digital financial transactions. We will then be completely dependent. And, above all, this will *no longer be reversible*. There will be no easy way back. We will have turned into a kind of colony and our freedom will be lost forever. How on earth would we protest and revolt against this order, if the new feudal lords fully control our public sphere?

Perhaps now we are beginning to understand why digital monopolies are causing such dangerous, toxic damage to our society. We hopefully recognise the creepy affinity between *specific* monopolies in the field of media or markets and autocracy itself. To a certain extent, autocracy implies the total monopolisation of political power and similar laws apply. As is the case with specific monopolies, also here a return to the *status quo ante* is very difficult to envisage once the digital monpolies have fully taken over. Once the separation of powers, checks and balances, pluralism, open and fair access have been lost, it is very hard to get them back, especially as there will no longer be any free media in which to denounce digital autocracy.

10.
THE BITTER END

Revolt or surrender?

As you will have noticed by now, we are heading towards a dark ending. You can certainly criticise me for having changed my mind. In 2023, in the book *Big Tech Must Go!*, I estimated that the tipping point, beyond which any rescue of our democracy would become increasingly unlikely, would be the year 2029. In that book, I correctly predicted that the supremacy of Dark Tech would necessarily spill over into the field of politics. However, the new US government's coalition with tech companies has accelerated the momentum of this development to an extent that was unimaginable even for me in early 2023.

As I have outlined here, there are two options for Europe: we can either dare to revolt against Trump and tech (▶8) or we can surrender (▶9). We can also think of both scenarios as conceptual macroeconomic trajectories.

In the 'uprising' scenario, we would invest massively over a period of 2-4 years to achieve digital sovereignty but simultaneously accept major losses of prosperity at the beginning. We must bear in mind that the wide array of European problems caused by the reform backlog will not disappear: Ailing infrastructure, a weakening economy, growing social inequality, investment required to integrate refugees, the need to improve the healthcare system, education and science. We need to completely rebuild European defence and cover the costs of a radical digital reboot.

And we must factor into this scenario all the additional costs that the terrible revenge of Trump and tech will bring with it. They are

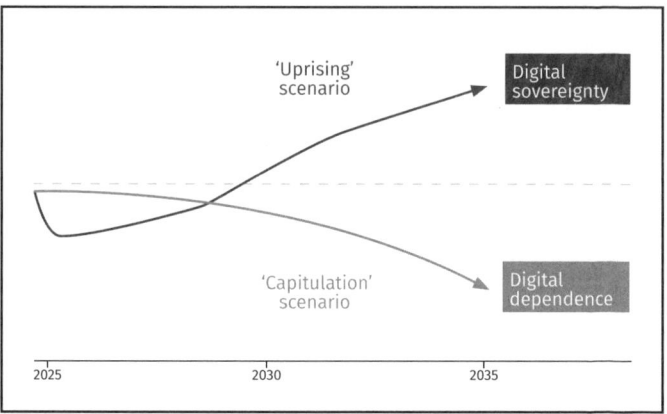

Fig. 12: Conceptual economic development of the scenarios 'The uprising' (Chapter 8) versus 'The capitulation' (Chapter 9)

extremely close to their goal of leading us into total dependency and turning Europe into a dependent 'digital colony' of their libertarian empire. Being so close to achieving their goal, we can be sure that they will respond to any resistance, however slight, with highly aggressive measures.

We also have to consider that, in the digitalocratic attention economy, it is precisely the important, long-term policy areas that are falling by the wayside. We can also see this when it comes to climate change. As we are constantly being bombarded with ever new, spectacular distractions on the platforms, global warming is 'no longer that important to us' any more. Just as the platforms amplify polarisation, hatred, turmoil and malice, as a society, we are also pushing one outrageous political spectacle after another through the digital agenda. If we really wanted to give our revolt a serious go, then we would have to be prepared, as a society, to make sacrifices over a period of around 2 to 4 years. But in which country would the people give the government that much time?

This is especially true, as, during the first 2 to 4 years, the 'capitulation' scenario is not so bad for us compared to the 'uprising' scenario. Even though, of course, every thinking person should understand that, along this route, circumstances will only deteriorate for us year by year. In this scenario, the digitalocratic rulers will continue to maximise our dependency over time. And the greater our dependency, the more they can exploit us, and, above all, the more they can rob us of our freedoms.

We're in a mess: the 12 reasons

Although all of this is more than obvious, I believe that the chances of us daring to revolt, i. e. courageously and resolutely asserting our own digital and democratic sovereignty in the long term, are less than ten percent.

Here are the reasons for my scepticism:

1. Lack of awareness of the problem

As mentioned in the introduction to this book, there is still a lack of general awareness of the problem. People continue to locate their problems in 'real issues' — such as the war in Ukraine, migration, national security, education, the economy, poverty, social inequality and so on. Compared to these, the threat to media freedom posed by digital monopolies is not perceived as a problem of the same magnitude. On the contrary, ironically, the conspiracy-theory type ANTI-narrative of Dark Tech and populists is widely supported: 'freedom of expression' is supposedly being threatened by the interventions of the 'tyrannical State' (▶7). The same lack of awareness of the problem applies to the issue of 'digital sovereignty'. But, as long as the broad public is not aware of the massive dangers lurking here, it is currently difficult to convey to people that considerable sacrifices are necessary to fundamentally reshape this field for all of us. Behind closed doors, many experts who understand what is happening are telling me: "It's too late anyway. There's nothing more we can do."

2. A return to the old world is impossible

The established elites have kept on outdoing each another in coming up with grandiose descriptions of the various problems for society concerning the digital world. But, so far, they have not managed to develop their own successful alternative visions and solutions. Even worse: In current debates, intellectuals, journalists and academics typically criticise the digital situation as if some sort of 'return' were possible, after which the old rules of discourse would apply again and a functioning public sphere could be 'restored'. As a media researcher, I would question this, at least the simplistic version of it. In thousands of years of media history, new media could never be stopped and this is exactly what Dark Tech and Trump are banking on. And one thing is for sure: we will never return to a culture of the printed word, of rational discourse, of enlightenment, which we have had under the conditions of analogue media. The digitalocratic age has long since dawned and the old elites will not rise again. This is why their criticism is also perceived as 'anti-progressive nagging' from outdated 'luddites' who are doomed for failure anyway. Sure, for a few more years, they can complain bitterly about this or that. They can still feel very important when interviewed by the press or in television, but in the medium term their fate is sealed.

Indeed, in its origins, the internet was still in sync with the forces of enlightenment. But as a society, we have allowed the Dark Tech corporations to steal the internet from us and to now control it. And we have been unable to implement or at least come up with a common vision of a democratically legitimised digital world. This is precisely the problem with most critics of the digital world: they have expressed their outrage at length but have not presented a gripping vision and, above all, have not implemented a better digital order. As a rule, 'resistance' only flares up selectively when individual areas of the long-outdated, old media world fall victim to the digital transformation. When the operation of a newspaper, a TV station or a cultural programme, a museum, a theatre, a library, an institution for 'media literacy', a radio station, etc. is to be discontinued, minor forces of resistance flare up for a few weeks in order to protect the *status quo*. The aim is to preserve vested interests to maintain niches and forms of discourse that are less and less relevant for society as a whole. But, in doing so, the demise of rational discourse and the upsurge of digitalocracy is even accelerated.

3. Extreme dependence on Dark Tech

Dark Tech is already fully penetrating society and all its systems and discourses. As a critic of big tech, you can quickly recognise that: Wherever I appear somewhere in politics or organisations, the digital corporations have already been active with these same stakeholders for many years. They have their 'partnerships', 'sponsorships' and 'collaborations' everywhere: In the government, in ministries, in trade associations, in the media, with political parties. And all areas within our society are completely dependent on Dark Tech in the digital sphere. Due to the monopolies, criticism of Dark Tech will only be possible via Dark Tech platforms in the future. I also sell my books on Amazon (because the majority of all digital book sales take place there). I also criticise Dark Tech via their own platforms, such as LinkedIn (Microsoft) or YouTube (Alphabet). It is hard to imagine that, in the future, tech giants would allow critical debates to take place on their platforms if they threaten their very existence. Perhaps they are already actively dimming these discourses — they would surely have the power to do so (this 'dimming' and 'boosting' is certainly the easiest way for Dark Tech to influence our discourses in their favour in the future, especially since it is not recognisable to those affected). I have personally experienced how big tech uses its power to put pressure on and blackmail conference organisers who have brought me on as a speaker, for example. Why shouldn't they do the same where it is easiest for them — on their own platforms?

4. There are no signs of real resistance anywhere in the world

I cannot see a single powerful stakeholder in the western world who is currently resisting this technolibertarian bid for supremacy with real determination. There is no successful case anywhere that we could use as a model. At one point, for example, it might have been possible that companies such as Apple, Alphabet (Google) or Meta would have resisted Trump's autocratic agenda. Together, they could have threatened the Trump government, saying: "Should you dare to establish autocratic conditions in the US, we will immediately move our global headquarters from the US to free, democratic Europe instead. Because we don't do deals with autocrats." They would have had enough money to take such a stand for democracy. There would have been a battle between Dark Tech and 'shady tech'. Of course, anyone who knows the anti-democratic, aggressively libertarian history of these corporations knows that this is an extremely naïve idea on my part. The point is that it could have happened, but it didn't.

However, there could also have been a huge uprising *within* these Dark Tech companies. Apparently the most brilliant superbrains of our time work there and they are supposedly doing this primarily to make the world a better place. So why don't they come together to arrange a fun general strike, across all the 'Dark Tech empires'? Along the lines of: "We won't do ANYTHING until our management ensures that our companies become 100 % democracy-compliant in the future." That would also be conceivable. But it isn't happening.

5. The power of Dark Tech extends to business, media and politics

We must bear in mind that the current concentration of power is unparalleled in human history. Dark Tech concentrates unimaginable amounts of economic power. On top of that, it has a huge amount of control and power in terms of public opinion via its platforms. This has never happened before in this form. This domination of the political public sphere is even further accelerated by the massive investments in lobbying activities. Thus, even the remaining media and public spaces that are not yet directly controlled by Dark Tech are also being brought 'into line' in terms of Dark Tech's agenda. This supremacy is probably already 'too big to fail'.

6. Our decision-makers lack digital competence

Another problem is the digital incompetence of our decision-makers. We can also recognise this in the way in which we frame the public discourse. How many tens of thousands of times in the last ten years have European intellectuals, journalists and academics snobbishly made fun of the 'embarrassing dolt, moron and idiot' Trump, who again and again made a fool of himself? It's too bad that Trump turned out to be damn clever and successful. Not only did he completely see through the dynamics of digital monopoly formation for years while European intellectuals didn't even realise that there was a problem in the first place. He even managed to immunise and emancipate himself from the digital monopolies by not only designing but completely developing his own platform and successfully going live with it in early 2022, at the age of 76. What a huge achievement — I'd love to see any one of his European critics accomplish something like that! Meanwhile our vain decision-makers and smart alecks were still in a 'digital slumber', even 2022. When Musk bought Twitter in October 2022, we sleepily mused something like: "Hey, we don't think it's a good idea that a billionaire is just able to buy himself a platform like that." But we haven't achieved much more since then. *It's a fatal mistake not to show your opponents any respect and to overestimate yourself so excessively even when your own performance is substandard.* Unfortunately, all too often, we have made it easy for Dark Tech and the populists by not taking them seriously enough. And instead, we have taken ourselves too seriously.

7. The occupation of the digital world was only possible thanks to our cooperation

On top of that, we have allowed ourselves to be fooled by regulations. This is because our experts have waved through all the 'feudalistic privileges' and preferential treatments without resistance. Only these privileges have made the current reign of Dark Tech possible in the first place and then even secured it (▶5). Anyone who acts 'stunned' now and rants furiously against politicians as well as legal experts should also be fair in their appraisal and take into account that activities under the banner of supposed 'net freedom' and in the fight 'against internet censorship' have also made significant contributions. Those involved have created a wonderful ideological and political shield for Dark Tech, possibly without even realising that they have allowed themselves to be instrumentalised. On disputed topics, these groups were able to mobilise tens of thousands of people who, just a few years ago, were demonstrating on the streets in all seriousness, trying to prevent that 'the free internet as we know it would be abolished by Brussels bureaucrats'. This was the prevalent narrative still in 2018 (!!) in the context of copyright regulation. The 'feudalistic Dark Tech bros' must have been laughing their heads off: Their own vassals were out on the streets, actively demonstrating for the purpose of keeping up the 'feudalistic oppression'. Today, however, we cannot see anybody out there demonstrating on the streets, which is very puzzling indeed.

8. Existing EU regulations such as DMA and DSA do not provide solutions

Due to the weakness of our decision-makers, even the EU's Digital Markets Act (DMA) and Digital Services Act (DSA) are so weak that they cannot solve our root problems. The DMA does not allow monopolies to be broken up or unbundled in an effective way. The DSA does absolutely nothing to address the core problems (intermediary privilege, liability privilege, criminal privilege) and creates an ill-defined, second legal standard, which will inevitably lead to restrictions on freedom of expression by the platforms, which would for example *not* be covered by the laws in Germany or the EU (in plain language: in case of doubt, platforms will then also block legal content that would actually be allowed as free speech). Of course, it is completely misleading and unfair to call this 'censorship', as Dark Tech, Trump & co. do. After all, the DSA is only a kind of stopgap measure that attempts to eliminate the worst damage caused by the *fundamental problems*, which are: (A) the 'opening of the floodgates' for hate speech and fake news (due to the regulatory flaw of the liability privilege) in combination with (B) the additional 'rewarding' of particularly radical, polarising or emotional content by the platforms' algorithms. The fact that Trump and tech are talking about 'censorship' and a threat to 'freedom of speech' is of course cynical, especially as the platforms are full of insults, lies and slander, not least because all content gets published immediately WITHOUT being (pre-)censored or getting 'checked' (e. g. by fact-checkers). Steve Bannon's 'Flood the zone with shit' is still our internet reality. However, instead of eliminating the core problem (liability of platforms when monetising specific content), the EU regulations have created a second and, above all, ill-defined standard for evaluation. Although this is well-intentioned, it is implemented weakly. And, unfortunately, it provides an unnecessary target for 'liberators' such as Vance, Musk & co. We can assume that Trump and tech will tear these regulations to pieces in the coming months and years anyway.

9. Dark Tech and populists are winning right now

For these reasons, the movement tipping the balance of power to Dark Tech and the populists is in full swing. They are currently winning this game. And our society sympathises with winners: *might is right*. We have been witnessing the gradual rise of anti-democratic political 'alternatives' for years. These are no longer marginalised groups in politics. With Trump, the AfD and other right-wing populist parties, they have long since entered national politics and parliaments and have strong positions there. This trend is ongoing and is also visible on the platforms, which of course boost and reinforce such content. The anti-democratic and conspiracy theory narratives of Dark Tech and Trump ('Freedom of speech is threatened by a cartel of Deep State and State media — we will liberate you') are no longer only represented at the margins of our societies. They are increasingly voiced also by people that are more positioned towards the centre. Whilst moderate in the past, conservative parties in Europe are now also experimenting with these libertarian positions. This shows that they recognise future opportunities here and that they are willing to tolerate the unmistakable anti-democratic side effects of this transformation.

10. Dark Tech occupies the most important utopias of the future

At another level, it is striking that Dark Tech and their populist partners have currently occupied many future utopias for our society. We have long since accepted this type of agenda-setting on the big stages of the digital world anyway. The grandiose menu of our own future is presented to us year after year at the world's leading tech conferences: Artificial Intelligence, the Internet of Things, smart cities, augmented reality, NFTs (Non-Fungible Tokens), Web 3.0, cryptocurrencies, blockchain, robotics and so on. Here they are in the spotlight on stage, the 'digital evangelists', telling us what new temptations and redemptions the Dark Tech corporations have in store for us. All of this is adorned with the rainbow-like shimmer of their political narrative, according to which these platforms, of all things, will 'liberate' us and serve us this 'better, technolibertarian future'. And the tech preachers are always bringing new, ever more spectacular gifts along with them. Aren't they the ones who will soon provide us with AGI, i.e. Artificial General Intelligence, an AI so hyper-intelligent that it will solve all the problems that we humans have so far been unable to solve ourselves due to our 'sad limitations'? Then there are visions of 'transhumanism', which will further develop humans towards superintelligence by linking them with technology, for example through brain-computer interfaces. The future belongs to these 'Tech bros', who want to bring human intelligence even to Mars and eventually populate the entire universe. They have been enchanting us with so many utopias at once that they have recently been summarised in the acronym TESCREAL (i.e. Transhumanism, Extropianism, Singularitarianism, Cosmism, Rationalist ideology, Effective Altruism, Longtermism). And let's not forget: the tech oligarchy also has the financial power to pump hundreds of billions of dollars into the development and implementation of each of these ideas. Their financial power alone will determine what our future will look like. And let's remember the second argument I made: By contrast, the critics of the digital sphere appear to be detached, 'luddite party poopers', 'paper tigers' who won't stop grumbling and try to take away the pretty pink plush bunnies that the nice tech bros want to give to all of humanity.

11. No resistance from young people

There is no movement of young people in Europe, the US or anywhere else in the western world that is revolting against the 'digitalocratic takeover' of our democracy. Indeed, we seem to overlook how very surprising this is. Let's remember the climate crisis and movements such as 'Fridays for Future', for example. When I speak in schools or at universities, I often ask how they feel about this. Typically, I will lay the situation out like this to young people: "Look, the problem is less significant for old people like me. I'm 54 years old. I have been extremely fortunate to have spent my life in a democracy. You, on the other hand, still have your life ahead of you. What will you do when you're caught in the 'digital monopoly trap' in a few years' time? Above all, if Dark Tech owns the entire digital public sphere? Then the situation becomes more or less irreversible. How and, above all, where will you call for resistance if all communication channels, all platforms and all the infrastructure are dominated and controlled by your opponents?"

It is particularly fascinating that this situation is very different if we compare it to the times before the emergence of the internet in the second half of the twentieth century. During those days, there was a critical resistance movement against the State monopoly on broadcasting at the time (even if the threat against media freedom at the time was nothing in comparison to today). There were even activists who hijacked radio frequencies and started illegal pirate stations. Felix Guattari is an example of this, which is significant in that he and Gilles Deleuze presented a kind of postmodern 'theory of the internet' in the book 'Rhizome' as early as 1976, no less than 13 years before Tim Berners-Lee's invention of the 'World Wide Web'.[1] These actvists even went to prison for such actions and for their media freedom convictions.[2]

You could describe people like Guattari as something like 'hackers' back then. In fact, they 'hacked' the structures of one significant media genre of those days, the radio. At some point, their underlying ideas about media freedom gave rise to the free internet, which was then taken over and occupied by the monopolies of Dark Tech in the noughties. But where would we locate a similar movement today, in which figures (comparable to Guattari back then) would 'hack' the platforms in the same way as the pirate radio stations did in the case of State-monopoly broadcasting? In our times, a similar liberation movement would have to 'hack' the digital monopolies and conceptualise a new, better media world. Unfortunately, there is currently no sign of such a young grassroots movement anywhere in the world.

We can take the argument a step further by considering that becoming an influencer is still one of the most popular future prospects for young people. And there are young influencers, streamers and creators in all kinds of fields — for example on the topic of climate protection, politics, self-optimisation, fitness and sports, finance and banking, beauty and in every other field imaginable. But there is hardly anyone who has gained a strong following by advocating the liberation of the internet from the domination of Dark Tech. When I ask young people in schools or universities if they know anyone who has turned this topic into their mission, they say 'no' every time. When I ask them why, in the extremely overcrowded market of influencers, no one is successfully covering this important topic, I regularly get the same worrying answer — namely: "If you want to become an influencer, you need a strong following. And anyone who criticises the platforms has to expect to get punished by the platforms for doing just that — they won't be able to build up a large number of followers in the first place." And that makes sense.

Is there no glimmer of hope at all? Yes, there is certainly a small residual chance that the anti-democratic forces could fail on their own. Trump and Musk could self-destruct due to their own monstrous egos. Trump's irrational actions could lead the US economy into a deep recession and he could be penalised by a massive plunge in the polls. Elon Musk could drive Tesla into bankruptcy. But even in scenarios like these, there would be setbacks, individuals would be replaced, formations would shift in the short term and the transformation towards the new, digitalocratic order would be slowed down. But the fundamental analysis would remain exactly the same:

Our European digital dependency on the US monopolies would remain the same (▸4/5). We would continue to have no voice to form and shape our digital public sphere as the basis of our democracy according to our own desires. The tech platforms would remain the very same habitats of polarisation that they already are now (▸6). The 'overcoming' of our democracy through a new, digitalocratic order would still continue unabated (▸3). The 'grand narrative' of rightwing technolibertarians and their conspiracy theory of 'threatened freedom of speech' would remain intact, as would the lack of a political programme among the Democrats in the US, for example, but also among moderate, conservative as well as economically liberal parties in Europe (▸7). Should Trump, Musk & co. fail on their own, this too would probably only be a temporary blip. No, despite all my appreciation for him, Bernie Sanders will not be able to save us. Under no circumstances should we put our hopes in such scenarios. Hope is a bad advisor anyway. We can only really change the situation if we get back into action ourselves and dare to rise up (▸8).

The digitalocratic apocalypse

Let's refer back to the deeper meaning of our observation on the first pages of this book: the media are not really an issue for us, people are mainly concerned with 'things'. We don't even notice the media themselves. They seem 'natural' to us.

Let's take the perspective of young people who are just finishing school, for example. They are fully immersed in a digital media universe and, above all, spend a lot of their time on digital platforms.

They hardly ever leave these digital platforms (especially since platforms like TikTok no longer have any outlinks). That's just the way it is. It just seems 'natural' to everyone. And no other media order is conceivable.

We see similar tendencies if we check out what politicians are doing. Members of moderate parties are shocked by the success of the radical parties on digital platforms. What is their reaction? They turn to digital consultants and attend coaching sessions that are meant to transform them into successful influencers. And all of this is then accompanied in the public sphere by new digital-savvy 'social media experts' who grade them: "Who's doing the coolest stuff on Tiktok?" Again, all of this fits in with the current way of thinking, namely: "This is what today's media are like. You have to step up to the challenge and adapt yourself to it." And that's what we are all doing instead of waking up and realising that this is our very last chance to step in and shape our digital media reality by our own interventions. We are just dancing to the tune of tech algorithms in total dependence.

There could be a choice. On the one hand, there is the current, internet of lies and hate, which is controlled and dominated by US billionaires in cooperation with the anti-democratic Trump administration. On the other hand, imagine a free, safe and peaceful European internet that belongs to us humans and is co-designed by all of us through democratic co-determination. Unfortunately, the latter, i.e. the 'better internet' doesn't yet exist. We would first have to create it by ourselves, directly confronting the overpowering alliance of Trump and Dark Tech. And that's why, even now, our choice only exists in a rather hypothetical way.

Now let's assume that we don't make it. What happens then?

In Germany, at the time of me writing these words, our new government is being set up. Once again, the topic of 'digital sovereignty' does not play the central role that it needs to. There is likely to be a drastic increase in the defence budget. The military threat in the east and the topic of migration are likely to be the dominant issues.

So we will continue to meander along. Meanwhile, Trump and

Dark Tech will continue to expand their links to the right-wing populist scene in Europe. They will continue to incite the populations to rise up against their own governments and, if they like, incite the people to 'overthrow' them. Europe will be asked to make considerable sacrifices regarding the war and, later on, the reconstruction of Ukraine. Russia, meanwhile, will extend its aggressive actions towards Georgia, Moldovia and further.

Trump and Dark Tech will continue to put Europe under maximum pressure. The 'war game' is one in which the US currently dominates all aspects of the digital economy almost completely, right up to the new technology of generative AI. They will defend this monopolistic dominance tooth and nail. Meanwhile, they will impose tariffs on Europe in all other areas of the analogue economy (automobiles, etc.). The US has already announced that it will consider the EU's existing (far too weak) tech regulation as 'tariffs' and will also 'respond' with tariffs. In this way, they will blackmail Europe against implementing the regulations from the DMA and DSA, which are already far too weak.

At the same time, the dynamics in Ukraine and the Middle East are unlikely to lead to a reduction in the influx of refugees and may even lead to a massive increase. Governments in Europe will be under extreme pressure to find solutions due to the rise of right-wing populists, which in turn will drastically increase conflicts within the EU.

Meanwhile, the authoritarian-libertarian Trump administration will present its own destabilisation of democracy as huge progress and highlight its own 'track record', which in turn helps the right-wing populists, who will add fuel to the fire to their heart's content: "Look what Trump and DOGE have achieved in such a short time — and you're getting NOTHING done!"

This will be boosted by the digital platforms, which is why the right-wing populists will continue to gain popularity. The question is how long major western democracies will be able to withstand this constant bombardment — perhaps two or three years. In the course of this time, more and more previously moderate forces will succumb to the opportunistic temptations that Trump and Dark Tech are dangling in front of them: some 'cooperation' here, 'partnerships' there, particularly great 'deals', exclusive 'access' and so on.

The more Trump and tech advance the libertarian restructuring of the US through tax breaks, deregulation, deals and other incentives, the more investments and capital will shift there, with Europe losing out. Perhaps the whole thing will be exacerbated by the emergence of a libertarian opposition in the UK. This opposition might, for example, agree to an opportunistic 'partnership' with the USA in order to strive for a deregulated low-tax zone right on Europe's doorstep. Companies would then emigrate, more opportunists could follow and millionaires would increasingly move their residence and money outside Europe.

We could then see new right-wing populist governments within Europe, while Putin exerts military pressure from the east. Over the next few years, the EU would be weakened further and further (in the worst-case scenario, a large country would leave the EU). The right-wing populists would also behave and act in Europe in the same way as in the US currently: Ever new, horrific 'revelations' would expose the 'shocking' connections between the supposedly 'corrupt elite' and the European 'Deep State', along the lines of stories told by Musk and the Department of Government Efficiency (DOGE).

The libertarian mastermind Peter Thiel calls the strategy behind this approach *apokalypsis* (referring back to his ideological mentors, James Dale Davidson and William Rees-Mogg), which in Greek means 'unveiling'. In other words: apocalyptic revelations are seen as accelerators of the libertarian apocalypse.

> "Trump's return to the White House augurs the *apokálypsis* of the ancien regime's [!] secrets. The new administration's revelations need not justify vengeance — reconstruction can go hand in hand with reconciliation. But for reconciliation to take place, there must first be truth. The apokálypsis is the most peaceful

means of resolving the old guard's war on the internet, a war the internet won. My friend and colleague Eric Weinstein calls the pre-internet custodians of secrets the Distributed Idea Suppression Complex (DISC) — the media organizations, bureaucracies, universities and government-funded NGOs that traditionally delimited public conversation." [3]

In the context of this apocalypse actively brought about by Dark Tech, the pressure in the social cauldron will continue to rise. On the one hand, there will be weak economic growth caused by high defence costs and, on the other, an increasing shift of value creation to the digital sphere, in which US Dark Tech companies are the main beneficiaries. For Europe, this will mean stagnation, mass lay-offs, an explosion of social conflicts and the migration of wealth and companies abroad. As a result of the increasing pressure and growing populism, ever more drastic measures and deportations of immigrants could take place, with ever more escalating violence and renewed spirals of populism and radicalisation.

This apocalypse would again be boosted by the platforms' algorithms, triggering unrest, attacks, riots and bloody protests. At the same time, more and more acts of violence would be taking place in which members of the supposedly 'tyrannical elites' would fall victim to violent attacks, such as hate figures doing climate research, 'left-wing' politicians, members of the LGBTQ+ community, trans people, and others.

Europe could break apart as part of this process. Right-wing populist governments would come to power in more and more countries. This would close the trapdoor for good, because, as a result, we would see self-reinforcing processes similar to those currently taking place in the US. The libertarian 'CEO kings' would do away with checks and balances, push forward with a barrage of initiatives that supposedly fulfill 'what the people want', while dissenting voices would be muted, intimidated or incriminated as 'enemies of the people' via alleged 'revelations'. Once again this would come with a tremendous and dizzying amount of amplification on the digital platforms, where the agenda-setting always comes from the libertarians. No one would be able to tell what is true and what is false, what is real and what is fake.

This is precisely when the final libertarian lock-in would begin: We would witness the incarceration of democracy itself. After all, it is difficult to imagine how such libertarian governments could be overcome or voted out of office in the future. We can grasp this if we look at the current situation in the US. The ruling oligarchs have far reaching control in terms of agenda-setting (consider the hundreds of presidential decrees by Trump and, on top of that, the barrage of ever new 'revelations' and actions by DOGE). And, in addition, we have the continuous support from the digital platforms, which are part of the libertarian machinery.

If we keep in mind how far the control of the public by the tech oligarchs has already progressed, then a future election victory of the Democrat party in the US is unlikely. But even if this were to happen, protests by the libertarians against 'electoral fraud' or 'sabotage' by the 'reactionary leftist forces' would certainly get infinitely louder than what we have already experienced on 6 January 2021 with the Storming of the Capitol. Such reactions would be accompanied by violent protests, riots, unrest, uprising — again the 'civil war' scenario that Musk considers to be inevitable.

Then, too, we will get caught up in the autocratic trap — because the libertarians will not only 'own' political power but also our public sphere. As they see it, they will have 'liberated' us from the 'tyranny of democracy' so that they can rule over us forever. It is obvious that the supposed 'liberation' is just a pretext in order to further enrich themselves and continue to exploit us all.

The fact that the oligarchs themselves are fully aware of the kind of apocalypse that they are preparing is demonstrated by the 'billionaire bunkers', which US digital expert Douglas Rushkoff has reported on in detail. Five billionaires sought his advice. They asked him: "New Zealand or Alaska?" What would be the ideal location for a bunker that would offer them security if the *'event'* occurred: "That was their euphemism for the environmental collapse, social unrest, nuclear explosion, solar storm, unstoppable virus, or malicious computer hack that takes everything down."[4]

The 'billionaire bunkers' have been widely discussed in public but Rushkoff has not disclosed the names of his clients. To quote from a press report:

> "But what he [Rushkoff] experienced is not just a crazy story about a few excessively rich people with doomsday fantasies. Tech bosses like Mark Zuckerberg, Jeff Bezos and Elon Musk have also long been developing exit strategies. [Rushkoff:] 'I think what they're actually running from are the consequences of their own actions. They want to earn enough money to escape the reality that they themselves have created'."[5]

After the media war is over, we might face the apocalypse the libertarians have predicted. The billionaires will be well prepared.

But one thing is certain: there will be no space for us in their bunkers.

ENDNOTES

Media War — Introduction

1 Cf. Durkee, Alison: "Who Is Tommy Robinson? Elon Musk Champions Far-Right UK Activist-And Splits With Farage." In: *Forbes*, 6.1.2025; https://www.forbes.com/sites/alisondurkee/2025/01/02/who-is-tommy-robinson-why-elon-musk-is-posting-about-far-right-british-activist/

2 Cf. for example n.a.: "Tommy Robinson profile: Convicted criminal is one of UK's most prominent far-right activists." In: *The Irish Times*, 17.2.2023; https://www.irishtimes.com/ireland/social-affairs/2023/02/17/tommy-robinson-profile-convicted-criminal-is-one-of-uks-most-prominent-far-right-activists/

3 Cf. n.a.: "Tommy Robinson begs Trump for US asylum." In: *The Guardian*, 10.7.2019; https://theweek.com/102186/tommy-robinson-pleads-with-trump-for-asylum

4 Cf. Young, Andrew: "On-the-run Tommy Robinson suns himself at an all-inclusive five-star hotel in Cyprus." In: *Daily Mail*, 4.8.2024; https://www.dailymail.co.uk/news/article-13707385/tommy-robinson-five-star-hotel-cyprus-foot-soldiers-run-riot-violent-protests-britain.html

5 Jochecová, Ketrin: "Steve Bannon: Musk's money will help us make Europe a populist haven." In: *Politico*, 8.1.2025; https://www.politico.eu/article/us-steve-bannon-elon-musk-wealth-and-influence-are-weapons-to-advance-maga-aligned-goals-in-europe/

6 Hoey, Joan (ed.): "Democracy Index. What's wrong with representative democracy?" In: *The Economist Intelligence Unit Limited* (2025), p. 15—16; https://image.b.economist.com/lib/fe8d13727c61047f7c/m/1/609fbc8d-4724-440d-b827-2c7b7300353d.pdf?utm_campaign=MA00001514&utm_medium=email-owned&utm_source=eiu-marketingcloud&RefID=&utm_term=20250226&utm_id=2064759&sfmc_id=00QWT00000J2uGH2AZ&utm_content=cta-button-1&id_mc=279801853

7 The Press Freedom Index is published annually by the organization "Reporters Without Borders"; cf. https://rsf.org/en/index

8 Cf. Kilander, Gustaf: "JD Vance says US could drop support for NATO if Europe tries to regulate Elon Musk's platforms." In: *The Independent*, 17.9.2024; https://www.independent.co.uk/news/world/americas/us-politics/jd-vance-elon-musk-x-twitter-donald-trump-b2614525.html

9 Thiel, Peter: "A time for truth and reconciliation." In: *Financial Times*,

10.1.2025; https://www.ft.com/content/a46cb128-1f74-4621-ab0b-242a76583105
10 Sutton, Ricky: "US sues Google for deleting key evidence in bad faith." In: *Mi-3*, 14.1.2025; https://www.mi-3.com.au/14-01-2025/us-sues-google-deleting-key-evidence-bad-faith
11 Cf. Reuter, Markus: "Wer jetzt bei Peter Thiel Software kauft, hat wirklich nichts verstanden." In: *Netzpolitik*, 24.3.2025; https://netzpolitik.org/2025/palantir-wer-jetzt-bei-peter-thiel-software-kauft-hat-wirklich-nichts-verstanden/
12 Cf. Krempl, Stefan: "'Erpressbarkeit': Informatiker gegen Cloud-Kooperation zwischen BSI und Google." In: *Heise Online*, 21.3.2025; https://www.heise.de/news/Erpressbarkeit-Informatiker-gegen-Cloud-Kooperation-zwischen-BSI-und-Google-10324992.html
13 JD Vance's speech at the Munich Security Conference is available here: https://www.YouTube.com/watch?v=pCOsgfINdKg
14 Musk, Elon, and Alice Weidel in an interview, 9.1.2025; Self-transcription according to https://www.YouTube.com/watch?v=bY-KmcP64hE
15 Cf. Andree, Martin, and Timo Thomsen: *Atlas der digitalen Welt*. Frankfurt/M.: Campus 2020.
16 Many of these scientific studies, publications, regulations, proposals and initiatives are attached at the bottom of the website accompanying this book, www.media-war.com (see section 'Bonus Tracks'). Unfortunately, they are not translated into English yet — but depending on international interest, I will start to make these works available in English on the very same website in the upcoming months.

1. The combat zone

1 While many academics have, in the past, highlighted the harmful effects of disinformation and social media on the quality of public discourse, there is also a strand of academic research that repeatedly emphasises that fake news were "overrated" and that a harmful influence on democracy or public discourse was "not scientifically proven". It is beyond the scope of this book (or would require a book of its own) to answer these questions in detail. However, here are a few objections from the perspective of my own research:
- The empirical studies on which these studies are based are often methodologically based on the analysis of content on websites or independent domains and then usually find that only a tiny proportion of the population uses them or that the reach is very low. This is certainly true but has nothing to do with the relative importance of fake news and can be explained by the massive concentration of traffic on the internet, where it is almost entirely concentrated on the

- platforms. Based on our own measurements of traffic distribution, the findings of these studies are therefore not surprising. However, the conclusion is obviously wrong.
- This directly leads us to the next methodological problem of such studies: the majority of digital traffic is on the social networks, but we have no scientific access to the black boxes of the platforms. We cannot therefore make a differentiated assessment of their impact. But the platforms are certainly responsible for a large proportion of the fake news and misinformation consumed online.
- In addition, there is the considerable methodological difficulty of precisely defining disinformation in the scientifically analysed corpora. Courts need at best months, but often years, to clarify whether individual statements are violating the law. However, in such studies, the task is not about classifying individual statements, but potentially many billions of individual contributions. This methodological problem has arisen on a massive scale in my own research efforts on the subject.
- Other studies are based on surveys and then find, for example, that the respondents state that they obtain their news information from traditional editorial media providers. Methodologically, however, such arguments are built on sand because we observe massive satisficing distortions in this field in particular, i. e. respondents often give socially desirable answers (to put it bluntly: they barely watch porn and read a lot of books). For example, in survey-based investigations of newspaper reach, we see results that can be a factor of 10 (!) higher than the actual printed circulation of the same newspaper. By contrast, our scientific measurement of real usage in the digital sphere has enabled us to prove, down to the smallest detail, that the proportion of usage by editorial providers is only microscopically small.
- Moreover, the mechanisms of media influence should not be over-simplified. To put it bluntly, the consumption of a single piece of misinformation certainly does not lead to an immediate change in voting behaviour. Incidentally, this complexity of human decision-making behaviour also applies to other fields. People do not watch an advertising video and then go and buy the product. Certainly, dozens of reasons can be identified for each decision to buy something (for example: The need has existed for some time, a friend recommended it to me, the product was on sale, etc.). One could also deduce from this: "The effect of advertising on purchasing decisions is overrated." Nevertheless, it is obvious that companies invest billions of euros on advertising.
- The same principle applies to our political realities. If fake news is "overrated", how do we explain the storming of the Capitol, for exam-

ple? It is well known that the perpetrators believed that Trump had won the election. Is a critical view of such phenomena unfounded?
- In recent years, various stakeholders have made huge efforts (and also invested considerable sums) to use digital disinformation for their propagandistic purposes — and if we assess the current situation with regard to Western support for the war in Ukraine (or the false statements regarding the economic consequences of Brexit, for example), we can see that they have often been very successful. Are all of them wrong? Above all, how do you explain the success of these campaigns if fake news is "overrated"?
- In empirical surveys, large sections of the population regularly express considerable concern about the increasing spread of misinformation and disinformation. Scientific research should take people's concerns seriously and not trivialise them or downright disempower the respondents (e.g. that people's concerns are completely "unfounded", that it is just a misjudgment as a result of the "hysterical" media coverage of fake news, because the harmfulness of misinformation has "not yet been scientifically proven", and so on)
- The proponents of these views ("fake news is overrated") would then also have to question their own findings with regard to the serious implications for the normative foundations of media regulation and democracy, for example. Until now, there has been a general democratic consensus that the mass media dissemination of information enables citizens to form their political opinions and therefore forms the basis of our democracy. In the long evolution of this political public sphere, Western democracies have therefore developed complex mechanisms of media moderation and curation, which generally serve to identify, correct and highlight false information (up to legally enforceable corrections as well as penalties, and so on). This has been done whilst ensuring that freedom of expression is respected.

The question here would therefore be whether such tried and tested mechanisms should be thrown overboard (because it has not been "scientifically proven" that false information is harmful).

Incidentally, my own scientific approach to the topic is different. It is based on researching and measuring digital opinion power on the basis of real usage measurements on the one hand and on analysing the digital attention economy and platform structures on the other (as carried out here in chapter 6, for example). From my own academic perspective, in view of the methodological limitations mentioned above, I would ask academics who put forward such arguments whether the core question in the study designs they use can be proven in a strictly methodological way at all. Or to put it another way: The harmful influence of misinformation on democracy would then be "not scientifically proven" to date simply because scientifically proving it is actually impossible, at least under current conditions (especially also taking into account the black boxes of the platforms that are spreading fake news). However, in view of the massive political collateral damage currently being caused, it would be misleading to leave the public thinking that there is no danger.

Furthermore, in their treatment of the topic, the representatives of this scientific research strand completely ignore the central aspect of the power and domination structures that result from the massive bundling of opinion power, but also from the monopolistic control of digital access and the massive asymmetry of economic and lobbyist power (and these are findings that, to my knowledge, are not only very clearly "scientifically proven", but are also not seriously questioned in any area of research). Unfortunately, it is in the nature of things that representatives of tech corporations, as well as right-wing parties and ideologies, love to use precisely this argument in public debates, i.e. that fake news is "overrated" and its harmful influence on democracy "has not yet been scientifically proven", that it is merely a matter of "media alarmism" and "scaremongering", etc. In view of the massive damage done to Western democracies, which has become obvious to everyone, the persistence with which the aforementioned scientific position is being defended fills me with concern. Nevertheless, for the sake of completeness, I would like to append a small selection of academic references to this thesis so that interested readers can form their own opinions. These authors are very active in the media, and there are hundreds of interviews and articles on the subject online.

2 Oborne, Peter, and Tom Roberts: *How Trump Thinks. His Tweets and the Birth of a New Political Language.* London: Head of Zeus 2017, p. vii.
3 Cf. in detail McIntyre, Lee: *Post Truth.* Cambridge, Mass., London: MIT Press 2018.
4 Cf. the original article at: https://x.com/elonmusk/status/149997696 7105433600. Musk, Elon: "Starlink has been told by some governments (not Ukraine) to block Russian sources. We will not do so unless at gunpoint. Sorry to be a free speech absolutist." Twitter, 5.3.2022. Cf. Dorlijski, Vanessa: "Nach massiven Entlassungen: Elon Musks X verstärkt Teams für Sicherheit und Content-Moderation." In: *Forbes*, 5.9.2024; https://www.forbes.at/artikel/nach-massiven-entlassungen-elon-musks-x-verstaerkt-teams-fuer-sicherheit-und-content-moderation; Stolton, Samuel et. al.: "Elon Musk triggers Twitter chaos with mass firings worldwide." In: *Politico*, 4.11.2022; https://www.politico.eu/

article/twitter-fires-employs-worldwide/; cf. Krause, Daniel: "'Der Vogel ist frei': Was Elon Musk unter Meinungsfreiheit versteht." In: *Der Tagesspiegel*, 20. 12. 2022; https://www.tagesspiegel.de/wirtschaft/der-vogel-ist-frei-was-elon-musk-unter-meinungsfreiheit-versteht-9067603.html

5 Goodkind, Nicole: "Elon Musk apologizes for antisemitic tweet but tells advertisers 'go f**k yourself'." In: *CNN*, 30. 11. 2023; https://edition.cnn.com/2023/11/29/investing/elon-musk-dealbook-summit

6 Cf. Ritscher, Anna and Eva Hoffmann: "Nach dem Sturm auf das US-Kapitol. Im Hass vereint." In: *Taz*, 8. 1. 2021; https://taz.de/Nach-dem-Sturm-auf-das-US-Kapitol/!5738598/

7 Almost every key publication in the history of cyberlibertarian discourse makes this comparison; an excellent synopsis and analysis can be found in Golumbia, David: *Cyberlibertarianism. The Right-Wing Politics of Digital Technology.* Minneapolis, London: University of Minnesota Press, 2024, p. 189—226 ("Digital Technology and the Printing Press").

8 Based on a survey, it was determined that 56 % of media consumption was on digital channels in the year 2023 in Germany; Cf. Kupferschmitt, Thomas and Thorsten Müller: "ARD/ZDF-Massenkommunikation Trends 2023: Mediennutzung im Intermediavergleich." In: *Media Perspektiven*, 21 (2023): 1–20, here p. 4. A similar finding can be reached by analysing the allocation of advertising investments — because advertising companies spend money where they assume the audience will pay attention (which, incidentally, they optimise through highly granular analyses). During the Covid pandemic, digital channels overtook analogue ones. Cf. e. g. Janke, Klaus: "Digitale Spendings liegen erstmals über nicht-digitalen Investments." In: *Horizont online*, 7. 10. 2021; https://www.horizont.net/medien/nachrichten/werbemarkt-2021-digitale-spendings-liegen-erstmals-ueber-nicht-digitalen-investments-194918; Janke, Klaus: "Warum die Mediaagenturen so viel Wachstum bei den digitalen Plattformen erwarten." In: *Horizont online*, 14. 2. 2022; https://www.horizont.net/medien/nachrichten/werbemarkt-warum-die-mediaagenturen-so-viel-wachstum-bei-den-digitalen-plattformen-erwarten-197781

9 For Europe, cf. Navarro, J. G.: "Advertising Expenditure in Western Europe from 2017 to 2024, by Medium." In: *Statista*, checked on 6. 1. 2025; https://www.statista.com/statistics/799801/ad-spend-in-western-europemedia/. For 2024, the study puts the share of digital media at 63.3 % for Europe. If we extrapolate the growth rates of the last eight years for all individual channels into the future, this results in a share of 76.1 % for digital media and 23.9 % for analog media in 2029.

10 A detailed derivation of the substitution of analog media by digital media can be found in Andree, Martin: *Big Tech Must Go! Digital Giants*

are Destroying our Democracies and Economies — We Will Stop Them. Frankfurt/M.: Campus 2023, Chapter I.

11 The finding of the 'grand narrative' is remarkable in a double sense: firstly, Jean-François Lyotard famously assumed the *end* of grand narratives in 1979; and secondly, many elements of this new, 'grand narrative' of the libertarians have been shaped by postmodern ideas and concepts of all things. On the end of the grand narratives, cf. Lytotard, Jean-François: *The Postmodern Condition: A Report on Knowledge.* Minneapolis, MN.: University of Minnesota Press 1984. Transl. Geoff Bennington, and Brian Massumi. The media theorist Evgeny Morozov also comes to the conclusion of a new grand narrative; cf. Morozov, Evgeny: "The New Legislators of Silicon Valley." In: *The Ideas Letter,* 37, 3.4.2025; https://www.theideasletter.org/essay/silicon-valleys-new-legislators/

12 Pollytix (ed.): "AfD voters in focus. Findings from the research." Data collection April/May 2024, n = 1,512. https://pollytix.de/wp-content/uploads/2024/08/pollytix_AfD-Waehlende-im-Fokus-Erkenntnisse-aus-der-Forschung_August-2024.pdf; here p. 10 f.

13 The Bloomberg Billionaires Index is updated daily. The figure shows the status on November 7, 2024. Current data can be viewed here: Bloomberg Billionaires Index; https:// www.bloomberg.com/billionaires/

14 Cf. e.g. the overview in https://www.allaboutmarketresearch.com/internet.htm

15 Of course, we should not be too quick and confuse correlation with causality — there may also be other reasons for the decline in democracy. But it should still come as a surprise to us that the stated connection between the implementation of Web 2.0 and a democratising effect is not only completely absent — but that a consistent decline in democracy can even be observed.

16 The data from the Swedish V-Dem Democracy Index is taken from https://ourworldindata.org/grapher/liberal-democracy-index-popw-vdem

17 Democratic societies generally use open public spaces such as streets, squares and parks as forums for exchange. They are open to all participants in the community to express their opinions there, for example through speeches, demonstrations, the distribution of leaflets, etc.; the public ownership element of these places is key.; cf. Golumbia, David: *Cyberlibertarianism. The Right-Wing Politics of Digital Technology.* Minneapolis, London: University of Minnesota Press 2024, p. 304.

18 Golumbia, David: *Cyberlibertarianism. The Right-Wing Politics of Digital Technology.* Minneapolis, London: University of Minnesota Press 2024, p. 306.

19 Cf. on lock-in and network effects and other factors that trigger them Kenneth A. Bamberger, and Orly Lobel: "Platform Market Power." In: *Berkeley Technology Law Journal* 32, no. 3 (2017): 1051–1092; https://heinonline.org/HOL/P?h=hein.journals/berktech32&i=1095

2. The warlords

1 Cf. Igel, Leon: "Was Donald Trumps Inaugurationsfeier über die neue Weltordnung verrät." In: *Neue Züricher Zeitung*, 21.1.2025; https://www.nzz.ch/pro/trumps-inauguration-tech-giganten-und-zeichen-einer-neuen-weltordnung-ld.1867161
2 N. a.: "Musk soll angeblich seit 2022 regelmäßig Kontakt zu Putin haben." In: *Spiegel Online*, 25.10.2024; https://www.spiegel.de/ausland/elon-musk-soll-seit-2022-regelmaessig-kontakt-zu-wladimir-putin-haben-a-e769b376-1966-4e67-a22d-a03d83ad6561
3 Cf. Schmidt, Holger, and Hamidreza Hosseini: "Plattformökonomie: Künstliche Intelligenz treibt den Wert der Plattformen auf neue Höchststände." In: *Frankfurter Allgemeine Zeitung*, 2.1.2025; https://www.faz.net/pro/digitalwirtschaft/plattformen/kuenstliche-intelligenz-treibt-den-wert-der-plattformen-auf-neue-hoechststaende-110203874.html
4 Schmidt, Holger, and Hamidreza Hosseini: "Plattformökonomie. Künstliche Intelligenz treibt den Wert der Plattformen auf neue Höchststände." In: *Frankfurter Allgemeine Zeitung*, 2.1.2025; https://www.faz.net/pro/digital-economy/platforms/artificial-intelligence-drives-the-value-of-platforms-to-new-highs-110203874.html
5 The data is taken from the US polling aggregator RealClear Polling; cf. https://www.realclearpolling.com/polls/president/general/2024/trump-vs-harris
6 Cf. Lipton, Eric and Kirsten Grind: "Elon Musk's Business Empire Scores Benefits Under Trump Shake-Up." In: *The New York Times*, 11.2.2025; https://www.nytimes.com/2025/02/11/us/politics/elon-musk-companies-conflicts.html
7 Thiel, Peter: *Zero to One. Notes on Startups, or How to Build the Future.* New York: Currency 2014, p. 173.
8 The digital policy expert rightly points out that the liability privilege enables tech companies to impose the many negative effects and, above all, the costs of their business models ('digital fallout') on society; this allows them to externalise costs and internalise profits; Herwig, Stefan: "Können wir Facebook zerschlagen?" In: *Frankfurter Allgemeine Zeitung*, 13.10.2021; https://www.faz.net/aktuell/feuilleton/medien-und-film/facebook-und-die-macht-der-netzwerke-wie-die-politik-versagt-17581650.html

9 Cf. in particular the "Report On The Investigation Into Russian Interference In The 2016 Presidential Election" by Robert S. Mueller from March 2019; https://www.justice.gov/archives/sco/file/1373816/dl?inline=; Myre, Greg: "Intelligence Report: Russia Tried To Help Trump In 2020 Election." In: *NPR*, March 16, 2021; https://www.npr.org/2021/03/16/977958302/intelligence-report-russia-tried-to-help-trump-in-2020-election; Rutenberg, Jim: "The Untold Story of 'Russiagate' and the Road to War in Ukraine." In: *The New York Times*, 2.11.2022; https://www.nytimes.com/2022/11/02/magazine/russiagate-paul-manafort-ukraine-war.html?searchResultPosition=1; Watson, Kathryn: "U.S. imposes sanctions targeting Russia and Iran over 2024 election interference." *CBS News*, 31.12.2024; https://www.cbsnews.com/amp/news/russia-iran-sanctions-2024-election-interference/

10 Cf. Bensmann, Marcus, David Schraven et al: *Europas Brandstifter. Putins Krieg gegen den Westen*. Essen: Correctiv 2024, pp. 92—121; Heil, Georg, and Markus Pohl: "Scholz ist noch der Beste der Bösen." In: *Tagesschau Online*, 18.10.2024; https://www.tagesschau.de/investigativ/kontraste/russland-geheimdossier-deutschland-100.html

3. The objectives of the warlords

1 The end of democracy will be achieved through the digital "process of disintermediating governments", as formulated with crystal clarity in the libertarian blueprint by Davidson and Rees-Mogg as early as 1997; Davidson, James Dale, and William Rees-Mogg: *The Sovereign Individual. Mastering the Transition to the Digital Age*. New York et al.: Touchstone 2020 [1997], p. 179.

2 Cf. e.g. Mildenberger, Carl David: "Libertarismus." In: *Handbuch Liberalismus*. Edited by Michael G. Festl. Stuttgart: J.B. Metzler, 2021, pp. 361–368.

3 Cf. e.g. Cooper, Melinda: "The Alt-Right: Neoliberalism, Libertarianism and the Fascist Temptation." In: *Theory, Culture & Society*, 38(6) (2021), pp. 29—50; https://doi.org/10.1177/0263276421999446; here p. 34.

4 Against the backdrop of current developments in the USA, it is particularly interesting that various earlier positions of libertarianism have been 'overlooked' at the same time. In the past, libertarians had been sceptical about restrictions on migration and were often supporters of open borders. Furthermore, libertarians in the past had always been supporters of free trade and opponents of tariffs. Cf. van der Vossen, Bas: "Libertarianism." In: *Oxford Research Encyclopedia of Politics*. Edited by William Thompson. Oxford: Oxford University Press, 2017; https://doi.org/10.1093/acrefore/9780190228637.013.86

5 This chapter is strongly inspired by the relevant study on the subject by

David Golumbia, which reconstructs in great detail both the emergence of the (cyber)libertarian movement and the fascinating entanglements between business, the digital economy, publicists and digital evangelists, net-activist NGOs and so on. Golumbia, David: *Cyberlibertarianism. The Right-Wing Politics of Digital Technology*. Minneapolis, London: University of Minnesota Press 2024.

6   Cf. Moll, Sebastian: "Rechter Blogger Curtis Yarvin. Der dunkle Königsmacher." In: *taz*, 15. 3. 2025; https://taz.de/Rechter-Blogger-Curtis-Yarvin/!6072620/

7   Hern, Alex: "Occupy founder calls on Obama to appoint Eric Schmidt 'CEO of America'." In: *The Guardian*, 20. 3. 2014; https://www.theguardian.com/technology/2014/mar/20/occupy-founder-obama-eric-schmidt-ceo-america

8   Cf. Taplin, Jonathan: *The End of Reality. How Four Billionaires are Selling Out Our Future*. Dublin: Penguin 2023.

9   Cf. in detail Rushkoff, Douglas: *Survival of the Richest. Escape Fantasies of the Tech Billionaires*. London: Scribe Publications 2022, p. 10 ff.

10 That is what it seemed like at first glance; a closer look reveals the stylistic elements to be an amalgamation of depictions of a Roman gladiator and elements of "Pepe, the frog", a meme that in the past has often been used by right-wing extremist groups.

11 Cf. Turner, Fred: *From counterculture to cyberculture. Stewart Brand, the Whole Earth Network, and the rise of digital utopianism*. Chicago et al.: Univ. of Chicago Press 2006; Steven Levy: *Hackers. Heroes of the Computer Revolution*. Doubleday, 1984.

12 Cf. Facebook: "The Hacker Way". Available at https://www.facebook.com/HackerWayPhilosophy/posts/hacker-way-focus-on-impact-be-fast-be-boldthe-hacker-way-often-called-the-hacker/1838301603165221/

13 Barlow, John Perry: "A Declaration of the Independence of Cyberspace." In: *Electronic Frontier Foundation (EFF)*, 8. 2. 1996; https://www.eff.org/cyberspace-independence

14 On exit as a central metaphor of the libertarian Silicon Valley "mindset", cf. in detail Rushkoff, Douglas: *Survival of the Richest. Escape Fantasies of the Tech Billionaires*. London: Scribe Publications 2022, p. 10.

15 Cf. Davidson, Rees-Mogg: *Sovereign Individual*, p. 312.

16 — p. 321, p. 330.

17 The various offers and further contacts and addresses, for example in the Bermuda Islands, can be found at the end of the book under self-explanatory headings, such as "To Create Your Wealth Offshore"; Davidson, Rees-Mogg: *Sovereign Individual*, p. 402 f.

18 Thiel, Peter: "The Education of a Libertarian." In: *Cato Unbound. A Journal of Debate*, 13. 4. 2009; https://www.cato-unbound.org/2009/04/13/peter-thiel/education-libertarian/

19. I use the term here consistently in a more general sense to characterize the old "elites" from the libertarians' point of view, analogous to Golumbia (cf. e. g. Golumbia, David: *Cyberlibertarianism. The Right-Wing Politics of Digital Technology.* Minneapolis, London: University of Minnesota Press 2024, p. 373).
20. Cf. a book by one of Thiel's students on the libertarian revolt against the universities: Gibson, Michael: *Paper Belt on Fire: How Renegade Investors Sparked a Revolt Against the University.* New York: Encounter Books 2022; here the term 'paper belt' is only used to describe the university elites.
21. Land, Nick: *The Dark Enlightenment.* Perth: Imperium Press 2023 [2012], p. 10.
22. For the various aspects of long-termism and Musk's statements on these aspects, cf. Torres, Emile P.: "How Elon Musk sees the future: His bizarre sci-fi vision should concern us all." In: *Salon*, 17. 7. 2022; https://www.salon.com/2022/07/17/how-elon-musk-sees-the-future-his-bizarre-sci-fi-vision-should-concern-us-all/; Kulish, Nicholas: "How a Scottish Moral Philosopher Got Elon Musk's Number". In: *New York Times*, 8. 10. 2022; https://www.nytimes.com/2022/10/08/business/effective-altruism-elon-musk.html; Troy, Dave: "No, Elon and Jack are not 'competitors'. They're collaborating." In: *Medium*, 29. 10. 2022; https://davetroy.medium.com/no-elon-and-jack-are-not-competitors-theyre-collaborating-3e88cde5267d
23. Lobo, Sascha: "Wenn der Staatsapparat durch eine Staats-KI ersetzt wird." In: *Der Spiegel*, 5. 3. 2025; https://www.spiegel.de/netzwelt/netzpolitik/elon-musk-wenn-der-staatsapparat-durch-eine-staats-ki-ersetzt-wird-kolumne-a-c0b62a8f-345e-4011-9de0-482d22d80b2f
24. Cf. Torres, Emile P.: "How Elon Musk sees the future: His bizarre sci-fi vision should concern us all." In: *Salon*, 17. 7. 2022; https://www.salon.com/2022/07/17/how-elon-musk-sees-the-future-his-bizarre-sci-fi-vision-should-concern-us-all/
25. Cf. Bews, Katharina: "Städte ohne Regeln: Tech-Giganten plädieren bei Trump für unkontrollierte 'Freedom-Cities'." In: *Frankfurter Rundschau*, 12. 3. 2025; https://www.fr.de/wirtschaft/staedte-ohne-regeln-tech-giganten-plaedieren-bei-trump-fuer-unkontrollierte-freedom-cities-zr-93621284.html
26. https://www.praxisnation.com/news/network-state-cryptos-end-game
27. Cf. Land, Nick: *The Dark Enlightenment.* Perth: Imperium Press 2023 [2012], p. 21 ff.
28. Cf. Nagle, Angela: *Kill All Normies: Online Culture Wars from 4chan and Tumblr to Trump and the Alt-Right.* Winchester, UK: Zero Books 2017.
29. This point leads to the innermost core of an old philosophical debate that Jürgen Habermas had with postmodern philosophy. As is well known, it

was precisely the postmodern philosophers who, in various spurts in the wake of Nietzsche, exposed truth, knowledge and rationality as mere constructs (Luhmann, Foucault, Derrida etc.). Today, however, this postmodern 'liberation' should make us a little queasy. Aren't Trump's lies the perfect realisation of this postmodern epistemology? Doesn't the replacement of authorship by generative AI technologies deliver the same result as the evocated 'death of the author' (Roland Barthes) that postmodern theorists were longing for? Lee McIntyre has already emphasised the far-reaching affinities between the new, right-wing populist post-factual knowledge order and postmodern theorists in 2018; cf. McIntyre, Lee: *Post Truth*. Cambridge, Mass., London: MIT Press 2018, pp. 133—150. For example, McIntyre quotes Mike Cernovich, a right-wing populist blogger with a penchant for conspiracy theories, among others: "I don't look like a guy who reads Lacan, do I?" (150). The 'grand narrative' of the libertarians is thus by no means epistemologically naïve; on the contrary, it can draw on more than a century of postmodern thought. Thus, the academic philosophical elite of the Western world is also confronted with the same LOSE-LOSE situation as the other participants in the discourse. To put it bluntly: Either such postmodernist authors continue to sit on the bandwagon of the supposedly cool, avant-garde, subversive 'deconstruction' of truth — in which case it must allow the Trump, Vance, Musk lies and fake news to "pass through" without any criticism (as it's all "just constructions"). Or it would have to leave the postmodern ivory tower, which in turn would mean honing core epistemological positions that it had painstakingly built up over the last few decades. It would mean admitting in retrospect that Habermas was right about his unease about postmodernism — and with his advocacy of a *critical* (as opposed to an affirmative, uninvolved) theory. Perhaps this LOSE-LOSE situation also explains why criticism of the new, digital platform realities from academic circles has remained so dull, so colourless, but above all so inactive in recent decades (as has also been the case in the sphere of journalism, by the way). Interestingly enough, the same circles have not shied away from active protests in other fields. On discourse ethics in the sense of Habermas, cf., above all, the essay Habermas, Jürgen: "Wahrheitstheorien." In: Helmut Fahrenbach (ed.): *Wirklichkeit und Reflexion. Walter Schulz zum 60. Geburtstag.* Pfullingen: Neske 1973, pp. 211–265; cf. also: *Theory of Communicative Action, Volume One: Reason and the Rationalization of Society.* Boston, Mass.: Beacon Press 1987 [1981]; *Theory of Communicative Action, Volume Two: Lifeworld and System: A Critique of Functionalist Reason.* Boston, Mass.: Beacon Press 1987 [1981]; *The Philosophical Discourse of Modernity. Twelve Lectures.* Cambridge, MA: MIT Press 1990. Transl. Frederick G. Lawrence.

30 Cf. Pörksen, Bernhard: *Zuhören. Die Kunst, sich der Welt zu öffnen.* München: Hanser 2025.
31 Daub, Adrian: *What Tech Calls Thinking. An Inquiry into the Intellectual Bedrock of Silicon Valley.* New York: FSG Originals x Logic: 2020, p. 91.
32 Nagle, Angela: *Kill All Normies. Online Culture Wars from 4chan and Tumblr to Trump and the Alt-Right.* Winchester, UK: Zero Books 2017, p. 117.
33 Davidson, Rees-Mogg: *The Sovereign Individual*, p. 330 a.o.
34 Cf. Amlinger, Carolin, and Oliver Nachtwey: *Gekränkte Freiheit. Aspekte des libertären Autoritarismus.* Frankfurt/M.: Suhrkamp 2022.
35 — p. 120.
36 — p. 330.
37 — p. 297.
38 — p. 273.
39 — p. 310.
40 — p. 345.
41 — p. 295—296.
42 Mike Bedigan: "See the first ad from Musk-backed PAC that highlights 'four long years of humiliation'." In: *The Independent*, 5.3.2025; https://www.independent.co.uk/news/world/americas/us-politics/elon-musk-america-pac-ad-b2709814.html
43 Davidson, James Dale, and William Rees-Mogg: *The Sovereign Individual. Mastering the Transition to the Digital Age.* New York et al.: Touchstone 2020 [1997], p. 227 and p. 231.

4. The invasion

1 Our simplified representation of feudalism is based on Bloch, Marc: *Die Feudalgesellschaft.* Stuttgart: Klett-Cotta 1999 [1939]; Duby, Georges: *Die drei Ordnungen. Das Weltbild des Feudalismus.* Frankfurt/M.: Suhrkamp 2016 [1979]; Patzold, Steffen: *Das Lehnswesen.* München: Beck 2023 [2012]. Patzold rightly points out the complexity of the very heterogeneous regional and epochal manifestations.
2 Bloch, Marc: *Die Feudalgesellschaft.* Stuttgart: Klett-Cotta 1999 [1939], p. 332.
3 Patzold, Steffen: *Das Lehnswesen.* München: Beck 2023 [2012], p. 15.
4 The economic *locus classicus* regarding our dependence on monopolised access can be found in the 25th chapter of Karl Marx's *Das Kapital*. Marx uses an episode about a British colonialist settler, Thomas Peel, as an illustration: "Mr. Peel […] took with him from England to Swan River, West Australia, means of subsistence and of production to the amount of £50,000. Mr. Peel had the foresight to bring with him, besides, 300 persons of the working class, men, women, and children. Once arrived at his

destination, 'Mr. Peel was left without a servant to make his bed or fetch him water from the river.'"; Marx, Karl: *Capital. A Critique of Political Economy*. Vol. 1: *The Process of Production of Capital*. Moscow: Progress Publishers 1887. Transl. Samuel Moore and Edward Aveling, edited by Frederick Engels, p, 541; https://www.marxists.org/archive/marx/works/download/pdf/Capital-Volume-I.pdf. What had happened? Quite simply: the settlers ran away from Peel and simply looked for a piece of land of their own. Or to put it the other way around: When capital (here: land) is available in abundance, the power of the capitalist instantly implodes. Central to this is the realisation of Marx that it is not the object itself (the land) that is capital — it is its *use* and, above all, the socially constructed scarcity that turns the object into capital. "We know that the means of production and subsistence, while they remain the property of the immediate producer, are not capital. They become capital only under circumstances in which they serve at the same time as means of exploitation and subjection of the labourer." (541–42) The specific problem case of the exploitation of settlers that Marx describes is a so-called monopsony, loosely translated as 'single buyer', which is the case for instance when there is only one leading supplier who bundles the entire demand for labour (p. 796). At the moment when — as in the case of Thomas Peel — the workers can look for uncultivated land and cultivate it themselves, the capitalist no longer has a monopoly on access and the entire mechanism of capitalist exploitation implodes. Marx described the contemporary presentation of the problem also from the capitalist's point of view: "Where land is very cheap and all men are free, where every one who so pleases can easily obtain a piece of land for himself, not only is labour very dear, as respects the labourer's share of the produce, but the difficulty is to obtain combined labour at any price." (p. 542). In other words, the more monopsonistic the labor market, the greater the exploitation of the workers. This correlation is still recognised in economics today: "The real wage is therefore lower in the monopsony than under competitive conditions" (Sell, Friedrich L.; Ruf, Ernst K. (2014): "Anmerkungen zum Monopson am Arbeitsmarkt II." In: *Volkswirtschaftliche Diskussionsbeiträge*, 2014,1, Universität der Bundeswehr München, Fachgruppe für Volkswirtschaftslehre, Neubiberg, p. 4).

5   A structural analysis of the feudalistic aspects of today's tech monopolies is delivered in Varoufakis, Yanis: *Technofeudalism. What Killed Capitalism*. Dublin: Penguin 2023, but without a more detailed historical comparison.

6   Thiel, Peter: "Competition Is for Losers." In: *The Wall Street Journal*, 12. 9. 2014; https://www.wsj.com/articles/peter-thiel-competition-is-for-losers-1410535536

7   The influential tech investor Peter Thiel has elaborated on his theses on

monopoly in Thiel, Peter: *Zero to One. Notes on Startups, or How to Build the Future*. New York: Currency 2014, p. 32 ff.

8   Rest, Jonas: "Markenfirmen stecken in der Amazon-Falle." In: *Manager Magazin*, 4. 3. 2024; https://www.manager-magazin.de/unternehmen/tech/amazon-wie-marken-firmen-in-die-falle-geraten-verkaeufe-mit-verlust-a-5e1d25e4-1573-48c4-9f0d-3faa5b15ef33

9   Fries, Trutz: "Amazons Eigenmarken 2022, Analyse und Liste." In: *Amalytix*, 1. 5. 2021; https://www.amalytix.com/blog/amazon-eigenmarken/

10 On Amazon's dominance of the book market, cf. Schmidt, P.: "Umsatzanteil von Amazon am Gesamtumsatz des Online-Handels in Deutschland im Jahr 2023." In: *Statista*, 8. 10. 2024; https://de.statista.com/statistik/daten/studie/831978/umfrage/anteil-von-amazon-am-gesamtumsatz-des-online-handels-in-deutschland/#:~:text=Im%20Jahr%202023%20wurden%2017,E%2DCommerce%2DRiesen%20erwirtschaftet; and Carollo, Laura: "Amazon dominiert den Onlinebuchhandel." In: Statista, 20. 5. 2015; https://de.statista.com/infografik/2271/umsatz-des-versandhandels-mit-buechern-in-deutschland/#:~:text=Amazon%20kontrolliert%2090%20Prozent%20des,lediglich%20300%20Millionen%20Euro%20erwirtschaftet.&text=Die%20Grafik%20zeigt%20den%20gesch%C3%A4tzten%20Umsatz%20des%20Versandhandels%20mit%20B%C3%BCchern%20in%20Deutschland

11 Bloch, Marc: *Die Feudalgesellschaft*. Stuttgart: Klett-Cotta 1999 [1939], p. 475.

12 The situation is different when monopolies are contained by the State, because the possibilities of exploitation by the monopolist are then limited by democratic checks and balances. This is often the case with natural monopolies (railroads, electricity, water supply, etc.).

13 Staab, Phlilipp: *Digitaler Kapitalismus. Markt und Herrschaft in der Ökonomie der Unknappheit*. Frankfurt/M.: Suhrkamp 2020, p. 30.

14 On Bell and AT&T, cf. Gertner, Jon: *The Idea Factory. Bell Labs and the Great Age of American Innovation*. New York: Penguin 2012, especially p. 368.

15 The most important characteristics of public goods are the low degree of exclusion (no one tends to be excluded), non-rivalrous consumption (the availability of the good is not reduced by consumption), as well as strong boundaries that prevent potential rejection. All of these aspects also apply to media, media genres and markets.; Cf. Deneulin, Severine, and Nicholas Townsend: "Public Goods, Global Public Goods and the Common Good." In: *International Journal of Social Economics* 34, no. 1–2 (2007), pp. 19—36; Kersten, Jens: *Die Verfassung öffentlicher Güter*. Baden-Baden: Nomos 2023; https://doi.org/10.5771/9783748942504; Priddat, Birger P.: "Öffentliche Güter als politische Güter." In: *Zeitschrift für öffentliche und gemeinwirtschaftliche Unternehmen / Journal for Public*

and Nonprofit Services, 31,2 (2008), pp. 152—173. In his book *Weaving the Web*, Tim Berners-Lee traces the lengthy process of the creation of the World Wide Web and thus provides a fascinating document on the challenges of developing various committees, processes, open protocols and checks and balances, which should protect and secure the web like a public good against private interests; cf. Berners-Lee, Tim: *Weaving the Web. The Original Design and Ultimate Destiny of the World Wide Web*. San Francisco: Harper 1999.

16   Here is a small selection of the many different attempts by dark tech to blackmail democratic governments through its monopoly power:

Chanel, Sheldon: "Facebook's Australia ban threatens to leave Pacific without key news source." In: *The Guardian*, 19. 2. 2021; https://www.theguardian.com/world/2021/feb/19/facebooks-australia-ban-threatens-to-leave-pacific-without-key-news-source

Kaye, Byron, Stephen Coates and Miral Fahmy: "Meta says it may block news from Facebook in Australia." In: *Reuters*, 28. 6. 2025; https://www.reuters.com/technology/meta-says-it-may-block-news-facebook-australia-2024-06-28/

Kaye, Byron: "When Facebook blocks news, studies show the political risks that follow." In: *Reuters*, 14. 4. 2025; https://www.reuters.com/technology/when-facebook-blocks-news-studies-show-political-risks-that-follow-2024-04-14/

Shead, Sam: "Meta says it may shut down Facebook and Instagram in Europe over data-sharing-dispute." In: *CNBC*, 7. 2. 2022; https://www.cnbc.com/2022/02/07/meta-threatens-to-shut-down-facebook-and-instagram-in-europe.html

pbe/dpa: "Apple bringt seine KI erst im April auf EU-iPhones." In: *Spiegel*, 29. 10. 2024; https://www.spiegel.de/netzwelt/gadgets/apple-intelligence-kommt-erst-im-april-2025-auf-eu-iphones-ac4bed812-4f5b-4b20-bd4b-6094de830e39

Derico, Ben and James Clayton: "Meta threatens to remove US news content if new law passes." In: *BBC*, 6. 12. 2022; https://www.bbc.com/news/technology-63869013

Guardian staff and agency: "Meta threatens to pull news content in California if law to pay publishers passes." In: *The Guardian*, 1. 6. 2023; https://www.theguardian.com/us-news/2023/jun/01/california-news-publishers-law-meta-google

Kafka, Peter: "If Elon Musk's X threatened a big ad company with government interference, that's very bad." In: *Business Insider*, 20. 2. 2025; https://www.businessinsider.com/elon-musk-linda-yaccarino-x-twitter-threaten-advertisers-government-ipg-2025-02

Momtaz, Rym: "Taking the Pulse: Is Elon Musk Meddling in European Politics?" In: *Carnegie Endowment for International Peace*

(*CEIP*), 23. 1. 2025.; https://carnegieendowment.org/europe/strategic-europe/2025/01/taking-the-pulse-is-elon-musk-meddling-in-european-politics?lang=en

Henley, Jon: "How Elon Musk has meddled in European affairs." In: *The Guardian*, 11. 1. 2025; https://www.theguardian.com/technology/2025/jan/11/how-elon-musk-has-meddled-in-european-affairs

Smiszek, Krzysztof: "Musk's DSA denial could harm European citizens." In: *The Parliament*, 18. 2. 2025; https://www.theparliamentmagazine.eu/news/article/oped-musks-dsa-denial-could-harm-european-citizens

5. The occupation

1 Wolf, Martin: *The Crisis of Democratic Capitalism.* Dublin: Penguin 2023; cf. in particular Chapter 5: "Rise of Rentier Capitalism".
2 An examination of the aspirations of this supposed 'sect' for sovereignty from medieval feudalism can be found in Duby, Georges: *Die drei Ordnungen. Das Weltbild des Feudalismus.* Frankfurt/M.: Suhrkamp 2016 [1979], p. 477ff., here p. 482.
3 — p. 484.
4 Luther's writing "An Open Letter to The Christian Nobility of the German Nation" ["An den christlichen Adel deutscher Nation von den Christlichen Standes Besserung"] provides a detailed analysis of how the papal monopolization of access to salvation is secured by "three walls" of ideological settlements (this is almost reminiscent of Warren Buffet and the idea of 'moats', which are supposed to protect monopolies from competition). The popes, according to Luther, "assume for themselves sole authority" (13). Above all, he shows exactly how huge extractions of indulgences, benefices, levies, interest, fiefs and conditions are derived from this, i. e. how "thievery and robbery" (21) are made possible in the first place; Luther, Martin (transl.: C.M. Jacobs): *An Open Letter to The Christian Nobility of the German Nation Concerning the Reform of the Christian Estate*, 1520. Works of Martin Luther: With Introductions and Notes Volume II. Philadelphia: A. J. Holman Company 1915.; https://www.onthewing.org/user/Luther%20-%20Nobility%20of%20the%20German%20Nation.pdf. Luther also clearly understands the dangers of economic monopolies: "Furthermore, there are some who buy up altogether the goods or wares of a certain kind in a city or country, so that they alone have such goods in their power, and then fix prices, raise and sell as dear as they will or can." Such "monopolies" are "not to be suffered in the land and city, and princes and rulers should check and punish it if they wish to fulfil their duty." (27); he also describes the same

technique of establishing monopolies that Big Tech uses today: "they proceed to sell these goods so cheap that the others cannot meet them" and adds: "These people do not deserve to be called men or to live among people" (28); Carruth, W. H.: "On Trade and Usury." A Sermon by Dr. Martin Luther; In: *The Open Court* Vol. 1897: Iss. 1, Article 2 (1897), pp. 27—28. On the protection of monopolies, cf. OECD, Directorate for Financial and Enterprise Affairs, Competition Committee: "Monopolisation, Moat Building and Entrenchment Strategies — Background Note." 11. 6. 2024.

5   Further information on the attitude of the 'Chicago School' towards monopolies and the key political role of this network in establishing the current digital monopoly economy can be found in Wu, Tim: *The Curse of Bigness. Antitrust in the New Gilded Age*. New York: Columbia Global Reports 2018, pp. 78—118.

6   Cf. Pistor, Katharina: *Der Code des Kapitals. Wie das Recht Reichtum und Ungleichheit schafft*. Frankfurt/M.: Suhrkamp 2023 [2021].

7   — p. 66.

8   Cf. Heath, Alex: "Ex-Google CEO says successful AI startups can steal IP and hire lawyers to 'clean up the mess'." In: *The Verge*, 15. 8. 2024; https://www.theverge.com/2024/8/14/24220658/google-eric-schmidt-stanford-talk-ai-startups-openai

9   Pistor: *Code des Kapitals*, p. 47.

10 The platforms only have to become active after 'notice & takedown' procedures have started. As long as the content does not go through a notice & takedown procedure, platforms are not liable. As a rule, however, the full communicative effect of criminal content unfolds so quickly (within hours) that this process usually starts too late. Platforms can only be held liable under the European DSA if they have been notified of criminal content but still do not delete or block it.

11 On the deals between Spotify and Joe Rogan, cf. Sisario, Ben: "Joe Rogan Apologizes for 'Shameful' Past Use of Racial Slur." In: *The New York Times*, 2. 5. 2022; https://www.nytimes.com/2022/02/05/arts/music/joe-rogan-spotify-apologyslur.html; the follow-up deal was even more attractive for Joe Rogan: Steele, Anne: "Joe Rogan Gets New Spotify Deal Worth Up to $250 Million." In: *The Wall Street Journal*, 2. 2. 2024; https://www.wsj.com/business/media/joe-rogan-podcast-spotifydeal-28eb5f74

12 For the sake of precision, it should be added that platforms have multi-sided business models. On the one customer side, content is offered to end users free of charge; on the second customer side, the attention of users is sold to advertisers for the promotion of their products. The structure is similar to that of private television (customer side 1: viewers / customer side 2: advertisers). In contrast to private television, however, platforms are allowed to monetize punishable content contained

in the overall mix of the offer without being liable as long as no notice & takedown procedure has taken place. The argument I have put forward, on the other hand, is *not* about advertising for illegal activities (such as selling narcotics); this would also not be permitted for platform operators.

13 Data basis: AI Tools; here March 2025, subcluster "Text Generators"; https://aitools.xyz/popular-ai-tools/2025/march.
14 Cf. Holzgraefe, Moritz, and Nils Ole Oermann: *Digitale Plattformen als Staaten. Legitimität, Demokratie und Ethik im digitalen Zeitalter.* Herder 2023, p. 184 f.

6. The weapons

1 Cf. Habermas, Jürgen: *The Structural Transformation of the Public Sphere. An Inquiry into a Category of Bourgeois Society.* Cambridge: MIT Press 1962; on the effects of the digital transformation, cf.: *A New Structural Transformation of the Public Sphere and Deliberative Politics.* Cambridge: Polity 2023.
2 Cf. McLuhan, Marshall: *Understanding Media. The Extensions of Man.* London, New York: Routledge 2001 [1964].
3 The metaphor of the hall of mirrors is adapted here from Robertson, Claire E., Kareena del Rosario, Jay J. Van Bavel: "Inside the Funhouse Mirror Factory: How Social Media Distorts Perceptions of Norms." In: *Current Opinion in Psychology* 60 (2024); https://www.sciencedirect.com/science/article/abs/pii/S2352250X24001313. It also states: "When people stare into the [digital] mirror they do not see the true version of reality, but instead one that has been distorted by a small but vocal minority of extreme whose opinions create illusory norms. In turn, these outliers are often amplified by design features and algorithms that prioritize engaging content."
4 On the various factors that determine news value, cf. Engelmann, Ines: "Nachrichtenfaktoren und die organizationsspezifische Nachrichtenselektion. Eine Erweiterung der Nachrichtenwerttheorie um die Meso-Ebene Journalistischer Organisationen." In: *Medien & Kommunikationswissenschaft*, 60 (2012), pp. 41–63; Fürst, Silke: "Öffentlichkeitsresonanz als Nachrichtenfaktor. Zum Wandel der Nachrichtenselektion." In: *Medien-Journal, Zeitschrift für Kommunikationskultur*, 37 (2017), pp. 4—15; Kepplinger, Hans Mathias: "Der Nachrichtenwert der Nachrichtenfaktoren", in: — (ed.): Journalismus als Beruf. Wiesbaden 2001, pp. 61—75; —: "Der prognostische Gehalt der Nachrichtenwerttheorie", —, pp. 77—99; Shoemaker, Pamela J.: *Gatekeeping. Communication Concepts.* Newbury Park, CA 1991.
5 Cf. Morant, Lyndon: "The Truth Behind 6 Second Ads." In: *Medium,*

8.2.2018; https://medium.com/@Lyndon/the-tyranny-of-six-seconds-592b94160877; the figure mentioned, which has since been cited in many scientific studies, is certainly outdated and comes from a Facebook source, but I would trust Facebook and Meta in particular to answer this question based on their data access.

6   Cf. among others, Schnaack, Greta and Anja Weber: "Nachrichtenflut im Netz." In: *Bitkom*, 2024; https://www.bitkom-research.de/news/nachrichtenflut-im-netz-jeder-und-jede-zweite-fuehlt-sich-ueberfordert

7   Cf. e.g. Lorenz-Spreen, Philipp et al: "Accelerating Dynamics of Collective Attention." In: *Nature Communications* 10, 1759 (2019), pp. 1—9; https://doi.org/10.1038/s41467-019-09311-w

8   Cf. Malone, Clare: "The Meme-ification of American Politics." In: *The New Yorker*, 25.1.2024; https://www.newyorker.com/news/annals-of-communications/the-meme-ification-of american-politics

9   Cf. Oremus, Will, and Drew Harwell: "Musk accused Reuters of 'social deception'. The deception was his." In: *Washington Post*, 15.2.2025; https://www.washingtonpost.com/technology/2025/02/15/musk-doge-deception-reuters/

10 Cf. Mau, Steffen, Thomas Lux, and Linus Westheuser: *Triggerpunkte. Konsens und Konflikt in der Gegenwartsgesellschaft*. Frankfurt/M.: Suhrkamp 2023; for the taxonomy of triggers used here, cf. p. 276.

11 Cf. Michelis, Daniel: "Social-Media-Modell." In: *Social Media Handbuch. Theorien, Methoden, Modelle und Praxis*. 3., erw. Aufl. Baden-Baden: Nomos 2015, pp. 23—37.

12 Elsner, Mark, Oliver Heil and Atanu Sinha: "How Social Networks Influence the Popularity of User-Generated Content." In: *Marketing Science Institute Special Report* 10-206, 2010; https://thearf-org-unified-admin.s3.amazonaws.com/MSI/2020/06/MSI_SR_10-206.pdf

13 Wojcik, Stefan, and Adam Hughes: "Sizing Up Twitter Users." In: *Pew Research Center*, April 2019; https://www.pewresearch.org/internet/2019/04/24/sizing-up-twitter-users/; Hughes, Adam, and Nida Asheer: "National Politics on Twitter: Small Share of U.S. Adults Produce Majority of Tweets." In: *Pew Research Center*, October 2019; https://www.jstor.org/stable/resrep63051?seq=1; McClain, Colleen, Regina Widjaya, Gonzalo Rivero and Aaron Smith: "The Behaviors and Attitudes of U.S. Adults on Twitter." In: *Pew Research Center* (2021); https://www.pewresearch.org/internet/2021/11/15/the-behaviors-and-attitudes-of-u-s-adults-on-twitter/; this strong asymmetry was also confirmed in a separate empirical study with 500 respondents on viral advertising videos; cf. Andree, Martin, and Niklas van Husen: *Digital Bootcamp*. Frankfurt/M.: Campus 2021, p. 94f.

14 N.a.: "Studie: Knapp die Hälfte aller Abiturienten will 'Influencer' oder 'Creator' werden." In: *News for Teachers*, 20.8.2023; https://www.

news4teachers.de/2023/08/studie-knapp-die-haelfte-aller-abiturienten-will-influencer-oder-creator-werden/; Bitkom (ed.) "Jeder Fünfte folgt Online-Stars in sozialen Netzwerken", 2018; https://www.bitkom.org/Presse/Presseinformation/Jeder-Fuenfte-folgt-Online-Stars-in-sozialen-Netzwerken.html

15 Briggs, Ellyn: "Gen Zers Still Really Want to Be Influencers." In: *Morning Consult*, 4.10.2023; https://pro.morningconsult.com/analysis/gen-z-interest-influencer-marketing

16 Cf. Engels, Barbara: "Traumjob Influencer. Likes, Views und das große Geld?" Edited by the Institute of the German Economy. IW-Report 46, 2023; https://www.iwkoeln.de/fileadmin/user_upload/Studien/Report/PDF/2023/IW-Report_2023-Traumjob-Influencer.pdf; Hoose, Fabian and Sophie Rosenbohm: "Entgelte von sog. UGC-Plattformen für künstlerisch/ publizistische Leistungen und deren Einbeziehung in die Künstlersozialabgabe." Edited by Bundesministerium für Arbeit und Soziales (BMAS). Forschungsbericht 640 (2024); https://www.bmas.de/SharedDocs/Downloads/DE/Publikationen/Forschungsberichte/fb-640-entgelt-ugc-plattformen-kuenstlerisch-leistung-kuenstlersozialabgabe.pdf?__blob=publicationFile&v=2

17 Cf. Ingham, Tim: "Spotify Dreams of Artists Making a Living. It Probably Won't Come True." In: *Rolling Stone*, 3.8.2020; https://www.rollingstone.com/pro/features/spotify-million-artists-royalties-1038408/

18 Cf. e.g. Primack, Brian A. et al: "Social Media Use and Perceived Social Isolation Among Young Adults in the US." In: *American Journal of Preventive Medicine*, Volume 53, Issue 1 (2017), pp. 1—8; DOI: 10.1016/j.amepre.2017.01.010

19 Bousquet, Kristen: "What's An Influencer And How Can I Make Money As One?" In: *Forbes*, 14.7.2024; https://www.forbes.com/sites/kristenbousquet/article/how-to-become-aninfluencer/; Bousquet, Kristen: "How Much Are Creators With Under 10,000 Followers Getting Paid?" In: *Forbes*, 11.4.2024; https://www.forbes.com/sites/kristenbousquet/2024/04/11/how-muchare-creators-with-under-10k--followers-getting-paid/; Payas, Steph, Madelyn Ormond, Serena Ngin, Brianna Borik and Katie Kammerdeiner: *NeoReach Industry Report: Creator Earnings 2023*; https://neoreach.com/quarterly-reports/2023-creator-earnings-report/; Needleman, Sarah E. and Ann-Marie Alcántara: "Social-Media Influencers Aren't Getting Rich — They're Barely Getting By." In: *The Wall Street Journal*, 17.6.2024; https://www.wsj.com/tech/social-media-influencers-arent-getting-richtheyre-barely-getting-by-71e0aad3?mod=hp_lead_pos7; Bertoni, Steven, Matt Craig, Zoya Hasan, Alexandra S. Levine and Alexandra York: "Forbes Top Creators 2024." In: *Forbes*, 28.11.2024; https://www.forbes.com/sites/stevenbertoni/2024/10/28/top-creators-2024-the-

influencers-turning-buzz-into-billions; Ingham, Tim: "Spotify Dreams of Artists Making a Living. It Probably Won't Come True." In: *Rolling Stone*, 3.8.2020; https://www.rollingstone.com/pro/features/spotify-million-artistsroyalties-1038408/; Jin, Li: "The Creator Economy Needs a Middle Class." In: *Medium*, 17.12.2020; https://medium.com/@wunderlichvalentin/the-creator-economy-needs-a-middleclass-5e80be85382c

20 Gabbatt, Adam: "Value of X has fallen 71% since purchase by Musk and name change from Twitter." In: *The Guardian*, 2.1.2024; https://www.theguardian.com/technology/2024/jan/02/x-twitter-stock-falls-elon-musk

21 Getahun, Hannah, and Erin Snodgrass: "Elon Musk drohte Twitter-Mitarbeitern mit Kündigung, wenn sie seine Tweets nicht erfolgreicher als die von Joe Biden machen würden." In: *Business Insider*, 15.2.2023; https://www.businessinsider.de/wirtschaft/twitter-musk-drohte-mit-kuendigung-wenn-seine-tweets-nicht-sichtbarer-werden/

22 Merrill, Jeremy B., Trisha Thadani, and Kevin Schaul: "Musk's influence on X eclipses all members of the incoming Congress, combined." In: *Washington Post*, 17.12.2024; https://www.washingtonpost.com/business/interactive/2024/see-how-elon-musks-online-audience-dwarfs-donald-trumps/

23 Cf. e.g. Knutson B, Hsu TW, Ko M, Tsai JL: "News source bias and sentiment on social media." In: PLoS ONE 19, 10, 2024; https://doi.org/10.1371/journal.pone.0305148; Robertson, C. et al: "Negativity drives online news consumption." In: *Nature Human Behavior* 7, 5 (2023), pp. 812—822; https://doi.org/10.1038/s41562-023-01538-4; Fan, R., Xu, K., & Zhao, J. (2020): "Weak ties strengthen anger contagion in social media." In: arXiv. https://doi.org/10.48550/arXiv.2005.01924

24 Cf. Andree, Martin: *Archäologie der Medienwirkung. Faszinationstypen von der Antike bis heute*. München: Fink 2005, pp. 209—250.

25 It is to Martin Doll's credit that he dedicated a thorough scientific study to this topic; cf. Doll, Martin: *Fälschung und Fake. Zur diskurskritischen Dimension des Täuschens*. Berlin: Kadmos 2012. It should also be mentioned that I use the term 'true' (as well as the counter-concept of 'lie') more naïvely here in the text than would actually be appropriate. Post-structuralist theories in particular would certainly emphasise that this truth does not 'exist' and that it is only ever present as a discursive construct. This is precisely why studies such as Martin Doll's are so useful: they can demonstrate that we should not understand the concept of truth 'essentially', but must operationalise it: "truth" only ever experiences its "practice-dependent flexible determination" in a "discourse-specific" way that is "conditioned by the respective historical point in time" (11). What is important to note, however, is that, even as

an operative illusion, truth (as a construction!) remains a central reflective value for functional systems. It is precisely here that there is great potential for a scientifically sound way to overcome a postmodern relativism of truth that is too short-sighted. This effort is overdue in view of the current social threat posed by fake news and disinformation. This would also be the epistemological position of this book.

26 Cf. Allcott, Hunt, and Matthew Gentzkow: "Social Media and Fake News in the 2016 Election." In: *Journal of Economic Perspectives* 31, 2 (2017), pp. 211—236.

27 Vosoughi, Soroush, Deb Roy, and Sinan Aral: "The Spread of True and False News Online." In: *Science*, 359, 6380 (9. 3. 2018), pp. 1146—1151; DOI: 10.1126/science.aap9559

This effect can even be empirically measured under editorial conditions on the internet — fake news from the Bild newspaper is disseminated on social media by a factor of 7.7 more than real news.

Nastjuk, Ilja et al: "Virality of fake news in social media. The influence of emotions"; University of Göttingen, September 2021; https://www.unigoettingen.de/de/document/download/9b64d4ace04f79f-263987d822a90f88d.pdf/Viralit%C3%A4t%20von%20Fake%20News%20in%20Social%20Media.pdf

28 Cf. Bell, David A.: "The Age of Trump and Musk: Reflections on the Election of 2024." In: *Society* (62): 109–111 (2025). DOI: https://doi.org/10.1007/s12115-024-01045-w

29 Bail, Chris: *Breaking the Social Media Prism. How to Make Our Platforms Less Polarizing*. Princeton, Oxford: Princeton University Press 2021, p. 66 f.

30 Cf. Osmundsen, Mathias, et al: "Partisan Polarization Is the Primary Psychological Motivation behind Political Fake News Sharing on Twitter." In: *American Political Science Review* 115.3 (2021), pp. 999—1015; doi:10.1017/S0003055421000290.

31 Cf. Frimer, Jeremy A. et al: "Incivility Is Rising Among American Politicians on Twitter." In: *Social Psychological and Personality Science*, 14, 2 (2022), pp. 259—269; https://doi.org/10.1177/19485506221083811

32 Cf. generally Mau, Steffen: *Das metrische Wir. Über die Quantifizierung des Sozialen*. Frankfurt/M.: Suhrkamp 2017.

33 On the connection between rank and ranking in the digital attention economy, cf. Andree, Martin: "Ranken." In: *Historisches Wörterbuch des Mediengebrauchs*, Bd. 3. Ed. by Heiko Christians, Matthias Bickenbach, Nikolaus Wegmann. Köln et al.: Böhlau 2022, pp. 333—350. Cf. on mechanisms of 'value formation' in various discursive contexts also beyond the economy in connection with system-theoretical concepts of symbolically generalized communication media (Luhmann) as well as with recourse to the model of 'success media' (Parsons) —: *Medien machen*

Marken. Eine Medientheorie des Marketing und des Konsums. Frankfurt/M.: Campus 2010.
34 Cf. De Carbonnel, Alissa: "Fake news fact-checks hobbled by low reach, study shows." In: *Reuters*, 11.7.2019; https://www.reuters.com/article/world/echo-chambers-fake-news-fact-checks-hobbled-by-low-reach-study-shows-idUSKCN1U60PG/; an early empirical study on the topic was already able to show that hardly any fact-checkers were ever consulted on the specific fake news consumed; cf. Allcott, Hunt, and Matthew Gentzkow: "Social Media and Fake News in the 2016 Election." In: *Journal of Economic Perspectives* 31, 2 (2017), pp. 211—236.
35 White, Nate: "British Writer Pens The Best Description Of Trump I've Read." In: *London Daily*, 24.4.2025; https://londondaily.com/british-writer-pens-the-best-description-of-trump-i-ve-read
36 Scholz, Jana: "Die AfD dominiert TikTok — Studie zur Sichtbarkeit der Parteien in den Sozialen Media." Universität Potsdam, 2.9.2024; https://www.uni-potsdam.de/de/medieninformationen/detail/2024-09-02-die-afd-dominiert-TikTok-studie-zur-sichtbarkeit-der-parteien-in-den-sozialenmedien
37 Cf. https://psmm.info/press-release-de
38 Cf. also the studies Tabia, Tanzen Prama et al: "Political Biases on X before the 2025 German Federal Election." In: *Zenodo*, 17.2.2025; DOI: https://doi.org/10.5281/zenodo.14880275; Global Witness: "X and TikTok algorithms push pro-AfD content to non-partisan German users: New analysis." In: *Global Witness*, 20.2.2025; https://globalwitness.org/en/campaigns/digital-threats/tiktok-and-x-recommend-pro-afd-content-to-non-partisan-users-ahead-of-the-german-elections/
39 Cf. Fox 4 Dallas-Fort Worth: "Elon Musk at Trump rally in Butler, PA: FULL SPEECH." YouTube, 6.10.2024.; https://www.youtube.com/watch?v=Asoq00GQ3BA
40 This legitimization of violence, even against supposedly 'parasitic' opponents of freedom, can be found again and again in the history of libertarianism; cf. e.g. Cooper, Melinda: "The Alt-Right: Neoliberalism, Libertarianism and the Fascist Temptation." In: *Theory, Culture & Society*, 38(6) (2021), pp. 29—50; https://doi.org/10.1177/0263276421999446, here p. 34.
41 Rathje, Steve, et al: "People Think That Social Media Platforms Do (but Should Not) Amplify Divisive Content." In: *Perspectives on Psychological Science* 19, 5 (2024), pp. 781—795; DOI: 10.1177/17456916231190392
42 Cf. in detail Morozov, Evgeny: "The New Legislators of Silicon Valley." In: *The Ideas Letter* 37, 3.4.2025; https://www.theideasletter.org/essay/silicon-valleys-new-legislators/

7. The trap

1. Reitman, Rainey: "Bitcoin — a Step Toward Censorship-Resistant Digital Currency." In: *Electronic Frontier Foundation (EFF)*, 20.1.2011; https://www.eff.org/deeplinks/2011/01/bitcoin-step-toward-censorship-resistant?language=fa; cf. also Golumbia, David: *Cyberlibertarianism. The Right-Wing Politics of Digital Technology*. Minneapolis, London: University of Minnesota Press 2024, p. 314.
2. Meineke, Michelle: "Can you answer these 3 questions about your finances? The majority of US adults cannot." In: *World Economic Forum*, 24.4.2024; https://www.weforum.org/stories/2024/04/financial-literacy-money-education/
3. Cf. Golumbia, David: *Cyberlibertarianism. The Right-Wing Politics of Digital Technology*. Minneapolis, London: University of Minnesota Press 2024, p. 393.
4. Golumbia, David: *Cyberlibertarianism. The Right-Wing Politics of Digital Technology*. Minneapolis, London: University of Minnesota Press 2024, p. 33.
5. In fact, the very phrase "absolutism of freedom of speech" is a contradiction in terms, because freedom and coercion have always been mutually dependent on each other in a paradoxical way — for the history of this problem, cf. the volume Fulda, Daniel, Hartmut Rosa, and Heinz Thoma (eds.): *Freiheit und Zwang. Studien zu ihrer Interdependenz von der Aufklärung bis zur Gegenwart*. München: Fink 2018. Christoph Menke, the leading theorist on the subject, begins his standard work "Theorie der Befreiung" [Theory of Liberation] with the memorable sentence: "All the liberations that have brought about modernity since its inception have — sooner or later — turned into their opposite"; Menke, Christoph: Theorie der Befreiung. Frankfurt/M.: Suhrkamp 2022, p 9. Nobody should know this better than the tech bros — who were originally liberators but now operate on the dark side of the force.
6. Cf. e.g. Debusmann, Bernd: "White House takes control of press pool that covers Trump." In: *BBC*, 26.2.2025; https://www.bbc.com/news/articles/ce30n52e6p1o; Stelter, Brian: "PBS and NPR are in a once-in-a-generation funding fight. They might well lose." *CNN*, 16.4.2025; https://edition.cnn.com/2025/04/16/media/pbs-npr-funding-fight/index.html; Garisto, Dan, Jeff Tollefson, and Alexandra Witze: "How Trump's attack on universities is putting research in peril." In: *Nature* 24.4.2025; https://www.nature.com/articles/d41586-025-01289-4
7. Gärditz, Klaus F.: "BVerfG zu Meinungsäußerung und Menschenwürde. Die Grenze des Sagbaren." In: *Legal Tribune Online*, 22.06.2020; https://www.lto.de/recht/hintergruende/h/bverfg-beschluss-1-bvr-2459-19-grundrechte-meinungsfreiheit-beleidigung-grenze
8. —

9   One example of many is the speech by AfD politician Tobias-Matthias Peterka on 14 December 2023 on "Freedom of expression in social networks" in the German parliament: "The digital revolution has democratised the flow of information to an unprecedented extent. And of course I'm not talking about Web 1.0 here, but about modern social media [...]. Oh, how you were celebrating what happened during the so-called Arab Spring. You were even right about how important such platforms are for working against oppressive regimes. Today, you can no longer put a watchdog official in front of the printing press or place your companions in public service broadcasting, as you liked to do. Fortunately, this dam has been broken almost everywhere. And that annoys you, it also annoys the EU and its Commissioner Breton quite bitterly. Out of pure self-empowerment, he famously wrote Elon Musk a letter warning him to be careful with Twitter and X, otherwise bad things could happen. Please reply within 24 hours. The Chinese Communist Party took the same action against internet billionaire Jack Ma. So this is your EU now. [...] It simply hurts him [Breton] that there are communication channels that are beyond his control."; Cf. https://www.bundestag.de/dokumente/textarchiv/2023/kw50-de-meinungsfreiheit-netzwerke-982830

10 "One should not speak of 'censorship' when the obstruction or suppression of an expression of opinion takes place within the framework of a 'factual quality assessment'" — for example, when articles are not selected by an editorial team; Buchloh, Stephan: "Überlegungen zu einer Theorie der Zensur. Interessen — Formen — Erfolgsfaktoren." In: *Die Kommunikationsfreiheit der Gesellschaft. Die demokratischen Funktionen eines Grundrechts.* Hrsg. von Wolfgang Langenbucher. Wiesbaden: Westdeutscher Verlag 2003, pp. 112—138, here p. 116.

11 Cf. Hobohm, Hans-Christoph: "Zensur." In: *Handbuch Sozialwissenschaftliche Gedächtnisforschung.* Edited by Berek, M., et al. Springer VS, Wiesbaden, 2021. https://doi.org/10.1007/978-3-658-26593-9_99-1, here p. 2 f.

12 Buchloh, Stephan: "Überlegungen zu einer Theorie der Zensur. Interessen — Formen — Erfolgsfaktoren." In: *Die Kommunikationsfreiheit der Gesellschaft. Die demokratischen Funktionen eines Grundrechts.* Edited by Wolfgang Langenbucher. Wiesbaden: Westdeutscher Verlag 2003, pp. 112—138, here p. 113.

13 —, p. 128.

14 Bernhard, Lukas, and Lutz Ickstadt: "Lauter Hass — leiser Rückzug. Wie Hass im Netz den demokratischen Diskurs bedroht. Ergebnisse einer repräsentativen Befragung." Published by Das NETTZ, Gesellschaft für Medienpädagogik und Kommunikationskultur, HateAid und Neue deutsche Medienmacher*innen als Teil des Kompetenznetzwerks gegen

Hass im Netz, Berlin 2024. https://kompetenznetzwerk-hass-imnetz.de/download_lauterhass.php, p. 40 f.
15 — p. 55.
16 — p. 54 f.
17 — p. 49.
18 — p. 50.
19 Großmann, Sven: "Nach Habeck-Debatte: Wann Beleidigungen strafbar sein sollten." In: *Beck Recht, Steuern, Wirtschaft*, 17. 12. 2024; https://rsw.beck.de/aktuell/daily/meldung/detail/habeck-beleidigung-strafbarkeit-politiker-demokratie
20 Chartier, Roger: *Die kulturellen Ursprünge der Französischen Revolution.* Frankfurt, New York: Campus 1995 [1991], p. 80.
21 Barbrook, Richard: *Media Freedom. The Contradictions of Communications in the Age of Modernity.* London, Ann Arbor: Pluto 1995.
22 Cf. Andree, Martin: *Archäologie der Medienwirkung. Faszinationstypen von der Antike bis heute.* München: Fink 2005, pp. 446 ff; Schneider, K.: "Acheiropoietos." In: *Reallexikon für Antike und Christentum. Sachwörterbuch zur Auseinandersetzung des Christentums mit der antiken Welt.* Vol. 1 ff. Edited by Theodor Klauser. Stuttgart: Hiersemann 1950 ff. vol. 1, pp. 68—72; Dobschütz, Ernst von: *Christusbilder. Untersuchungen zur christlichen Legende.* Leipzig: Hinrichs 1899, pp. 37 ff. as well as the extensive references in the appendix, pp. 118*—122*.
23 Cf. https://x.com/elonmusk/status/1870209985805799511?s=46
24 Amlinger, Carolin, and Oliver Nachtwey: *Gekränkte Freiheit. Aspekte des libertären Autoritarismus.* Frankfurt/M.: Suhrkamp 2022, p. 306.
25 Cf. https://x.com/elonmusk/status/1854206931256099056?s=46

8. The uprising

1 Cf. Burilkov, Alexandr and Guntram Wolff: "Europa ohne die USA verteidigen: eine erste Analyse, was gebraucht wird." In: *Kiel Policy Brief*, 183, 2025; https://www.ifw-kiel.de/de/publikationen/europa-ohne-die-usa-verteidigen-eine-erste-analyse-was-gebraucht-wird-33811/
2 Wehnes, Harald, and Martin Weigele: "Alarmzeichen: Deutschland demnächst im goldenen Microsoft-Käfig?" In: *Gesellschaft für Informatik*, 30. 10. 2024; https://gi.de/themen/beitrag/alarmzeichen-deutschland-demnaechst-im-goldenen-microsoft-kaefig
3 Wehnes, Harald: "Digitale Kolonie und Lock-in verhindern. Der Weg zur digitalen Souveränität mit Open Source." In: *INFORMATIK* 2024. Lecture Notes in Informatics (LNI), Gesellschaft für Informatik, Bonn 2024, pp. 651—662, here p. 651.
4 Krempl, Stefan: "Wegen Trump: Ruf nach ernsthaften Schritten in Richtung alternativer Software." In: *Heise*, 25. 2. 2025; https://www.heise.

de/news/Big-Tech-Abhaengigkeit-Trump-als-Booster-fuer-digitale-Souveraenitaet-in-der-EU-10294963.html

5   N. a.: "How the EU's DMA is changing Big Tech: all of the news and updates." In: *The Verge*, 24. 4. 2025; https://www.theverge.com/24040543/eu-dma-digital-markets-act-big-tech-antitrust

6   On the regional focus of dark tech in Germany, cf. Hoben, Anna et al.: "Silicon Valley mitten in München." In: *Süddeutsche Zeitung*, 3. 3. 2023; https://www.sueddeutsche.de/muenchen/muenchen-apple-campus-mitarbeiter-1.5761350?reduced=true ; Kerstholt, Marion: "Von der Kohle zur Künstlichen Intelligenz." In: *Tagesschau*, 18. 3. 2024; https://www.tagesschau.de/wirtschaft/unternehmen/microsoft-ki-deutschland-100.html; Hoffmann, Catherine: "Open AI eröffnet erstes Deutschland-Büro in München." In: *Süddeutsche Zeitung*, 7. 2. 2025; https://www.sueddeutsche.de/muenchen/open-ai-deutschland-buero-muenchen-li.3198078; Otte, Romanus: "25 Jahre Amazon Deutschland: Milliarden-Bilanz und große Pläne für Amazons wichtigsten Markt außerhalb der USA." In: *Business Insider*, 21. 11. 2024; https://www.businessinsider.de/wirtschaft/amazon-deutschland-25-jahre-bilanz-und-plaene-fuer-den-wichtigsten-auslandsmarkt/

7   Cf. Reuter, Markus: "Trump droht mit Zöllen gegen EU-Regulierung von Big Tech." In: *netzpolitik.org*, 24. 2. 2025; https://netzpolitik.org/2025/dma-dsa-und-dsgvo-trump-droht-mit-zoellen-gegen-euregulierung-von-big-tech/

8   Cf. Neuerer, Dietmar: "Ukraine unter Druck — Experten befürchten große Fluchtbewegung." In: *Handelsblatt*, 21. 2. 2025; https://www.handelsblatt.com/politik/deutschland/ukraine-unter-druck-experten-befuerchten-grosse-fluchtbewegung/100108847.html

9   Cf. et al.

Titcomb, James: "Tech will quit Britain over online safety crackdown, warn Musk and Google." In: *The Telegraph*, 16. 2. 2025; https://www.telegraph.co.uk/business/2025/02/16/tech-quit-britain-online-safety-act-warn-musk-google/

Chanel, Sheldon: "Facebook's Australia ban threatens to leave Pacific without key news source." In: *The Guardian*, 19. 2. 2021; https://www.theguardian.com/world/2021/feb/19/facebooks-australia-banthreatens-to-leave-pacific-without-key-news-source

Kaye, Byron, Stephen Coates and Miral Fahmy: "Meta says it may block news from Facebook in Australia." In: *Reuters*, 28. 6. 2025; https://www.reuters.com/technology/meta-says-it-may-block-newsfacebook-australia-2024-06-28/

Kaye, Byron: "When Facebook blocks news, studies show the political risks that follow." In: *Reuters*, 14. 4. 2025; https://www.reuters.com/

technology/when-facebook-blocks-news-studies-show-politicalrisks-that-follow-2024-04-14/

Guardian staff and agency: "Meta threatens to pull news content in California if law to pay publishers passes." In: *The Guardian*, 1. 6. 2023; https://www.theguardian.com/us-news/2023/jun/01/california-news-publishers-law-meta-google

Shalal, Andrea and Joey Roulette: "Exclusive: US could cut Ukraine's access to Starlink internet services over minerals, say sources." In: *Reuters*, 22. 2. 2025; https://www.reuters.com/business/us-couldcut-ukraines-access-starlink-internet-services-over-minerals-say-2025-02-22/.

9. The capitulation

1 Cf. Corlin, Peggy: "Which European Trump allies will be in Washington for inauguration?" In: *Euronews*, 20. 1. 2025; https://www.euronews.com/my-europe/2025/01/20/which-european-trump-allies-will-be-in-washington-for-inauguration
2 Cf.
Potter, Nicholas: "Der Payback-Präsident." In: *taz*, 4. 2. 2025; https://taz.de/Trump-verklagt-CBS/!6063588/
James, Katharina: "Donald Trump verklagt Meinungsforscherin und Regionalzeitung." In: *Zeit Online*, 18. 12. 2024; https://www.zeit.de/politik/ausland/2024-12/donald-trump-klagemeinungsforscherin-regionalzeitung-des-moines-register
Grynbaum, Michael M. and Alan Feuer: "ABC to Pay $15 Million to Settle a Defamation Suit Brought by Trump." In: *The New York Times*, 14. 12. 2024; https://www.nytimes.com/2024/12/14/business/media/trump-abc-settlement.html
Yang, Maya: "Trump sues for billions from media he says is biased against him." In: *The Guardian*, 15. 11. 2024; https://www.theguardian.com/us-news/2024/nov/15/trump-sues-media-outlets-bias
Grynbaum, Michael and Benjamin Mullin: "'60 Minutes' Chief Resigns in Emotional Meeting: 'The Company Is Done With Me'." In: *The New York Times*, 22. 4. 2025; https://www.nytimes.com/ 2025/04/22/business/media/cbs-60-minutes-trump-bill-owens.html
3 Cf. de Koning, Marloes: "X weigert Nederlander inzage in zijn persoonsgegevens en verliest kort geding." *NRC Handelsblad*, 27. 3. 2025; https://www.nrc.nl/nieuws/2025/03/27/x-weigert-nederlander-in-zage-in-zijn-persoonsgegevens-en-verliest-kort-geding-a4887864
4 Cf. Kreye, Andrian: "Die Rache beginnt." In: *Süddeutsche Zeitung*, 19. 12. 2024; https://www.sueddeutsche.de/kultur/usa-donald-trump-klage-des-moines-register-demokratie-lux.B3BR5joEwvpUnBZJZgj-Toj?reduced=true

5 Cf. Korecki, Natasha, und Sahil Kapur: "Kash Patel once said he would 'come after' journalists. It now hangs over his FBI candidacy." In: *NBC News*, 4.12.2024; https://www.nbcnews.com/politics/donaldtrump/kash-patel-said-come-journalists-now-hangs-fbi-candidacyrcna182661

6 Cf. e. g. Cadwalladr, Carole: "The great British Brexit robbery: how our democracy was hijacked." In: *The Guardian*, 7.5.2017; https://www.theguardian.com/technology/2017/may/07/the-great-british-brexit-robbery-hijacked-democracy; and Dachwitz, Ingo: "Abschlussbericht der Datenschutzbehörde: Nein, der Cambridge-Analytica-Skandal fällt nicht in sich zusammen." In: *Netzpolitik*, 23.10.2020; https://netzpolitik.org/2020/abschlussbericht-der-datenschutzbehoerde-nein-der-cambridge-analytica-skandal-faellt-nicht-in-sich-zusammen/

7 Cf. Meier, Dominik: "Trumpf gegen Trump: Schweiz betont Nicht-Mitgliedschaft in der EU. Im Kampf gegen US-Zölle betont die Schweiz ihre Vorteile als Nicht-EU-Mitglied." In: *SRF*, 1.4.2025; https://www.srf.ch/news/schweiz/vor-us-zollankuendigung-trumpf-gegen-trump-schweiz-betont-nicht-mitgliedschaft-in-der-eu

8 N. a.: "Apple will 500 Milliarden Dollar in den USA investieren." In: *Der Spiegel*, 24.2.2025; https://www.spiegel.de/netzwelt/gadgets/donald-trump-trifft-tim-cook-apple-will-500-milliarden-dollar-in-den-usa-investieren-a-6ec32c2b-5f1b-4a54-a9ba-bce10709dba8

9 N. a.: "Politico's owner praises JD Vance for 'inspiring message'." In: *Financial Times*, 19.2.2025; https://www.ft.com/content/cb1cc264-84b9-40da-a484-ff897cd386e4

10 N. a.: "Polen schließt KI-Abkommen mit Google." In: *Polskie Radio*, 14.2.2025; https://www.polskieradio.pl/400/7764/artykul/3484147,polens chlie%C3%9Ft-kiabkommen-mit-google

11 N. a.: "Meta wird Trump-kompatibel. Zuckerberg wirft Biden Zensur vor und stampft Diversitätsprogramme ein." In: *N-TV*, 11.1.2025; https://www.n-tv.de/wirtschaft/Zuckerberg-wirft-Biden-Zensur-vor-und-stampft-Diversitaetsprogramme-ein-article25481678.html

12 Kelly, Makena: "The Who's Who of MAGA Influencers You Should Know About by Now." In: *Wired*, 23.1.2025; https://www.wired.com/story/maga-influencers-content-creators/

13 Mayer, Jane: "Pete Hegseth's Secret History." In: *The New Yorker*, 1.12.2024; https://www.newyorker.com/news/news-desk/pete-hegseths-secret-history

14 Cf. Robertson, Katie: "Trump Administration to Remove 4 Major News Outlets From Pentagon Office Space." In: *The New York Times*, 1.2.2025; https://www.nytimes.com/2025/02/01/business/media/pentagon-press-corps.html

15 Self-transcription based on: https://x.com/realalexjones/status/1877856585059283308?s=48&t=X49AcxPs1E9FjmZPwjwPOg

16 Isaacson, Walter: *Steve Jobs*. New York: Simon & Schuster 2011. ProQuest Ebook Central, http://ebookcentral.proquest.com/lib/ubkoeln/detail.action?docID=4934365, Chapter Thirty-five: Round One Memento Mori.
17 N. a.: "Russischer Rohkost-Blogger ließ Baby verhungern." In: *Der Spiegel*, 17. 4. 2024; https://www.spiegel.de/panorama/justiz/russland-rohkost-blogger-maxim-ljutyj-liess-baby-kosmos-verhungern-acht-jahre-haft-a-79272f0e-4849-4ce0-aaae-6e1f0261a6e2
18 His detailed guest article in the FAZ is instructive, in which he names the catastrophic state of affairs with complete openness: "Today you no longer need to be afraid of Google. The matter has been settled for the time being. Google, perhaps the smartest company in the world, has simply won across the board." Döpfner, Mathias: "Warum wir Google nicht mehr fürchten." In: *Frankfurter Allgemeine Zeitung*, 16. 4. 2024; https://www.faz.net/aktuell/feuilleton/debatten/mathias-doepfner-warum-wir-google-nicht-mehr-fuerchten-19657527.html
19 Simon, Ulrike: "Springer sahnt bei Facebook gleich doppelt ab." In: *Horizont*, 17. 5. 2021; https://www.horizont.net/medien/nachrichten/folgen-bald-google-microsoft--apple-springer-sahnt-bei-facebook-gleich-doppelt-ab-191598
20 Bovermann, Phillip: "In Chat-GPT steckt künftig die 'Bild'-Zeitung." In: *Süddeutsche Zeitung*, 14. 12. 2023; https://www.sueddeutsche.de/medien/ki-springer-openai-deal-doepfner-1.6319701?reduced=true
21 Cf. Bargel, Vicky and Anton Rainer: "Zwei Milliardäre und der Kampf um die 'Welt'." In: *Spiegel*, 3. 1. 2025; https://www.spiegel.de/wirtschaft/elon-musk-und-mathias-doepfner-die-verbindung-hinter-dem-afd-beitrag-in-der-welt-a-87e73e0f-d8f8-48e6-aa0f-d3e4f0cbbabe
22 Cf. Schade, Marvin: "So viele Abos hat die Welt mit Elon Musks AfD-Beitrag gemacht." In: *Media Insider*, 29. 12. 2024; https://medieninsider.com/so-viele-abos-hat-die-welt-mit-elon-musks-afd-beitrag-gemacht/24595/

10. The bitter end

1 Deleuze, Gilles, and Félix Guattari: *A Thousand Plateaus*. London: Bloomsbury Academic 2013.
2 Cf. Barbrook, Richard: *Media Freedom. The Contradictions of Communications in the Age of Modernity*. London, Ann Arbor: Pluto 1995, p. 107 ff.
3 Thiel, Peter: "A time for truth and reconciliation." In: *Financial Times*, 10. 1. 2025; https://www.ft.com/content/a46cb128-1f74-4621-ab0b-242a76583105; the idea is almost identical to Davidson, James Dale, and William Rees-Mogg: *The Sovereign Individual. Mastering the Transition to the Digital Age*. New York et al.: Touchstone 2020 [1997], p. 14.

4 Cf. Rushkoff, Douglas: *Survival of the Richest. Escape Fantasies of the Tech Billionaires*. London: Scribe Publications 2022, p. 3—4.
5 Mehringer, Jella: "Die 'Broligarchie'. Das gefährliche Mindset der Tech-Milliardäre — Douglas Rushkoffs 'Survival of the Richest'." In: *Das Erste*, 9.2.2025; https://www.daserste.de/information/wissen-kultur/ttt/sendung/sendung-februar-hr-ttt-100.html

ACKNOWLEDGEMENTS

In recent years, I have attended hundreds of events in Germany and abroad, where I have spoken to many inspiring people about the topic discussed here. I was particularly struck by the finding that all areas of our society are equally affected by the problem of domination by tech monopolies — including the digital economy, media companies, private and public broadcasting, journalism, retail, start-ups, SMEs, global brands, manufacturing, publishing, bookshops, creative and media agencies, authors, artists, musicians, political parties and many more. I have learned a great deal about the various fields in all these encounters and would like to extend my heartfelt thanks to all supporters, colleagues, discussants and interested parties for all the enriching exchanges.

I would also like to express my sincere thanks to graphic designer Verena Bönniger for designing the illustrations and to Julian Hale for checking and correcting the English translation of this book.

In addition, I would like to thank Prof. Nikolaus Peifer, Director of the Institute for Media and Communication Law at the University of Cologne, for providing me with insights into the field of media regulation over the past few years — insights that have been invaluable to me. I would like to thank Prof. Stephan Packard for his selfless and continuous encouragement, as well as Prof. Peter Marx and Prof. Benjamin Beil for their support. I am also grateful to Prof. Martin Gläser, editor of the journal *MedienWirtschaft*, for his encouragement and interest in my texts.

My special thanks also go to the *Initiative Nachrichtenaufklärung* (News Clarification Initiative), which awarded the book *Big Tech muss weg!* (Big Tech Must Go!) the 'Günter Wallraff Special Prize for Press Freedom and Human Rights' in 2024, as well as the *German Journalists' Association*, which had previously nominated the book for this award; and the University of Cologne, which awarded the same book the 'Beatrice Primus Research Prize' in 2025.

I would also single out Björn Staschen, Marc-Uwe Kling, Hanna Möllers and all other partners of our Save Social petition for their partnership and cooperation. And I would like to thank Constantin Krückels for his expert sparring on the subject, Maja Göpel for her support in the real and digital world, Dr. Dominik Waßenhoven for the professional exchange, Ms. Waltraud Berz and Dr. Judith Wilke-Primavesi from Campus-Verlag for their competent support and the editor, Andrea Dietrich.

Above all, I would like to thank my family, my children and especially my wife, who have always been understanding about the fact that valuable weekends and holidays together had to be sacrificed for this project.